VEGETARIAN
MICROWAVE
COOKING

COMPILED BY PATRICIA PAYNE
DESIGNED BY PHILIP CLUCAS
PHOTOGRAPHED BY PETER BARRY
STYLED BY BRIDGEEN DEERY
AND WENDY DEVENISH
EDITED BY JILLIAN STEWART

CLB 2461
© 1990 Colour Library Books Ltd., Godalming, Surrey.
Typeset by The Ikthos Studios, Andover, Hants.
Printed and bound in Cordoba, Spain by Graficromo, S.A.
All rights reserved.
ISBN 0 86283 793 6

VEGETARIAN MICROWAVE COOKING

Colour Library Books

·Contents·

·FOREWORD·

There is nothing weird and wonderful about the pattern of vegetarian eating; vegetarians are not cranks, they simply prefer to eat dishes which do not contain meat, poultry, game or fish. A vegetarian diet can be just as varied and interesting as one based on meat and fish. Vegetarians have long been aware of the need to eat a balanced range of different foods and those who do so will happily tell you that they feel perfectly healthy, have plenty of energy, and, above all, that they really enjoy their food.

Variety is very much the keynote of vegetarian eating: different pastas, rices, cheeses, nuts and pulses are just a selection of the many different ingredients of a good vegetarian diet. Most important of all, vegetarian dishes are every bit as nutritious as their meat-rich counterparts. The main difference lies in the types of food that provide us with the necessary nutrients. In a typical vegetarian dish, the protein usually comes from pulses, nuts or cheese, or from a combination of these ingredients. Essential minerals, vitamins, fats and carbohydrates come from a host of basic foods such as wholemeal flour, grains and, of course, fresh vegetables and fresh and dried fruit.

The microwave oven is a wonderful asset to the vegetarian cook and is particularly useful for cooking vegetables. Low evaporation means vegetables require very little water to cook, so they retain all those essential vitamins and minerals. Fast cooking times also mean vegetables keep their fresh colour and crisp texture. Fresh vegetables cook as quickly as frozen vegetables do by conventional methods, and frozen vegetables are cooked beautifully in almost the blink of an eye.

Vegetarian menus have suffered from the image that they are composed solely of nut cutlets and baked potatoes, an image which is far from accurate. As this book will show, vegetarian menus cover a whole spectrum of foods. Eating 'the vegetarian way' has many points in its favour. A balanced meatless diet is a very healthy one, since it is nutritious, low in fat and high in bulk and fibre. Vegetarians rarely need to watch their weight, as a diet that is high in natural fibre and low in fat is also comparatively low in calories. The traditional pattern of Western eating is relatively expensive to follow, whereas vegetarian dishes are more economical and adapt wonderfully to microwave cooking methods.

Vegetarian food really can be exciting and delicious and, even if you are not a committed vegetarian, many of the ideas in this book are well worth trying. This imaginative collection of delicious recipes will enable the cook to produce exciting, well-balanced and delicious vegetarian meals in no time at all. All of which goes to prove that, vegetarian or not, everyone can enjoy more creative meals thanks to the versatility and variety of such natural produce as fruit, vegetables, grains and pulses.

·INTRODUCTION·

People are usually of two minds about microwave ovens: experienced cooks are sceptical; inexperienced cooks are mystified. Most people who don't own one think a microwave oven is an expensive luxury. Those of us who have one, though, would find it difficult to give it up. Great advances have been made in the design and capabilities of microwave ovens since the demand for them first began in the Sixties. With so many kinds of oven available, both beginners and advanced cooks can find one that best suits their particular needs.

How Microwave Ovens Work

Microwave ovens, whatever the make or model, do have certain things in common. The energy that makes fast cooking possible is comprised of electromagnetic waves converted from electricity. Microwaves are a type of high frequency radio wave. The waves are of short length, hence the name microwave.

Inside the oven is a magnetron, which converts ordinary electricity into microwaves. A wave guide channels the microwaves into the oven cavity, and a stirrer fan circulates them evenly. Microwaves are attracted to the particles of moisture that form part of any food. As the microwaves are absorbed, to a depth of about 4-5cm /1½ – 2 inches, they cause the water molecules in the food to vibrate about 2,000 million times a second. This generates the heat that cooks the food. The heat reaches the centre of the food by conduction, just as in ordinary cooking. However, this is accomplished much faster than in conventional cooking because no heat is generated until the waves are absorbed by the food. All the energy is concentrated on cooking the food and not on heating the oven itself or the baking dishes. Standing time is often necessary to allow the food to continue cooking after it is removed from the oven.

Most microwave ovens have an ON indicator light and a timer control. Some timer controls look like minute timers, while others are calibrated in seconds up to 50 seconds and minutes up to 30 minutes. This can vary slightly; some models have a 10 minute interval setting. Some ovens have a separate ON-OFF switch, while others switch on with the timer or power setting. Almost all have a bell or buzzer to signal the end of cooking time.

Microwave Oven Features

Although all microwave ovens operate on the same basic principles, there are marked differences in features between the various makes and models. Different terms are used for the same power setting depending. on what brand of oven you buy. Some ovens have a wider range of different settings as well. Chart No. 1 on power settings reconciles most of the popular terms.

CHART 1 Power Setting Comparison Chart

	Other Terms and Wattages	Uses
Low	ONE or TWO, KEEP WARM, 25%, SIMMER, DEFROST. 75-300 watts	Keeping food warm. Softening butter, cream cheese and chocolate. Heating liquid to dissolve yeast. Gentle cooking.
Medium	THREE or FOUR, 50%, STEW, BRAISE, ROAST, RE-HEAT, MEDIUM-LOW, FIVE, 40%, MEDIUM-HIGH, SIX, 60-75%. 400-500 watts	Cooking Hollandaise sauces. Baking cakes and custards.
High	SEVEN, FULL, ROAST, BAKE, NORMAL, 100%.	Quick cooking. Vegetables, biscuits, pasta, rice, breads, pastry, desserts.

Some ovens come equipped with a temperature probe which allows you to cook food according to its internal temperature instead of by time. It is most useful for roasting large cuts of meat. The probe needle is inserted into the thickest part of the food and the correct temperature set on the attached control. When that internal temperature is reached, the oven automatically turns off, or switches to a low setting to keep the food warm. Special microwave thermometers are also available to test internal temperature and can be used inside the oven. Conventional thermometers must never be used inside a microwave oven, but can be used outside.

A cooking guide is a feature on some ovens, either integrated into the control panel or on the top or side of the oven housing. It is really a summary of the information found in the instruction and recipe booklet that accompanies every oven. However, it does act as a quick reference and so can be a time saver.

Turntables eliminate the need for rotating baking dishes during cooking, although when using a square of loaf dish you may need to change position from time to time anyway. Turntables are usually of glass or ceramic and can be removed for easy cleaning. Of all the special features available, turntables are one of the most useful.

Certain ovens have one or more shelves so that several dishes can be accommodated simultaneously. Microwave energy is higher at the top of the oven than on the floor and the more you cook at once the longer it all takes. However, these ovens have the advantage of accommodating larger baking dishes than those with turntables.

If you do a lot of entertaining, then an oven with a KEEP WARM setting is a good choice. These ovens have a very low power setting that can keep food warm without further cooking for up to one hour. If you want to programme your oven like a computer, choose one with a memory control that can switch settings automatically during the cooking cycle.

Browning elements are now available built into microwave ovens. They look and operate in much the same way as conventional electric grills. If you already have a grill, you probably don't need a browning element. Some of the most recent ovens allow the browning element to be used at the same time as the microwave setting, which is a plus.

Combination ovens seem to be the answer to the problem of browning in a microwave oven. While the power settings go by different names in different models, generally there is a setting for microwave cooking alone, a convection setting with conventional electric heat, and a setting which combines the two for almost the speed of microwave cooking with the browning ability of the conventional cooker. However, the wattage is usually lower than in standard microwave ovens, and so cooking time will be slightly longer.

Safety and Cleaning

One of the questions most commonly asked is 'Are microwave ovens safe to use?' They are safe because they have safety features built into them and they go through rigorous tests by their manufacturers and by independent agencies.

If you look at a number of microwave ovens you will see that the majority of them are lined with metal, and metal will not allow microwaves to pass through. The doors have special seals to keep the microwaves inside the oven, and there are cut-out devices to cut off the microwave energy immediately the door is opened. There are no pans to upset, no open flames or hot elements and the interior of the oven stays cool enough to touch. Although microwave ovens don't heat baking dishes, the heat generated by the cooking food does, so it is a good idea to use oven gloves or pot holders to remove dishes from the oven.

It is wise periodically to check the door of your oven to make sure it has not been bent. Check latches and hinges, too, to make sure that they are in good working order. Don't use baking dishes that are too large to allow the turntable to rotate freely; this can cause the motor to over-heat or cause dents in the oven sides and door, lowering efficiency and affecting safety of operation.

Microwave ovens are cleaner and more hygienic to cook with than conventional gas or electric ovens. Foods do not spatter as much and spills do not burn, so clean-up is faster. The turntables and shelves can be removed for easier cleaning. Use non-abrasive cleansers and scrubbers, and be sure to wipe up any residue so that it does not build up around the door seals. Faster cooking times and lower electricity consumption combine to make microwave ovens cheaper to run, especially for cooking small amounts of food, than conventional ovens.

Once you have chosen your oven and understand what makes it work, the fun of cooking begins. As with conventional cooking, there are some basic rules to remember, but most of them are common sense.

Quantity

Food quantities affect cooking times. For example, one baked potato will take about 3-4 minutes, two will take about 6-7 minutes, four will take 10-11 minutes. Generally, if you double the quantity of the recipe, you will need to increase the cooking time by about half as much again.

Size

The smaller the piece of food the quicker it will cook. Pieces of food of the same kind and size will cook at the same rate. Add smaller or faster-cooking foods further along in the cooking cycle, such as mushrooms to a stew. If you have a choice of cooking heights, put food that is larger and can take more heat above food that is smaller and more delicate.

Covering

Most foods will cook, re-heat or defrost better when covered. Use special covers that come with your cookware or simply cover with cling film. This covering must be pierced to release steam, otherwise it can balloon and possibly burst.

Equipment and Cookware

The number of different baking dishes and the range of equipment for microwave cooking is vast. There are so many highly specialised dishes for specific needs that to list them all here is impossible.

Explore cookware departments and find your own favourites. Follow your microwave oven instruction booklet carefully since it will give you good advice on which cookware is best for your particular oven. Some dishes, lightweight plastics and even some hard plastics can't be used on combination settings – the temperature is too high and the dishes will melt or break. Most metal cookware can be used successfully in combination ovens, following the manufacturer's guidelines, but must not be used in ordinary microwaves ovens. Paper bags can catch fire on HIGH settings, and the same is possible with silicone coated paper, although its use is often recommended. Microwave energy penetrates round shapes particularly efficiently, so round dishes and ring moulds work very well. The turntable can also be cooked on directly for such foods as meringues, or used for re-heating foods like bread of coffee cakes.

CHART 2 Cooking Vegetables

Type	Quantity	Water	Mins. on High	Mins. Stdg. Time
Artichokes	4	430ml/¾pt	10-20	5
Asparagus	450g/1lb	140ml/¼pt	9-12	5
Aubergine	2 med.	30ml/2 tbsps	7-10	5
Beans	450g/1lb	140ml/¼pt		
Green, French			8	3
Broad			10	3
Beetroot	2	60ml/2fl oz	4-5	3
Broccoli	450g/1lb	140ml/¼pt	4-5	3
Brussels Sprouts	450g/1lb	60ml/2fl oz	8-10	3-5
Cabbage	450g/1lb	140ml/¼pt		
Shredded			7-9	3
Quartered			9-12	5
Carrots	225g/8oz	140ml/¼pt		
Whole			10	6
Sliced			7	5
Cauliflower	450g/1lb			
Whole		280ml/½pt	11	3
Florets		140ml/¼pt	7	3
Chicory	4	60ml/2fl oz (water or stock)	5	3
Corn-on-the-Cob	2 ears	60ml/2fl oz	6	3
Courgettes	450g/1lb	60ml/2fl oz	5	3
Fennel	1 bulb	280ml/½pt		
Sliced		boiling water	2-8	3
Quartered			10-12	3
Leeks, sliced	450g/1lb	140ml/¼pt	7-10	3
Mushrooms	225g/8oz	30ml/2 tbsps	2	3
Okra	225g/8oz	60ml/2fl oz	4	3
Onions, small	225g/8oz	30ml/1fl oz	7-8	3
Sliced	2	60ml/2fl oz	10	3
Parsnips	225g/8oz	40ml/¼pt	8-10	3
Peas, shelled	450g/1lb	140ml/¼pt	10-15	5
Mange tout	225g/8oz	140ml/¼pt	3	3
Peppers	2 sliced	60ml/2fl oz	3	3
Potatoes				
New	450g/1lb	140ml/¼pt	10-12	5
Baked	2		9-12	10
Boiled	450g/1lb	140ml/¼pt	6-7	5
Spinach	225g/8oz		4-5	3
Turnips	225g/8oz	60ml/2fl oz	12	3

Cooking Vegetables

Microwave cooking is ideal for vegetables. Very little water is needed, so they keep their colour and nutrients. They are best cooked loosely covered, and whole vegetables like corn-on-the-cob, aubergines, artichokes and chicory can be completely wrapped in cling film and cooked without any water. Cooking bags are another alternative.

Break broccoli into even-sized pieces and, if cooking a large quantity, be sure to put the flower ends in towards the centre of the dish. Trim down the tough ends of asparagus and peel the ends of the stalks, this will help the stalks cook quickly before the tips are overcooked. Some vegetables, like cucumbers, spring onions and button onions cook very well in butter or margarine alone, if well covered. Chart No. 2 lists suggested cooking times for vegetables.

Cooking Fruit

Poach, bake and preserve fruit with ease in a microwave oven. Sterilise jars for preserving by adding a little water and heating on HIGH for about 2-3 minutes and then draining. Metal lids and rubber seals are best sterilised outside the microwave oven. Paraffin wax for sealing jars cannot be melted in a microwave oven. The great advantage of microwave preserving is that jams and jellies can be made in small amounts and the job is much less messy and time-consuming. Whole preserved fruit and pickled vegetables can't be heated long enough to kill bacteria, so they must be refrigerated after bottling.

Cooking Rice, Pasta, Grains and Pulses

Rice and pasta need nearly as much cooking by microwave methods as by conventional ones. However, both pasta and rice cook without sticking together and without the chance of overcooking. This is because most of the actual cooking is accomplished during standing time. All kinds of rice and shapes of pasta benefit from being put into hot water with a pinch of salt and 5ml /1 tsp oil in a deep bowl. There is no need to cover the bowl during cooking, but, during standing time, a covering of some sort will help retain heat. Ease long spaghetti into the bowl gradually as it softens. Drain rice and pasta and rinse under hot water to remove starch. Both rice and pasta can be re-heated in a microwave oven without loss of texture. Fresh pasta doesn't seem to take to the microwave oven successfully.

CHART 3 Cooking Rice, Pasta, Grains and Pulses

Type	Quantity	Water	Mins. on High	Mins. Stdg. Time
Brown Rice	120g/4oz	570ml/1pt	20	5
White Rice (long grain)	120g/4oz	570ml/1pt	10-12	5
Quick Cooking Rice	120g/4oz	430ml/¾pt	6	5
Macaroni	225g/8oz	1litre/1¾pts	6	10
Quick Cooking Macaroni	225g/8oz	1litre/1¾pts	3	10
Spaghetti	225g/8oz	1litre/1¾pts	6-10	10
Tagliatelle /Fettucine	225g/8oz	1litre/1¾pts	5-9	10
Pasta Shapes	225g/8oz	1litre/1¾pts	6	10
Lasagne Ravioli Cannelloni	180g-225g	1litre/1¾pts	6	10
Barley	120g/4oz	570ml/1pt	20	10
Bulgur (cracked wheat)	225g/8oz	570ml/1pt	4	10
Dried Beans	180g/6oz	1litre/1¾pts	55-60	10
Dried Peas	225g/8oz	1litre/1¾pts	45-60	10
Lentils	225g/8oz	1litre/1¾pts	20-25	15

NOTE: Add a pinch of salt and 5ml /1 tsp oil to grains and pasta.

There is a great time saving with dried peas, beans and lentils – pulses. Cover them with water in a large bowl and heat on a HIGH setting to bring to the boil, which takes about 10 minutes. Allow the pulses to boil for about 2 minutes and then leave to stand for one hour. This cuts out overnight soaking. The pulses will cook in about 45 minutes to one hour depending on what variety is used. This is about half the conventional cooking time. Make sure pulses are cooked completely; it can be dangerous to eat them undercooked. Refer to Chart No. 3 for cooking times.

Cooking Eggs and Cheese

When poaching eggs, always pierce the yolks with a skewer or fork to prevent them from bursting. Use individual ramekins or patty pans with a spoonful of water in each. Alternatively, bring water to the boil in a large dish and add a pinch of salt and 5ml /1 tsp vinegar to help set the whites. Slip the eggs in one at a time. Cook just until the whites are set. To stop the cooking and to keep the eggs from drying out, keep them in a bowl of cold water. For frying eggs choose a browning dish, and for scrambling use a deep bowl or glass measuring jug. Always remove scrambled eggs from the oven while they are still very soft. Stir during standing time to finish cooking. Hollandaise sauce is easy to make. Choose the same kind of containers as for scrambled eggs and have a bowl of iced water ready. Use a MEDIUM setting and cook the sauce at short intervals, whisking vigorously in between times. Put the sauce bowl into the iced water at the first sign of curdling, or briefly when it has thickened, to stop the cooking process.

Cheese will get very stringy if it overcooks or gets too hot. When preparing a cheese sauce, stir finely grated cheese into the hot sauce base and leave to stand. The cheese will melt without further cooking. Cheese toppings will not brown except in a combination oven. A MEDIUM setting is best for cheese.

Baking

Baking is one of the most surprising things a microwave oven does. Quick breads, those leavened with baking powder or soda and sour milk, rise higher than they do in a conventional oven and bake faster. If using a square or loaf dish, cover the corners with foil for part of the cooking time to keep that part of the bread or cake from drying out before the middle is cooked. Cakes also rise much higher, and a single layer will bake in about 6 minutes on a MEDIUM setting.

Microwave ovens can cut the rising time for yeast doughs almost by half, and a loaf of bread will bake in an astonishing 8-10 minutes.

Biscuits will not usually crisp in a microwave oven except in one with a combination setting. However, they bake to a moist, chewy texture which is just as pleasing. A batch of 3 dozen will cook in about 10 minutes.

Pastry is not as much of a problem as most people believe. Prick the base and sides of the pastry well after lining a pie or flan dish. It is essential to bake the pastry shell 'blind' – without filling – in order to dry the base. Pastry will not bake to an even brown. The exception is, of course, pastry baked in a combination oven. Pastry and filling can be baked at the same time in these ovens.

To let air and heat circulate underneath breads, cakes and pastry shells, place them on a rack or inverted saucer. This allows the base to cook faster and more evenly. Once baked and cool, keep microwave-baked goods well covered. They seem to dry out faster than those conventionally baked.

Defrosting and Re-heating

With the defrosting and re-heating abilities of a microwave oven, menu planning can become crisis-free. Most ovens incorporate an automatic defrosting control into their setting programmes. If your oven does not have this facility, use the lowest temperature setting and employ an on /off technique. In other words, turn the oven on at 30 second – 1 minute intervals and let the food stand for a minute or two before repeating the process. This procedure allows the food to defrost evenly without starting to cook at the edges. The times given in Chart Nos. 4 and 5 apply to ovens of 600-700 watts.

Always cover the food when defrosting or re-heating. Plastic containers, plastic bags and freezer-to-table ware can be used to freeze and defrost food in. Meals can be placed on paper or plastic trays and frozen. Cover with cling film or greaseproof paper. Usually, foods are better defrosted first and cooked or re-heated second. There are exceptions to this rule, so be sure to check instructions on pre-packed foods before proceeding. Food frozen in blocks, such as spinach or casseroles, should be broken up as they defrost.

Breads, rolls and coffee cakes can be placed on paper plates or covered in paper towels to re-heat or defrost. These materials will help protect the foods and absorb the moisture which will come to the surface and could make these foods soggy. If you want a crisp crust on re-heated bread, slip a sheet of foil under the paper towel and don't cover completely.

Foods can be arranged on plates in advance and re-heated very successfully, an advantage when entertaining. A microwave oven allows you to spend more time with your guests, and less time preparing food in the kitchen!

CHART 4 Defrosting

	Mins. on Low /Defrost. Setting per 450g/1lb	Mins. Stdg. Time	Instructions
Vegetables	1-8	3-5	Cover loosely. Break up or stir occasionally.
Bread Loaf	2-4 (per average loaf)	5-10	Cover with paper towels. Turn over once.
1 Slice Bread	20 seconds	1	Cover in paper towels.
Rolls 6	1½-3	3	Cover in paper towels,
12	2-4	5	and turn over once.
Cake	1½-2	2	Place on serving plate. Some icings not suitable.
Fruit Pie 23cm/9"	8-10	6	Use a glass dish. Place on inverted saucer or rack.

Recipe Conversion

Experiment with your favourite recipes and you will probably find that many of them can be converted for microwave cooking with only a few changes. Things that don't work are recipes which call for whipped egg whites, such as angel food cake and crisp meringue shells. Soft meringues for pies will work, and one of the most amazing recipe conversions is that for crisp meringues. These meringues triple in size as they cook and are made from a fondant-like mixture.

Batters for pancakes, waffles or Yorkshire pudding are impossible to cook successfully.

To convert your own recipes, the following rules will help:

✱ Look for similar microwave recipes with the same quantities of solid ingredients, dish size, techniques and times.

✱ Reduce liquid quantities by one quarter. More can always be added later in cooking.

✱ Reduce the seasoning in your recipe; microwave cooking intensifies flavours.

✱ Microwave cooking takes approximately a quarter of the time of conventional cooking. Allow at least 5 minutes standing time before checking to see if the food is cooked. You can always add more time at this point if necessary.

CHART 5 Re-heating

	Quantity	Setting	Time from room temp. (mins.)	Special Instructions
Spaghetti Sauce	225g/8oz 450g/1lb	MED.	5-6 7-8	Stir several times. Keep loosely covered
Pasta	120g/4oz 225g/8oz	MED. or HIGH	2-3 5-6	Stir once or twice. Add 5ml / 1 tsp oil. Use shorter time for HIGH setting.
Rice	120g/4oz 225g/8oz	MED. or HIGH	2-3 4-5	Stir once or twice. Add 5ml / 1 tsp oil or butter. Use shorter time for HIGH setting.
Potatoes	120g/4oz 225g/8oz 450g/1lb	HIGH	1-2 2-3 3-4	Use the shorter time for mashed potatoes. Do not re-heat fried potatoes. Cover loosely.
Corn-on-the-Cob	2 ears 4 ears	HIGH	2-3 4-6	Wrap in cling film
Carrots	225g/8oz 450g/1lb	HIGH	1-2 2-4	Cover loosely. Stir once.
Turnips	225g/8oz 450g/1lb	HIGH	1-2 2-4	Cover loosely. Stir carefully.
Broccoli Asparagus	120g/4oz 225g/8oz	HIGH	2 2	Cover loosely. Rearrange once.
Peas Beans	120g/4oz 225g/8oz	HIGH	1-1½ 1½-2	Cover loosely. Stir occasionally

Altering Times

All recipes in this book were prepared in a 700 watt microwave oven. If you are using an oven with a lower maximum output, adjust the cooking times as follows:

500 WATT OVEN - add 40 seconds for each minute stated in recipe.
600 WATT OVEN - add 20 seconds for each minute stated in recipe.
650 WATT OVEN - only a slight increase in the overall time is necessary.

VEGETARIAN MICROWAVE COOKING

CHAPTER ~ 1

· VEGETARIAN · SOUPS ·

CHESTNUT SOUP

SERVES 4

This unusual soup is high in protein and dietary fibre, and is so delicious that it will soon become a firm family favourite.

30g /1oz vegetable margarine
2 sticks of celery, trimmed and finely chopped
2 large onions, peeled and chopped
225g /8oz unsweetened chestnut purée
900ml /1½ pints homemade vegetable stock
Salt and freshly ground black pepper
Wholemeal croutons for garnish

1. Put the margarine, celery and onions into a large, microwave-proof bowl. Cover with cling film and puncture this several times with the tip of a knife.

2. Cook on HIGH for 4 minutes. Remove the film and stir the vegetables to coat them evenly with the margarine.

3. In a jug or small bowl, blend the chestnut purée with 300ml /½ pint of the stock, stirring it well with a fork to blend it thoroughly.

Step 2 Stir the cooked vegetables in the butter to coat them all evenly.

Step 3 Using a fork or blender, gradually blend the stock into the chestnut purée, mixing it well to keep the mixture smooth.

Step 5 Add the remaining vegetable stock to the chestnut soup and mix well.

4. Stir the chestnut purée mixture into the celery and onions. Season with salt and pepper, re-cover and cook on HIGH for 7 minutes.

5. Stir in the remaining stock and microwave, uncovered, for a further 10 minutes. Allow the soup to stand for 10 minutes.

6. Reheat the soup for 5 minutes on HIGH, and serve garnished with the croutons.

Cook's Notes

PREPARATION: If unsweetened chestnut purée is unavailable, cook 225g /8oz shelled chestnuts in 140ml /¼ pint boiling water until they are soft, and purée these in a liquidiser or food processor.

FREEZING: This soup will freeze for 1 month.

VEGETARIAN SUITABILITY: This recipe is suitable for vegans.

TIME: Preparation takes about 15 minutes, microwave cooking time is about 24 minutes, with 10 minutes standing time.

VICHYSSOISE

SERVES 4

This classic French soup is both simple and economical to make.

3 large leeks
45g /1½oz butter
2-3 medium potatoes, peeled and sliced
850ml /1½ pints vegetable stock
140ml /¼ pint milk
Salt and freshly ground black pepper
90ml /3 tbsps sour cream

1. Cut the white part off the leeks. Trim the white parts and slice thinly. Wash thoroughly.

2. Trim the green parts of the leeks and shred them finely. Wash these thoroughly and set them aside.

3. Put the butter into a large microwave-proof bowl. Cook uncovered for about 1 minute on HIGH, or until the butter has melted.

4. Stir the potatoes and the white parts of the leeks into the melted butter, mixing well to ensure that they are evenly coated.

5. Cover the bowl with cling film and pierce this several times with the tip of a sharp knife.

Step 1 Cut the white parts off the leeks, trim and slice them thinly.

Step 4 Stir the potatoes and the white parts of the leeks into the melted butter, mixing well to ensure that they are evenly coated.

6. Cook the potatoes and leeks on HIGH for 5 minutes.

7. Stir the potatoes, add half the stock and re-cover the bowl. Continue cooking on HIGH for a further 14 minutes, or until the vegetables are very soft.

8. Allow the cooked vegetables to stand for about 5 minutes.

9. Pour the soup into a liquidiser or food processor and blend until smooth.

10. Whisk the remaining stock and the milk into the puréed soup with a balloon whisk.

11. Put the green parts of the leeks into a small bowl along with 2-3 tbsps of water. Cover with cling film, and pierce this with the tip of a knife.

12. Cook the shredded green leeks on HIGH for about 2 minutes, or until they have blanched.

13. Re-heat the puréed soup mixture for 3 minutes before serving topped with the sour cream and blanched green leek tops.

Cook's Notes

 TIME: Preparation takes about 12 minutes, microwave cooking takes about 25 minutes, plus 5 minutes standing.

SERVING IDEA: Serve this soup cold for a delicious change.

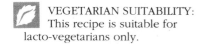 VEGETARIAN SUITABILITY: This recipe is suitable for lacto-vegetarians only.

GREEN PEA SOUP
SERVES 4

Pale green and creamy, this delicious soup is made with frozen peas, making it possible to enjoy the taste of summer all year round.

30g /1oz butter
1 shallot, finely chopped
450g /1lb frozen peas
30g /1oz plain flour
280ml /½ pint vegetable stock
430ml /¾ pint milk
1.25ml /¼ tsp dried marjoram
15ml /1 tbsp chopped fresh parsley
Salt and freshly ground black pepper
1 small bunch fresh mint
140ml /¼ pint single cream

1. Put the butter and shallot into a large bowl and cover with cling film. Pierce this several times with the tip of a sharp knife.

Step 2 The cooked shallot should be soft and pale gold in colour.

Step 6 Blend the soup in a liquidiser or food processor until it is smooth.

2. Cook on HIGH for 5 minutes until the shallot is soft.

3. Reserve 90g /3oz of the peas. Put the rest into the bowl along with the cooked shallot.

4. Stir the flour into the shallot and peas, mixing well until it is evenly blended.

5. Add the stock, milk, marjoram, parsley, salt and pepper. Cook uncovered on HIGH for 5 minutes, stirring once during cooking time.

6. Pour the soup into a liquidiser or food processor and purée until it is smooth.

7. Using a sharp knife, chop the mint finely. Stir this, along with the cream, into the puréed soup.

8. Stir the reserved peas into the soup and re-heat for 2 minutes on HIGH before serving.

Cook's Notes

 SERVING IDEA: Serve this soup with crusty rolls and a crumbly vegetarian Cheshire cheese.

COOK'S TIP: Liquidise the soup a little at a time to ensure a smooth texture.

TIME: Preparation takes about 10 minutes, microwave cooking time is about 12 minutes.

VEGETABLE SOUP

SERVES 4

This hearty vegetable soup makes the most of traditional and unusual vegetables.

2 tbsp vegetable oil
1 large carrot, peeled and diced
1 large turnip, peeled and diced
2 leeks, washed and thinly sliced
2 potatoes, scrubbed and diced
570ml /1 pint vegetable stock
450g /16oz can plum tomatoes, chopped
1 bay leaf
1.25ml /¼ tsp marjoram or savoury
60g /2oz soup pasta
Salt and freshly ground black pepper
90g /3oz fresh or frozen sliced green beans
120g /4oz okra, trimmed and sliced
60g /2oz frozen sweetcorn
60g /2oz frozen peas
15ml /1 tbsp chopped parsley

1. Put the oil into a large microwave-proof bowl. Add the carrot, turnip, leeks and potatoes. Stir to coat the vegetables with the oil.

2. Cover the bowl with cling film and pierce this several times with the tip of a sharp knife.

Step 1 Carefully stir the carrots, turnips, leeks and potatoes into the oil in the bowl to ensure that they are coated thoroughly.

Step 2 Cover the bowl with cling film, and pierce this several times with the tip of a sharp knife.

Step 4 Add the stock, tomatoes, bay leaf, marjoram, pasta and salt and pepper to the soup and stir well.

3. Cook the vegetables on HIGH for 10 minutes, or until they begin to soften.

4. Stir the vegetables and add the stock, tomatoes, bay leaf, marjoram or savoury, pasta, salt and pepper. Stir well and cover once again with the cling film. Cook on HIGH for 7 minutes.

5. Add the beans and okra to the bowl, re-cover and cook on HIGH for 2 minutes.

6. Remove the cling film and stir in the sweetcorn, peas and parsley. Cook, uncovered, on HIGH for a further 1 minute, or until the pasta is tender.

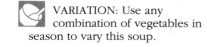

Cook's Notes

VEGETARIAN SUITABILITY: This recipe is suitable for lacto-vegetarians. The recipe can be adapted for vegans by omitting the soup pasta and replacing it with brown rice.

PREPARATION: If tinned tomatoes are not available, cook 340g /12oz fresh tomatoes in 140ml /¼ pint vegetable stock or water for 6 minutes on HIGH, and use these instead.

VARIATION: Use any combination of vegetables in season to vary this soup.

TOMATO AND DILL BISQUE
SERVES 4

*This sophisticated soup, with its delicate flavour,
is an elegant starter to serve at a summer lunch or dinner.*

900g /2lbs fresh tomatoes
1 onion, peeled and chopped
2 large sprigs of fresh dill
30ml /2 tbsps tomato purée
Salt and freshly ground black pepper
850ml /1½ pints vegetable stock
140ml /¼ pint double cream
10ml /2 tsps chopped fresh dill
60ml /2 fl oz natural yogurt
4 slices fresh tomato
4 small sprigs fresh dill

1. Cut the tomatoes in half over a bowl and remove the seeds. Reserve any juice that is produced.

2. Put the tomato flesh and any juice into a large bowl along with the onion, 2 dill sprigs, tomato purée, salt, pepper and vegetable stock.

3. Partially cover the bowl with cling film.

4. Cook on HIGH for 7 minutes, or until the tomatoes have broken down and the onions are soft.

Step 1 Cut the tomatoes over a bowl to collect any spilled juice.

Step 3 Partially cover the bowl containing the tomatoes with cling film.

Step 6 Gently push the puréed soup through a metal sieve to remove the tomato skins.

5. Remove the sprigs of dill and, using a liquidiser or food processor, purée the soup until it is smooth.

6. Strain the puréed soup back into the bowl through a metal sieve to remove the tomato skins.

7. Stir the double cream and chopped dill into the puréed tomato soup and mix well.

8. Cook on HIGH for 30 seconds to reheat

9. Garnish each serving with a spoonful of the yogurt, a tomato slice and a sprig of dill before serving.

Cook's Notes

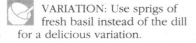 VARIATION: Use sprigs of fresh basil instead of the dill for a delicious variation.

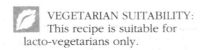 VEGETARIAN SUITABILITY: This recipe is suitable for lacto-vegetarians only.

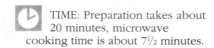 TIME: Preparation takes about 20 minutes, microwave cooking time is about 7½ minutes.

CREAM OF CUCUMBER
WITH MINT
SERVES 4

*This delicious summer soup can be eaten hot, or chilled
and served on ice for a refreshing change.*

---

3 large cucumbers
1 litre /1¾ pints vegetable stock
Salt and freshly ground black pepper
2-3 sprigs of fresh mint
280ml /½ pint single cream
60ml /2 fl oz natural yogurt

---

1. Cut one of the cucumbers in half and chop one half, unpeeled, into small dice. Set these small dice to one side.

2. Peel the remaining half and the other 2 cucumbers and roughly chop them into small pieces.

3. Put the peeled cucumber into a large bowl along with the stock, salt and pepper.

4. Remove the mint leaves from the sprigs and

Step 4 Remove the leaves from the sprigs of mint, putting the stalks only into the soup mixture.

Step 9 Using a sharp knife and a chopping board, chop the mint leaves finely.

put the stalks only into the bowl with the cucumber and stock.

5. Cover the bowl with cling film and pierce this several times with the tip of a sharp knife.

6. Cook the cucumber on HIGH for 6 minutes, or until it is tender.

7. Remove the mint stalks from the soup and, using a liquidiser or food processor, purée the soup until it is smooth.

8. Stir the single cream and the reserved cucumber dice into the puréed soup. Re-heat the soup on HIGH for 2 minutes.

9. Using a sharp knife, finely chop the mint leaves.

10. Sprinkle the chopped mint leaves over the soup just before serving, and stir a spoonful of yogurt into each serving for garnish.

Cook's Notes

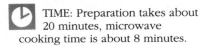 TIME: Preparation takes about 20 minutes, microwave cooking time is about 8 minutes.

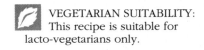 VEGETARIAN SUITABILITY: This recipe is suitable for lacto-vegetarians only.

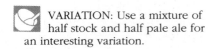 VARIATION: Use a mixture of half stock and half pale ale for an interesting variation.

SWEETCORN AND RED PEPPER SOUP

SERVES 4

This creamy soup has a definite bite to its flavour and can be made with either fresh or tinned sweetcorn kernels.

570ml /1 pint vegetable stock
4 medium potatoes, scrubbed and cut into
   even-sized pieces
1 bay leaf
Salt and freshly ground black pepper
15ml /1 tbsp butter or margarine
1 onion, peeled and chopped
1 large sweet red pepper
1 red chilli pepper
225g /8oz sweetcorn kernels
570ml /1 pint milk
Fresh chopped parsley for garnish

1. Put the stock into a large, microwave-proof bowl. Add the potatoes, bay leaf, salt and pepper.

2. Cover the bowl with cling film and pierce this several times with the tip of a sharp knife.

Step 5 Blend the potatoes and stock in a liquidiser or food processor until they make a smooth purée.

Step 7 Stir the onion, red pepper and chilli pepper into the melted butter, mixing well to ensure that they are evenly coated.

3. Cook the potatoes on HIGH for 10 minutes, or until they are tender.

4. Leave the potatoes to stand for 5 minutes.

5. Pour the potatoes and stock into a liquidiser or food processor, and purée until smooth.

6. Put the butter into the bowl and cook on HIGH for 30 seconds, or until melted.

7. Stir the onion, red pepper and chilli pepper into the melted butter and cook, uncovered, on HIGH for 2 minutes.

8. Add the puréed potatoes to the onions and peppers in the bowl along with the sweetcorn and the milk. Stir to blend thoroughly.

9. Re-heat the soup, uncovered, on HIGH for 2-3 minutes. Adjust the seasoning with a little more salt and pepper if desired, and garnish with the chopped parsley.

Cook's Notes

 COOK'S TIP: Great care must be taken when preparing fresh chilli peppers. Use clean rubber gloves and do not get the juice near eyes or mouth. Rinse eyes with lots of clear cold water should juice get into them.

SERVING IDEA: Serve with fresh, crusty rolls.

 TIME: Preparation takes about 20 minutes, microwave cooking time is about 14 minutes, with 5 minutes for standing.

VARIATION: Substitute soya milk for the fresh milk in this recipe to produce a soup which is suitable for vegans, but do not boil the soup after this addition .

PURÉE OF ASPARAGUS SOUP

SERVES 4

This thick and creamy soup makes full use of the delicate flavour of fresh summer asparagus.

1.3kg /3lbs asparagus, fresh or frozen, thawed
1 litre /1¾ pints vegetable stock
1.25ml /¼ tsp ground mace
Salt and freshly ground black pepper
280ml /½ pint single cream
140ml /¼ pint whipped cream
Sprinkling of ground mace

1. Trim the thick ends from the asparagus and cut away any tough outer skin.

2. Chop the spears into 2.5cm /1-inch pieces.

3. Put the chopped asparagus into a large, microwave-proof bowl along with the stock, mace, salt and pepper. Cover the bowl with cling film and pierce this several times with the tip of a sharp knife to allow the steam to escape.

4. Cook the asparagus on HIGH for 10 minutes, or until it is soft.

5. Leave the asparagus to stand for 5 minutes.

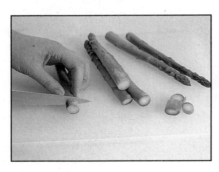

Step 1 Cut away the tough ends and any thick outer skin from the asparagus spears. Use a potato peeler or sharp knife to avoid cutting away too much of the tender, fleshy asparagus.

Step 2 Cut the asparagus into even-sized pieces approximately 2.5cm /1-inch in length.

Step 6 Blend the cooked asparagus pieces in a liquidiser or food processor until they become a smooth purée.

6. Using a liquidiser or food processor, blend the asparagus in the cooking liquid until it becomes a smooth purée.

7. Return the asparagus purée to the bowl and stir in the single cream.

8. Heat the soup for 3 minutes on MEDIUM to warm through. Do not boil the soup or the cream will curdle.

9. Garnish each serving with a spoonful of the whipped cream and a dusting of the ground mace.

Cook's Notes

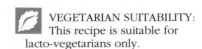 TIME: Preparation takes about 15 minutes, microwave cooking time is about 11 minutes, plus 5 minutes standing.

VEGETARIAN SUITABILITY: This recipe is suitable for lacto-vegetarians only.

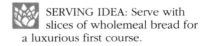 SERVING IDEA: Serve with slices of wholemeal bread for a luxurious first course.

BEETROOT AND SOUR CREAM SOUP WITH HORSERADISH

SERVES 4

This delicious and unusual soup
is worthy of any occasion

450g /1lb fresh beetroot
1 litre / 1¾ pints vegetable stock
225g /8oz turnips, peeled and cut into
    even-sized pieces
1 bay leaf
Salt and freshly ground black pepper
280ml /½ pint sour cream
15ml /1 tbsp grated fresh or bottled horseradish
Chopped chives for garnish

1. Put the unpeeled beetroots into a large bowl along with 60ml /2 fl oz of the stock.

2. Cover the bowl with cling film, and pierce this several times with the tip of a sharp knife.

3. Cook the beetroots on HIGH for 10 minutes, then leave them to stand for a further 10 minutes.

4. Carefully remove the skins from the cooked beetroots, using a small knife to cut away roots or rough skin.

Step 4 Carefully peel away the skins from the cooked beetroots.

Step 8 Blend the cooked soup in a liquidiser or food processor until it forms a smooth purée.

5. Cut the cooked beetroots into small pieces and put these, along with the turnips, remaining stock, bay leaf, salt and pepper back into the bowl.

6. Only partially cover the bowl this time with the cling film and cook on HIGH for 10 minutes, or until the turnip is tender.

7. Remove the bay leaf from the soup and discard this.

8. Using a liquidiser or food processor, blend the soup until it becomes a smooth purée.

9. Reserve 60ml /2 fl oz of the sour cream. Stir the remaining cream into the puréed soup along with the horseradish. Stir this mixture well to ensure that the horseradish is thoroughly blended.

10. Re-heat the soup, uncovered, on MEDIUM for 2-3 minutes, taking care not to boil the soup.

11. Serve the soup topped with the reserved cream and a sprinkling of fresh chives.

Cook's Notes

 TIME: Preparation takes about 20 minutes, microwave cooking time is about 23 minutes, with an extra 10 minutes for standing.

 FREEZING: This soup will freeze for up to 2 months.

 SERVING IDEA: Serve this soup with warm granary bread.

VEGETARIAN SUITABILITY: This recipe is suitable for lacto-vegetarians only.

MUSHROOM AND SHERRY CREAM SOUP

SERVES 4

This unusual soup is hearty and filling;
ideal for a cold day.

900g /2lbs mushrooms, trimmed and chopped
5-6 slices stale bread, crusts removed
700ml /1¼ pints vegetable stock
1 sprig fresh thyme
1 bay leaf
½ clove garlic, crushed
Salt and freshly ground black pepper
430ml /¾ pint single cream
60ml /2 fl oz sherry
140ml /¼ pint whipped cream
Grated nutmeg

1. Put the mushrooms into a large bowl and break the bread over them.

2. Add the stock, thyme, bay leaf, garlic, salt and pepper to the bowl. Partially cover the bowl with cling film and cook on HIGH for 7-8 minutes.

3. Stir the soup once or twice during the cooking time to break down the bread and blend the soup thoroughly.

Step 1 Break the bread into small pieces over the mushrooms in the bowl.

Step 3 Stir the soup with a wooden spoon 2 or 3 times during the cooking to blend it evenly.

Step 6 Add the cream and sherry to the soup purée, mixing it in to give a smooth finish.

4. Leave the soup to stand for 5 minutes.

5. Remove the bay leaf and the thyme. Using a liquidiser or food processor, blend the soup, little by little, until a smooth purée is produced.

6. Stir the cream and sherry into the soup purée, mixing it well with a balloon whisk.

7. Re-heat the soup, uncovered, on HIGH for 2-3 minutes.

8. Garnish each serving of soup with a spoonful of the whipped cream and a sprinkling of nutmeg.

Cook's Notes

TIME: Preparation takes about 20 minutes, microwave cooking time is about 11 minutes, plus 5 minutes standing time.

PREPARATION: If preferred, the bread can be made into breadcrumbs before adding to the soup.

VEGETARIAN SUITABILITY: This recipe is suitable for lacto-vegetarians only.

SPRING VEGETABLE SOUP

SERVES 4-6

*Early summer vegetables combine to produce a delightfully
light soup with a glorious fresh flavour.*

1 litre /1¾ pints vegetable stock
120g /4oz fresh shelled peas
3 large carrots, peeled and cut into thin
    5cm /2-inch strips
120g /4oz fresh French beans, cut into
    2.5cm /1-inch pieces
120g /4oz fresh asparagus, cut into 2.5cm /1-inch
    pieces
1 head green cabbage, finely shredded
3 spring onions, sliced
1 large red pepper, seeded and sliced
60ml /2 fl oz white wine, optional
Salt and freshly ground black pepper

1. Put the stock and the peas into a large
microwave-proof bowl.

Step 5 Stir the beans, asparagus and shredded cabbage into the soup mixture.

Step 6 Stir the red pepper slices and the wine into the soup.

2. Cover the bowl with cling film and pierce this
several times with the tip of a sharp knife.

3. Cook the peas on HIGH for 5 minutes.

4. Add the carrots to the peas and stock,
re-cover and cook for a further 5 minutes on
HIGH.

5. Add the beans, asparagus and cabbage,
re-cover and cook on HIGH for another 3
minutes.

6. Remove the cling film completely and stir in
the spring onions, red pepper slices and the
white wine, if used. Cook, uncovered, for 3
minutes on HIGH.

7. Season the soup with salt and pepper to taste
before serving.

Cook's Notes

 SERVING IDEA: Serve with
crunchy French toast.

 VEGETARIAN SUITABILITY:
This recipe is suitable for
vegans.

PREPARATION: Trim away
the hard core of the cabbage
and only use the finely shredded
leaves in this recipe.

TIME: Preparation takes about
25 minutes, microwave
cooking time is about 18 minutes.

TOMATO AND LEEK SOUP

SERVES 4-6

*This delicious combination of leeks and sweet tomatoes
is sure to become a firm favourite.*

2 large leeks, trimmed, washed and finely sliced
570ml /1 pint boiling water
570ml /1 pint fresh tomato juice
Dash of Tabasco or soy sauce
1.25ml /¼ tsp celery seeds
Shake of garlic powder
Salt and freshly ground black pepper
4 fresh tomatoes, skinned and sliced

1. Put the leeks and water into a large microwave-proof bowl, cover with cling film and pierce this several times with the tip of a sharp knife.

2. Cook the leeks for 5-6 minutes on HIGH.

3. Remove about half the leeks from the cooking liquid and set these aside.

4. Purée the remaining leeks and the cooking liquid in a liquidiser or food processor.

5. Pour the leek purée back into the bowl along with the tomato juice, Tabasco or soy sauce, the celery seeds and garlic powder.

Step 3 Carefully remove half the cooked leeks from the cooking liquid and set them aside.

Step 4 Using a liquidiser or food processor, purée the remaining leeks and the cooking liquid until smooth.

Step 8 Carefully stir the reserved leeks and the slices of tomato into the hot soup, making sure not to break the tomato slices too much.

6. Re-cover and cook for a further 3-4 minutes on HIGH until the mixture is hot. Stir this mixture once during the cooking time.

7. Season the soup with the salt and pepper.

8. Stir in the reserved leeks and the sliced tomatoes.

9. Cover the bowl once again with cling film and puncture as before. Cook on HIGH for 3-5 minutes, or until the soup is piping hot.

10. Stir the soup before serving.

Cook's Notes

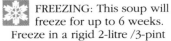 FREEZING: This soup will freeze for up to 6 weeks. Freeze in a rigid 2-litre /3-pint container.

 SERVING IDEA: Serve with crusty French bread and vegetarian Cheddar cheese.

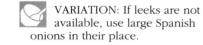 VARIATION: If leeks are not available, use large Spanish onions in their place.

PARSNIP AND CARROT SOUP

SERVES 4

A delicious and wholesome country soup which makes use of that favourite vegetable, the humble parsnip.

225g /8oz parsnips, peeled
225g /8oz carrots, peeled
280ml /½ pint vegetable stock or water
Salt and freshly ground black pepper
Pinch of nutmeg
570ml /1 pint milk
1 small bunch of chives, finely chopped
60ml /4 tbsps single cream

---

1. Grate the parsnips and carrots using a coarse cheese grater.

2. Put the grated parsnip and carrot into a large microwave-proof bowl along with the stock, salt, pepper and nutmeg.

3. Cover the bowl with cling film and pierce this several times with the tip of a sharp knife. Cook on HIGH for 10 minutes, stirring twice during the cooking time.

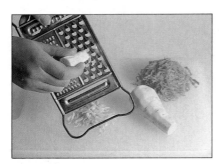

Step 1 Using a coarse cheese grater, grate the parsnips and carrots.

Step 5 Blend the soup to a smooth purée using a liquidiser or food processor.

Step 6 Stir the chives into the puréed soup, making sure that they are evenly distributed.

4. Stir the milk into the vegetables and stock and allow to stand for 1 minute.

5. Pour the soup into a liquidiser or food processor and blend to a smooth purée.

6. Return the soup to the bowl and stir in the chives. Cook on HIGH for 4-5 minutes, until the soup is very hot but not quite boiling.

7. Stir the cream into the soup just before serving.

Cook's Notes

PREPARATION: If a very smooth soup is required, the puréed soup can be strained through a metal sieve before the chives are added.

SERVING IDEA: Serve with crisp French sticks and vegetarian cheese.

VEGETARIAN SUITABILITY: This recipe is suitable for lacto-vegetarians only.

FREEZING: This soup will freeze for up to 3 months if frozen before the final addition of the cream. This can be added just before serving.

TIME: Preparation takes about 10 minutes, microwave cooking time is about 10 minutes, plus 1 minute standing time.

SALAD SOUP

SERVES 4-6

A delicious, unusual soup which is as refreshing as its name implies.

2-3 medium potatoes, peeled and diced
6 spring onions, finely chopped
½ head of lettuce, washed and shredded
120g /4oz fresh spinach leaves, washed, trimmed and shredded
1 bunch watercress, washed, trimmed and chopped
½ cucumber, peeled and grated or diced
30ml /2 tbsps chopped, fresh parsley
430ml /¾ pint vegetable stock
570ml /1 pint milk
Pinch nutmeg
Pinch cayenne pepper
Salt and freshly ground black pepper
140ml /¼ pint single cream
Natural yogurt and finely chopped parsley for garnish

1. Put the potatoes into a large, microwave-proof bowl. Cover the bowl with cling film and pierce this several times with the tip of a sharp knife.

2. Cook the potatoes on HIGH for 7 minutes, or until they are soft. Stir the potatoes twice during the cooking time.

Step 1 Cover the potatoes in the bowl with cling film and pierce this several times with the tip of a sharp knife to prevent the cling film from bursting.

Step 3 Stir the onions, lettuce, spinach, watercress, cucumber, parsley and stock into the bowl of cooked potatoes. Mix well with a wooden spoon.

Step 5 Using a liquidiser or food processor, blend the soup to a smooth purée. Purée a little of the soup at a time to ensure an even texture.

3. Add all the remaining vegetables, the herbs and the stock to the potatoes. Re-cover the bowl and continue cooking on HIGH for a further 5 minutes.

4. Stir the milk into the soup and sprinkle in the nutmeg and cayenne pepper. Season to taste with salt and pepper.

5. Pour the soup into a liquidiser or food processor, and blend until smooth.

6. Return the soup to the bowl and re-heat, uncovered, for a further 5-6 minutes on HIGH, making sure that the soup is very hot but does not boil.

7. Just before serving, stir in the natural yoghurt and sprinkle on the chopped parsley.

Cook's Notes

 TIME: Preparation takes about 10 minutes, microwave cooking time is about 18 minutes.

FREEZING: This soup will freeze well for up to 3 months.

 SERVING IDEA: Serve with hot garlic bread.

CREAMY SPINACH SOUP
SERVES 4-6

*The wonderful combination of spinach and cream in this soup
could not fail to please even the most fussy guest.*

900g /2lbs fresh spinach, trimmed and washed
30g /2 tbsps butter or margarine
1 shallot, finely chopped
30g /1oz plain flour
700ml /1¼ pints vegetable stock
1.25ml /¼ tsp dried marjoram
1 bay leaf
Pinch grated nutmeg
Salt and freshly ground black pepper
Squeeze lemon juice
430ml /¾ pint milk
140ml /¼ pint single cream
Thin slices of lemon, or chopped hard-boiled
    egg for garnish

1. Put the spinach into a large bowl. Cover with cling film and pierce this several times with the tip of a sharp knife.

2. Cook the spinach on HIGH for 5 minutes, until it is just wilting.

3. Put the butter into another large bowl along with the shallot. Cover as before, and cook for 5

Step 4 Stir the flour into the melted butter and onion with a wooden spoon, mixing it well to blend it thoroughly.

Step 9 Blend the soup in a liquidiser or food processor until it is smooth and thick. This may have to be done in several batches.

minutes on HIGH, until the shallot is soft and golden, but not brown.

4. Stir the flour into the onion and melted butter, blending it thoroughly with a wooden spoon.

5. Cook for 2 minutes on HIGH.

6. Gradually add the stock, marjoram, bay leaf and grated nutmeg, mixing well between additions to keep the soup smooth.

7. Cook, uncovered, for 2 minutes on HIGH, stirring occasionally until the soup has thickened.

8. Remove the bay leaf and add the spinach, salt, pepper and lemon juice. Cook for 3 minutes on HIGH.

9. Stir the milk into the soup, then pour the soup into a liquidiser or food processor and blend until smooth. This may have to be done in 2-3 batches.

10. Re-heat the soup on HIGH for 3 minutes, adjust the seasonings and stir in the cream.

11. Garnish with slices of lemon, or chopped hard-boiled egg.

Cook's Notes

 TIME: Preparation takes about 15 minutes, microwave cooking time is about 21 minutes.

VEGETARIAN SUITABILITY: This recipe is suitable for lacto-vegetarians only.

 FREEZING: This soup will freeze successfully for up to 3 months, without the garnish.

VARIATION: Use a mixture of watercress and spinach for a spicy variation.

SERVING IDEA: Serve with crunchy wholemeal croutons.

CHEDDAR CHEESE SOUP

SERVES 4

*An unusual soup which is ideal for using
up any pieces of leftover cheese.*

225g /8oz vegetarian Cheddar cheese, or mixture
  of different types of hard vegetarian cheeses
45g /1½oz butter
1 carrot, peeled and diced
2 sticks of celery, diced
30g /1oz plain flour
430ml /¾ pint vegetable stock
1 bay leaf
1.25ml /¼ tsp dried thyme
570ml /1 pint milk
Chopped parsley to garnish

Step 9 Blend the soup liquid and the cheese together to ensure even mixing.

1. Grate the cheese finely into a bowl and if more than one variety is used, mix them together.

2. Put the butter, carrot and celery into a bowl. Cover the bowl with cling film and pierce this several times with the tip of a sharp knife.

3. Cook for 5 minutes on HIGH.

4. Stir the flour into the vegetables, mixing well with a wooden spoon to blend thoroughly.

Step 4 Stir the flour into the cooked vegetables, mixing with a wooden spoon to blend thoroughly

5. Gradually mix in the stock, stirring well between additions to ensure a smooth mixture.

6. Add the bay leaf and the thyme, and cook, uncovered, on HIGH for 10 minutes, stirring twice during the cooking time to prevent lumps from forming.

7. Stir the milk into the vegetable and stock mixture and cook, uncovered, on HIGH for a further 5 minutes.

8. Pour 140ml /¼ pint of the soup liquid into the bowl of grated cheese.

9. Stir the cheese and soup liquid together to blend thoroughly.

10. Return the cheese mixture to the rest of the soup liquid and cook, uncovered, for 2 minutes on HIGH.

11. If the cheese has not completely melted after this time, cook for a further 1-2 minutes.

12. Sprinkle the chopped parsley over the soup and serve.

Cook's Notes

 TIME: Preparation takes about 10 minutes, microwave cooking takes about 23 minutes.

VEGETARIAN SUITABILITY: This recipe is suitable for lacto-vegetarians only.

SERVING IDEA: Serve with caraway or rye bread.

VEGETARIAN MICROWAVE COOKING

CHAPTER ~ 2

· VEGETARIAN · STARTERS ·

ASPARAGUS WITH ORANGE HOLLANDAISE

SERVES 4

*Simplicity is often the making of a classic dish, and serving fresh
asparagus in this way is certainly a classic combination.*

900g /2lbs fresh asparagus spears
60g /2oz butter
Grated rind and juice of ½ orange
Juice of ½ lemon
1 small bay leaf
1 blade of mace
3 egg yolks
Salt and freshly ground black pepper

1. Trim away any thick, tough ends from the asparagus and rinse them well.

2. Put the asparagus into a shallow casserole dish with 4 tbsps of water.

3. Cover the dish and cook the asparagus on HIGH for 7 minutes, or until just tender. Leave to stand whilst preparing the sauce.

4. Put some cold water into a shallow bowl along with several ice cubes to keep the water very cold.

5. Put the butter into a jug or small bowl and cook for 1 minute on HIGH until it has melted.

Step 9 Strain the juice mixture into the egg and butter mixture through a nylon sieve, to remove the bay leaf and mace.

Step 12
Immediately the sauce has reached the required consistency, stand it in its bowl in the iced water to prevent further cooking.

6. Put the orange juice, lemon juice, bay leaf and mace into another bowl and heat for 1 minute on HIGH.

7. In a larger bowl, beat together the egg yolks, orange rind and seasonings.

8. Pour the melted butter into the egg yolk mixture and mix well with a small whisk.

9. Strain the juice into the butter and egg mixture through a small nylon sieve and whisk well.

10. Put the sauce mixture into the oven and cook on HIGH for 15 seconds. Remove from the oven and whisk well.

11. Repeat this process until the sauce has thickened, this should take about 2 minutes.

12. Immediately the sauce has reached the required consistency, stand it in its bowl in the iced water to prevent further cooking.

13. Arrange the asparagus on serving plates and pour equal amounts of sauce over.

Cook's Notes

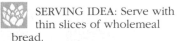 SERVING IDEA: Serve with thin slices of wholemeal bread.

TIME: Preparation takes about 10 minutes, microwave cooking time is about 11 minutes.

VEGETARIAN SUITABILITY: This recipe is suitable for lacto-vegetarians only.

STUFFED TOMATOES PROVENÇAL

SERVES 4

A refreshing starter, ideal as a first course to a rich meal.

4 large ripe tomatoes
30g /1oz butter or vegetable margarine
1 clove of garlic, crushed
1 shallot, finely chopped
225g /8oz mushrooms, finely chopped
15ml /1 tbsp white wine
45g /1½oz fresh white breadcrumbs
5ml /1 tsp freshly chopped parsley
5ml /1 tsp freshly chopped basil
1.25ml /¼ tsp dried thyme
1 tsp Dijon mustard
Salt and freshly ground black pepper
Parsley sprigs to garnish

1. Cut the rounded ends off the tomatoes to form caps. Remove the green cores from the other end.

2. Carefully scoop the flesh and seeds out of each tomato and strain this through a nylon sieve to remove excess juice.

3. Put the butter into a small bowl along with the garlic and the shallot. Cook for 2 minutes on HIGH.

Step 2 Carefully scoop the flesh and seeds out of each tomato.

Step 5 Put the breadcrumbs, herbs, seasonings, mustard and tomato pulp into the onion and mushroom mixture and mix well to prepare the stuffing.

Step 7 Arrange the filled tomatoes on a shallow dish with their caps placed over the stuffing at a slight angle.

4. Stir the mushrooms and wine into the shallot mixture and cook for a further 2 minutes on HIGH.

5. Add the breadcrumbs, herbs, mustard, seasonings and tomato pulp to the onion and mushroom mixture, and mix well.

6. Fill each tomato cavity with equal amounts of the stuffing mixture.

7. Arrange the filled tomatoes on a shallow dish and place the caps on at a slight angle.

8. Cook, uncovered, for 2 minutes on HIGH, and serve with a sprig of parsley.

Cook's Notes

 PREPARATION: If preferred, the skins can be removed from the tomatoes before the centres are scooped out.

TIME: Preparation takes about 10 minutes, microwave cooking time is about 6 minutes.

SERVING IDEA: Serve with a mixed salad.

CELERIAC À LA MOUTARDE

SERVES 4

*This delicious starter could also be used as a
light lunch or supper for two.*

1 large root of celeriac, peeled
30ml /2 tbsps white wine
45g /1½oz butter
45g /1½oz plain flour
570ml /1 pint milk
60ml /4 tbsps Dijon mustard
15ml /1 tbsp celery seed
Salt and freshly ground black pepper
30g /1oz butter
60ml /4 tbsps dry breadcrumbs

1. Cut the celeriac into 5mm /¼-inch slices and
then into sticks about 2.5cm /1-inch long.

2. Put the celeriac sticks into a bowl along with
the wine. Cover the bowl with cling film and
pierce this several times with the tip of a sharp
knife. Cook for 4 minutes on HIGH.

3. Put the butter into a small, deep bowl and
cook on HIGH for 1 minute to melt.

4. Stir in the flour and cook for a further minute
on HIGH.

5. Stir the milk, mustard, celery seed and
seasonings into the flour and butter mixture.

6. Drain the celeriac and reserve the cooking
liquor. Add this to the sauce mixture. Mix well

Step 1 Cut the
celeriac into
5mm /¼-inch slices
and then cut each
slice into
2.5cm /1-inch
strips.

Step 4 Add the
flour to the melted
butter and blend it
well with a wooden
spoon to form a
roux.

Step 6 Drain the
celeriac and reserve
the cooking liquor.

and cook the sauce for 3 minutes on HIGH,
stirring after each minute until it is thick and
smooth.

7. Put the celeriac slices into 4 serving dishes
and coat with equal amounts of the sauce.

8. Heat a browning dish in the microwave oven
on HIGH for 3-4 minutes.

9. Put the 30g /1oz of butter onto the dish to
melt, then add the dried breadcrumbs. Cook on
HIGH until the crumbs are golden brown.

10. Sprinkle the crumbs over the celeriac and
sauce and heat through for 2 minutes on HIGH
before serving.

Cook's Notes

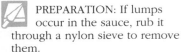 PREPARATION: If lumps
occur in the sauce, rub it
through a nylon sieve to remove
them.

 TIME: Preparation takes about
10 minutes, microwave
cooking time is about 15 minutes.

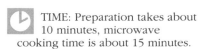 SERVING IDEA: Serve with a
small mixed salad.

VINAIGRETTE DE JARDIN

SERVES 4

*Healthy, fresh vegetables with a tangy dressing; this interesting
starter would make a delicious side dish, too.*

120g /4oz mange tout
2 courgettes, washed and sliced into rounds
120g /4oz broccoli florets
120g /4oz cauliflower florets
2 carrots, peeled and sliced into rounds
4 tomatoes
1 yellow pepper
4 spring onions, trimmed and cut into diagonal
   strips
90ml /6 tbsps olive oil
30ml /2 tbsps white wine vinegar
15ml /1 tbsp Dijon mustard
15ml /1 tbsp fresh, chopped herbs (eg chives,
   parsley, basil)
Salt and freshly ground black pepper

1. Cook each of the following vegetables on
HIGH, in 2 tbsps water, for the following times:
mange tout 2 minutes; courgettes 3 minutes;
broccoli 3 minutes; cauliflower 5 minutes; carrots
5 minutes. Drain each vegetable after cooking
and plunge into cold water to freshen. When
cool, drain them completely.

Step 5 Quarter the skinned tomatoes, remove and discard the seeds.

Step 11 Using a small whisk or fork, whisk the dressing ingredients together in a jug or bowl until they are thick and pale.

2. Put 570ml /1 pint water into a basin and
bring to the boil on HIGH for 4-5 minutes.

3. Cut a small cross in the rounded end of each
tomato and plunge them into the boiling water
for a few seconds.

4. Remove the tomatoes from the water and
carefully peel away the skins with a sharp knife.

5. Quarter the tomatoes and remove and discard
the seeds.

6. Cut the tomato flesh into thin slices.

7. Cut the pepper in half and remove the seeds.
Cut the flesh into thin slices.

8. Put the tomato and pepper strips and the
sliced spring onion into a large bowl.

9. Add the drained vegetables and mix well.

10. Put the oil, vinegar, mustard, herbs and
seasoning into a small bowl.

11. Whisk the dressing ingredients together
thoroughly with a small whisk or fork until thick
and pale.

12. Pour the dressing over the bowl of mixed
vegetables and stir well. Leave to marinate for
2-3 hours before serving.

Cook's Notes

 TIME: Preparation takes about
15 minutes, microwave
cooking time is about 20 minutes.

VEGETARIAN SUITABILITY:
This recipe is suitable for
vegans.

GARLIC MUSHROOMS

SERVES 4

An established favourite, this recipe is incredibly quick and easy to prepare when using a microwave oven.

30g /1oz butter or vegetable margarine
2 cloves of garlic, crushed
1.25ml /¼ tsp freshly chopped thyme
1.25ml /¼ tsp freshly chopped sage
1.25ml /¼ tsp freshly chopped parsley
45ml /3 tbsps white wine
Salt and freshly ground black pepper
675g /1½lbs mushrooms, cleaned and quartered
8 slices of French bread, 1.5cm /½-inch thick
30ml /2 tbsps chopped chives to garnish

---

1. Put the butter or margarine into a large bowl and heat for 1 minute on HIGH, until it melts.

2. Add the crushed garlic to the bowl and cook

Step 2 Cook the crushed garlic in the melted butter until it is soft and golden, but not browned.

Step 3 Using a wooden spoon, carefully stir the herbs, wine, seasonings and mushrooms into the cooked garlic, mixing well to ensure that the garlic flavour is evenly blended.

for 2 minutes on HIGH, or until it is soft and golden, but not browned.

3. Using a wooden spoon, stir the herbs, wine, seasonings and mushrooms into the cooked garlic, mixing well to spread the flavour evenly.

4. Cook, uncovered, on HIGH for 3 minutes, or until the mushrooms are cooked, but not soft. Stir the mushrooms once during this cooking time.

5. Put the bread onto a shallow dish or plate.

6. Heat on HIGH for 1 minute.

7. Pile equal amounts of the mushroom mixture onto each slice of warm bread.

8. Garnish with the chopped chives.

Cook's Notes

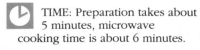 TIME: Preparation takes about 5 minutes, microwave cooking time is about 6 minutes.

 VEGETARIAN SUITABILITY: This recipe is suitable for vegans.

PREPARATION: This recipe can be prepared well in advance and reheated just before serving.

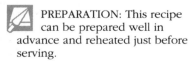 SERVING IDEA: Serve with sliced tomatoes.

VARIATION: Wild mushrooms are often available at good greengrocers or in supermarkets; they make a delicious variation to this recipe.

PASTA AND ASPARAGUS SALAD

SERVES 4

This elegant green salad is a wonderful way of making the most of asparagus, that most luxurious of vegetables.

120g /4oz tagliatelle
450g /1lb asparagus, trimmed and cut into
   2.5cm /1-inch pieces
2 courgettes, cut into 5cm /2-inch sticks
30g /2 tbsps freshly chopped parsley
30g /2 tbsps freshly chopped marjoram
1 lemon, peeled and segmented
Grated rind and juice of 1 lemon
90ml /3 fl oz salad oil
Pinch sugar, optional
Salt and freshly ground black pepper
1 head crisp lettuce
1 head endive or frisée lettuce

1. Put the pasta into a large bowl along with 570ml /1 pint of hot water, a pinch of salt and a teaspoon of vegetable oil.

2. Cover the bowl with cling film and pierce this several times with the tip of a sharp knife.

3. Cook the pasta on HIGH for 6 minutes, then leave to stand, still covered, for a further 8 minutes.

Step 8 Mix the pasta, cooked vegetables, herbs and lemon segments together in a large bowl, stirring carefully to avoid breaking the vegetables too much.

Step 10 Stir the lemon and oil dressing into the pasta and vegetables, taking great care not to break up any of the ingredients too much.

4. Drain the pasta and leave to cool completely.

5. Put the asparagus into a large bowl along with 140ml /¼ pint of water. Cook on HIGH for 3 minutes.

6. Add the courgettes to the asparagus and stir gently with a wooden spoon. Cook on HIGH for a further 3 minutes.

7. Drain the asparagus and courgettes into a collander and rinse them in cold water to refresh.

8. Put the pasta, cooked vegetables, herbs and lemon segments into a large bowl, and mix them together carefully to avoid breaking up the vegetables.

9. Mix together the lemon rind, juice, oil, sugar if used, salt and pepper.

10. Pour the lemon and oil dressing over the ingredients in the bowl and mix well to coat the vegetables and pasta evenly.

11. Arrange the lettuce and endive on serving plates and pile equal quantities of the asparagus and pasta mixture onto each plate.

Cook's Notes

TIME: Preparation takes about 15 minutes, microwave cooking time is about 11 minutes, plus 8 minutes standing time for the pasta.

COOK'S TIP: Put the ingredients for the lemon dressing into a clean screw top jar and shake vigorously to blend thoroughly.

VEGETARIAN SUITABILITY: This recipe is suitable for vegans.

DANISH EGG SALAD

SERVES 4

This delicious starter is also ideal for a light lunch or supper for two.

4 free-range eggs
30ml /2 tbsps single cream
Salt and freshly ground black pepper
30g /1oz butter
225g /8oz frozen peas, thawed
280ml /½ pint soured cream
60ml /2 fl oz mayonnaise
30ml/2 tbsps freshly chopped dill
Paprika
6 sticks of celery, trimmed and diced
120g /4oz diced vegetarian cheese of own choice
3 spring onions, chopped
1 head Chinese leaves, shredded

1. Beat the eggs and the cream together in a small bowl. Season with the salt and pepper.

2. Heat a browning dish for 5 minutes on HIGH.

3. Melt the butter in the browning dish for 1 minute on HIGH.

4. Pour half the egg mixture into the hot dish and cook the omelette on one side for 1 minute on HIGH.

5. Carefully turn the omelette over using a fish slice or spatula. Cook for a further minute on HIGH.

6. Repeat this procedure with the remaining egg mixture.

7. Put the peas into a small bowl and cook them

Step 11 Shred the cooked omelettes into 0.75cm /¼-inch wide, 5cm /2-inch long strips.

in 2 tbsps of water for 1 minute on HIGH. Drain and rinse under cold water to refresh.

8. Put the soured cream, mayonnaise, dill, paprika and a little salt into a bowl and whisk with a small balloon whisk until smooth and evenly blended.

9. Reserve 30ml /2 tbsps of the soured cream dressing. Mix the remaining dressing with the peas, celery, diced cheese, cucumber and spring onions.

10. Arrange the Chinese leaves onto serving plates and pile equal quantities of the vegetable salad on top of these.

11. Using a sharp knife, shred the omelettes into thin strips.

12. Arrange the omelette strips over the vegetable salad and drizzle the reserved soured cream dressing over to serve.

Cook's Notes

TIME: Preparation takes about 20 minutes, microwave cooking time is about 7 minutes.

VEGETARIAN SUITABILITY: This recipe is suitable for lacto-vegetarians only.

PREPARATION: If you do not have a browning dish, the omelette can be cooked in a shallow 17.5cm /7-inch round dish. This will not have to be pre-heated, but the omelette will not brown.

VARIATION: Use freshly chopped tarragon in place of the dill in this recipe and a mild vegetarian brie for a delicious French variation.

WARM SALAD WITH AVOCADO, GRAPES, BLUE CHEESE AND WALNUTS

SERVES 4

*This colourful salad is ideal as a
sophisticated starter for a gourmet meal.*

1 head curly endive
1 head chicory
1 head radicchio
1 bunch lamb's lettuce or watercress
1 head iceberg lettuce
2 avocados
150g /6oz black grapes
4 tbsps mixed chopped fresh herbs of choice
120g /4oz walnut pieces
120g /4oz vegetarian blue cheese, diced or
    crumbled
45ml /3 tbsps walnut oil and grapeseed oil,
    mixed
30ml /2 tbsps lemon vinegar
Pinch of sugar

1. Tear the endive, chicory and radicchio into
small pieces. Put these pieces into a large bowl.

2. If using lamb's lettuce, separate the leaves; if
using watercress, remove any thick stalks. Put
this into the bowl with the endive mixture.

3. Shred the iceberg lettuce with a sharp knife.
adding this to the bowl of salad ingredients.

4. Peel the avocados and cut into neat slices.
Carefully toss these slices into the bowl of mixed
salad.

Step 5 Remove the
pips from the
halved grapes using
the point of a sharp
knife.

5. Cut the grapes in half and remove any pips.
Add the grapes to the bowl of salad.

6. Finally, toss the chopped herbs, walnut
pieces and diced cheese into the salad, taking
great care not to break up the pieces of avocado.

7. Put the oils, vinegar and sugar into a clean
screw top jar. Screw the lid on tightly and shake
the jar vigorously until the dressing is well
blended.

8. Toss the salad dressing into the mixed salad
using two spoons.

9. Arrange the salad in equal amounts on 4
serving plates.

10. Heat each plate on HIGH for 1-2 minutes
just before serving.

Cook's Notes

VARIATION: For a delicious
vegan alternative, substitute
the blue cheese with 150g /6oz of
wild mushrooms that have been
cooked in 2 tbsps of white wine,
drained and then chilled.

PREPARATION: It is important
to tear the endive, chicory
and radicchio by hand as the
edges will discolour if they are cut
with a knife.

VEGETARIAN SUITABILITY:
This recipe is suitable for
lacto-vegetarians only. See
'Variation' for a vegan alternative.

COURGETTE AND CARROT TERRINE

SERVES 4-6

*This colourful terrine makes a sophisticated starter
which is sure to impress family or guests.*

6-8 large, green cabbage leaves
340g /12oz low fat vegetarian curd cheese
4 slices white bread, crusts removed
2 eggs, beaten
140ml /¼ pint double cream, lightly whipped
1 bunch chives, snipped
Salt and freshly ground black pepper
1-2 carrots, peeled and cut into thin strips
1-2 courgettes, washed and cut into thin strips
280ml /½ pint soured cream or natural yogurt
140ml /¼ pint mayonnaise
2 tomatoes, peeled, seeded and cut into small
  dice
30ml /2 tbsps lemon juice or white wine
Pinch of sugar (optional)

1. Trim the thick spines away from the cabbage leaves by cutting a triangular section out of each one.

2. Put the leaves into a shallow dish or bowl with 30ml /2 tbsps of water and a little salt. Cover the dish with cling film and pierce this several times with the tip of a sharp knife.

3. Cook the cabbage leaves for 1 minute on HIGH until they are wilting, but are not soft.

4. Put the cheese into a large bowl.

5. Either grate the bread to make crumbs, or use a food processor.

6. Put the breadcrumbs into the bowl with the cheese, eggs, cream, chives, salt and pepper. Mix these ingredients together thoroughly.

7. Put the carrots into a bowl with 30ml /2 tbsps water. Cover the bowl with cling film and pierce this several times with the tip of a sharp knife. Cook for 3 minutes on HIGH.

8. Remove the cling film and add the courgettes to the bowl. Cook, uncovered, on HIGH for a further 2 minutes.

9. Drain the carrots and courgettes and dry these vegetables well.

10. Leaving at least 5cm /2 inches of leaf hanging over the upper edges, carefully line a 450g /1lb loaf dish with the cabbage leaves, overlapping each leaf slightly to ensure that no gaps appear when the terrine is turned out.

11. Put one quarter of the cheese mixture into the loaf dish and spread this evenly.

12. Place one layer of carrot over the cheese layer.

13. Cover the carrots with a further quarter of the cheese mixture and top this with a layer of courgettes.

14. Repeat this procedure until all the cheese mixture and vegetables are used up.

15. Fold the cabbage leaves over the cheese and vegetables, making sure that they are completely covered by the overlapping leaves.

16. Cover the dish with cling film and puncture this several times as before.

17. Stand the loaf dish in another shallow dish of hot water.

18. Put the terrine into the microwave oven, still standing in the dish of water, and cook on MEDIUM for 10 minutes. Allow to stand for 10 minutes, then refrigerate before serving.

19. Put the soured cream, mayonnaise, tomatoes, lemon juice, sugar if used, salt and pepper, into a bowl and mix together thoroughly to make a sauce.

20. Serve the terrine in slices with a little of the sauce.

67

SPINACH-STUFFED ARTICHOKE HEARTS

SERVES 4

*This flavoursome way of serving an unusual vegetable
is made extra easy with the microwave oven.*

4 globe artichokes
450g /1lb fresh spinach, stalks removed and
    washed
15g /¹/₂oz butter or margarine
1 shallot, peeled and finely chopped
2 slices bread, made into fine breadcrumbs
1 egg, beaten
140ml /¹/₄ pint double cream
Pinch nutmeg
Pinch cayenne pepper
Salt
60g /2oz vegetarian Cheddar cheese, grated
60ml /4 tbsps double cream

1. Cut the tops off each artichoke to about
halfway down and trim the stalk end to allow
the artichokes to sit upright.

2. Trim away any tough, inedible leaves and cut
out as much of the fluffy 'choke' as possible to
form a firm shell.

3. Put the artichokes into a casserole dish with
some water and cook for 10 minutes on HIGH,
or until the hearts are tender.

4. Trim any remaining 'choke' away. Drain and
cool.

5. Put the spinach into a bowl and cover this
with cling film. Pierce this several times with the
tip of a sharp knife.

6. Cook the spinach on HIGH for 5 minutes.
Drain well, squeezing any excess water out of
the spinach with your hands.

Step 2 Trim away
any tough, inedible
leaves that remain
and cut out as
much of the fluffy
'choke' as possible,
to form a good
artichoke shell.

7. Put the butter into a bowl and cook on HIGH
for 30 seconds.

8. Cook the shallot in the melted butter for 1
minute until it is golden and soft, but not brown.

9. Mix the drained spinach into the shallot along
with the breadcrumbs, egg, cream, nutmeg,
cayenne pepper and the salt.

10. Pile equal amounts of this filling onto the
artichoke shells.

11. Arrange the filled artichokes in a circle on a
shallow dish or plate.

12. Cook the artichokes on MEDIUM for 5
minutes, or until the filling has set.

13. In a small bowl, mix the remaining cream
and the cheese together.

14. Divide this mixture evenly over the top of
each filled artichoke.

15. Cook for a further 2 minutes on MEDIUM to
melt the cheese, then sprinkle with a little grated
nutmeg before serving.

Cook's Notes

 TIME: Preparation takes about
25 minutes, microwave
cooking time is about 19-20
minutes.

VARIATION: Use any other
variety of vegetarian hard
cheese in the topping.

VEGETARIAN SUITABILITY:
This recipe is suitable for
lacto-vegetarians only.

AUBERGINE CAVIAR

SERVES 4

*This novel starter is an interesting and different way
of serving this delicious vegetable.*

1 large or 2 small aubergines
60ml /4 tbsps walnut oil
Juice of ½ lemon
1 clove garlic, minced or crushed
Pinch cayenne pepper
Freshly ground sea salt
2 hard-boiled eggs (optional)
1 small onion, finely chopped
30ml /2 tbsps freshly chopped parsley
4-8 slices French bread, toasted

Step 2 Score the cut half of each aubergine half using a sharp knife. Cut criss-cross lines deeply into the flesh in a diamond pattern, taking care not to cut through the skins.

1. Remove the stalk from the aubergine and cut it in half lengthways.

2. Using a small, sharp knife, score and cut the flesh on each half of the aubergine, at about 1.25cm /¼-inch intervals, diagonally, first in one direction, and then in the other.

3. Sprinkle each cut surface with a little salt and leave to stand for 30 minutes to draw out any bitterness and excess water.

4. Rinse the aubergines thoroughly and pat them dry with a clean cloth.

5. Put the aubergine halves into a covered casserole dish and cook on HIGH for 7-9 minutes, or until tender, but still retaining a good shape.

6. Cool the aubergines completely then chop them roughly.

7. Put the chopped aubergine into a food processor along with the lemon juice, garlic, cayenne pepper and salt. Blend together until smooth.

8. Very gradually, and with the food processor set on a moderate speed, pour the oil through the feed tube onto the aubergine purée.

9. Adjust the seasoning and chill the aubergine mixture.

10. Cut the eggs, if used, in half and separate the whites from the yolks.

11. Push the yolks through a nylon sieve.

12. Finely chop the egg whites.

13. Pile equal amounts of the aubergine caviar onto each slice of the French bread and top with the chopped onion, parsley and chopped egg white.

14. Sprinkle over the sieved egg yolk just before serving.

Cook's Notes

VARIATION: Use a 5cm /2-inch piece of cucumber instead of the eggs in this recipe, chopping this into very small dice and sprinkling it with a little black pepper before using it to garnish this dish.

 TIME: Preparation takes about 20 minutes, microwave cooking time is between 7 and 9 minutes.

 SERVING IDEA: Serve with a side salad.

VEGETARIAN SUITABILITY: This recipe is suitable for lacto-vegetarians, or for vegans if the eggs are omitted.

BROCCOLI AND HAZELNUT TERRINE

SERVES 4-6

This colourful, crunchy terrine is full of flavour and protein.

6-8 large whole spinach leaves
450g /1lb broccoli
2 eggs, beaten
180g /6oz low fat vegetarian curd cheese
280ml /$^1/_2$ pint double cream, lightly whipped
4 slices white bread, made into fine breadcrumbs
1 shallot, peeled and finely chopped
Pinch dried thyme
Pinch nutmeg
Salt and freshly ground black pepper
120g /4oz hazelnuts, lightly toasted then finely chopped
280ml /$^1/_2$ pint mayonnaise
140ml /$^1/_4$ pint natural yogurt
Grated rind and juice of 1 lemon
Pinch cayenne pepper
Salt

1. Trim away any coarse stalks from the spinach, taking care to leave the leaves whole. Wash the leaves and put them into a shallow dish with a pinch of salt.

2. Cover the dish with cling film and pierce this several times with the tip of a sharp knife. Cook the spinach leaves on HIGH for 1 minute, until they are just wilted.

3. Drain the leaves and carefully pat them as dry as possible.

Step 8 Spoon the broccoli and cheese mixture carefully into the lined loaf dish, pressing it down firmly with the back of a spoon.

Step 11 Stand the completed terrine on a tray along with a ramekin filled with water, before cooking.

4. Leaving at least 5cm /2 inches of leaf hanging over the upper edges, line a 450g /1lb loaf dish with the spinach. Overlap each leaf slightly to prevent gaps from forming when the filling is added.

5. Chop the broccoli finely.

6. Put the eggs, cheese, cream, breadcrumbs, shallot, thyme, nutmeg, salt and pepper into a large bowl and mix these ingredients together thoroughly.

7. Stir in the broccoli and hazelnuts, mixing well to incorporate evenly.

8. Spoon the cheese mixture into the lined loaf dish, packing it down well, but taking great care not to dislodge the lining of spinach leaves.

9. Carefully fold the spinach leaves over the top of the terrine.

10. Cover the dish with a double layer of cling film and pierce this several times as before.

11. Stand the loaf dish on a tray along with a ramekin of water.

12. Cook the terrine on MEDIUM for 10 minutes, or until barely set. Allow the terrine to cool in the dish before refrigerating and serving.

13. In a bowl, mix together the mayonnaise, yogurt, lemon rind and juice, cayenne pepper and the salt. Serve this sauce with slices of the chilled terrine.

SALAD OF WILD MUSHROOMS AND ARTICHOKES

SERVES 4

Wild mushrooms are becoming more readily available in supermarkets and greengrocers, and this recipe provides a delightful way of serving them.

2-3 globe artichokes, depending on size
1 slice of lemon
1 bay leaf
6 black peppercorns
225g /8oz oyster mushrooms, or other varieties of choice
30ml /2 tbsps vegetable oil
1 small head radicchio
1 small head iceberg lettuce
1 bunch watercress
1 small bunch fresh chives, snipped
90ml /6 tbsps olive or groundnut oil
30ml /2 tbsps white wine vinegar
15ml /1 tbsp Dijon mustard
Salt and freshly ground black pepper
Sprigs of fresh chervil or dill to garnish

1. Trim the pointed tips off the artichoke leaves with a sharp knife.

2. Put the trimmed artichokes into a microwave-proof bowl, along with the lemon, bay leaf, peppercorns and enough water to cover them.

3. Cook on HIGH for 7-8 minutes, or until one of the bottom leaves pulls away easily.

4. Stand each artichoke upside-down on a wire rack to drain completely.

5. Remove the stalks from the mushrooms and slice the caps thickly.

6. Put the mushroom slices into a bowl with the vegetable oil and stir to coat each slice with a little of the oil.

7. Cook the mushrooms on HIGH for 1-2 minutes. Set the mushrooms aside.

8. Tear the radicchio and lettuce leaves into small pieces and put them into a bowl. Remove the leaves from the watercress and add these to the lettuce in the bowl along with the snipped chives.

9. Whisk together the olive oil, vinegar, mustard and seasoning using a fork or small whisk. Continue whisking until the dressing is thick and pale coloured.

10. Remove the leaves from the drained artichokes, and arrange them attractively onto 4 plates.

11. Arrange the leaf salad over the artichokes.

12. Cut away and discard the fluffy chokes from each artichoke heart.

13. Trim the artichoke hearts and cut these into thin slices. Add the hearts to the bowl of sliced mushrooms and stir well.

14. Pour half of the prepared dressing over the mushrooms and the artichoke hearts and mix well.

15. Spoon equal amounts of the mushroom mixture over the leaves and salad on the plates.

16. Re-heat each serving for 1 minute on HIGH, garnish with the dill or chervil and the remaining dressing separately.

Cook's Notes

PREPARATION: The mushrooms and artichokes can be prepared well in advance and kept in a refrigerator until needed.

VARIATION: For a non-vegan variation, add 120g /4oz of cubed, mild vegetarian Wensleydale or Cheshire cheese.

SERVING IDEA: Serve with thin slices of wholemeal bread.

TOMATO CHARTREUSE

SERVES 4

This delicately flavoured starter is ideal for a warm summer's day.

30-45ml /2-3 tbsps agar agar
Juice of half a lemon
340ml /12 fl oz tomato juice
10ml /2 tsp tomato purée
1 bay leaf
Salt and freshly ground black pepper
90g /3oz mushrooms, sliced
3 spring onions, finely chopped
45ml /3 tbsps olive or vegetable oil
15ml /1 tbsp white wine vinegar
Salt and freshly ground black pepper
Pinch mixed dried herbs

1. Dissolve the agar agar in the lemon juice.

2. Combine the tomato juice, tomato purée, bay leaf and seasoning in a glass bowl. Cook on HIGH for 3-5 minutes, until it is boiling.

3. Allow to stand for 2 minutes and then remove the bay leaf.

4. Stir the dissolved agar agar into the tomato juice, whisk the mixture with a fork to make sure that the agar agar is evenly blended.

5. Dampen a 670ml /1¼-pint mould and pour in the tomato mixture. Chill in the refrigerator until it is set.

Step 1 Dissolve the agar agar in the lemon juice.

Step 8 Carefully loosen the sides of the set tomato chartreuse with a round-bladed knife, taking care not to cut into the jelly.

Step 9 Turn the inverted plate and the mould over completely to allow the chartreuse to drop out.

6. Put the mushrooms into a small bowl with the onions and the oil. Cook on HIGH for 1 minute.

7. Allow the mushrooms to cool completely, then combine them with the vinegar, seasoning and herbs.

8. Carefully loosen the sides of the tomato chartreuse with a round-bladed knife.

9. Invert a plate over the top of the mould and carefully turn both the plate and the mould over, shaking gently to drop the set tomato chartreuse onto the plate.

10. Arrange the mushroom mixture on the top before serving.

SPICY HOT GRAPEFRUIT

SERVES 4

*This simple starter makes an ideal first course,
or even a refresher between main courses.*

---

2 ruby grapefruits
5ml /1 tsp allspice
10ml /2 tsp caster sugar (optional)
Lemon balm or mint leaves to garnish

---

1. Cut the grapefruits in half.

2. Using a sharp, serrated knife or a grapefruit knife, cut around the edges of each half between the flesh and the pith.

3. Carefully cut down between each segment and inner thin skins.

4. Take hold of the inner pithy core and gently twist to remove this and the thin inner skins which have been cut away from the fleshy segments.

5. Remove any pips.

Step 2 Using a sharp serrated knife, or better still a curved grapefruit knife, carefully cut the grapefruit around the edges, between the flesh and the white pith.

Step 3 Cut between the fleshy segments and the thin inner skins.

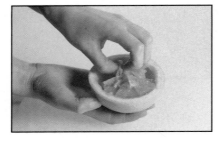

Step 4 Gently twist out the pithy inner core, pulling the inner segment skins out with it.

6. Sprinkle each grapefruit half with equal amounts of the allspice and the sugar, if used.

7. Arrange the grapefruit halves on a plate or shallow circular dish.

8. Cook the grapefruits on HIGH for 3-4 minutes, or until they are nice and hot.

9. Garnish with the balm or mint leaves and serve immediately.

Cook's Notes

TIME: Preparation takes about 10 minutes, microwave cooking time is about 3-4 minutes.

VEGETARIAN SUITABILITY: This recipe is suitable for vegans.

VARIATION: Sprinkle each grapefruit with powdered ginger instead of the allspice, and pour a teaspoon of ginger wine or sherry over each half.

PREPARATION: The grapefruit halves can be prepared well in advance and allowed to marinate in the spice before cooking and serving.

Vegetarian Microwave Cooking

CHAPTER ~ 3

· Lunches · Salads ·
and · Snacks ·

GRATIN OF VEGETABLES OLIVER

SERVES 4

*Fresh summer vegetables with a crunchy nut topping combine
to make a substantial lunch or supper dish.*

120g /4oz butter or vegetable margarine
225g /8oz black olives, pitted and chopped
120g /4oz dry breadcrumbs
180g /6oz vegetarian Cheddar cheese, grated
120g /4oz walnuts, chopped
10ml /2 tsps fresh chopped basil
Pinch cayenne pepper
4 medium carrots, peeled and sliced
4 courgettes, sliced
1 head broccoli, trimmed and cut into florets
225g /8oz French beans, trimmed
2 red peppers, seeded and sliced
8 spring onions, trimmed and sliced
Salt and freshly ground black pepper

1. Put the butter or margarine into a microwave-proof bowl. Melt on HIGH for 30 seconds.

2. Add the olives, breadcrumbs, cheese, walnuts, basil and cayenne to the melted butter

Step 2 Stir the olives, breadcrumbs, grated cheese, walnuts, basil and cayenne pepper into the melted butter or margarine and mix well to coat all ingredients thoroughly.

Step 7 Drain the cooked vegetables in a colander or with a slotted spoon, to remove any excess cooking liquid.

and stir well to coat all ingredients thoroughly. Set aside.

3. Put the carrots into a large, microwave-proof bowl along with 60ml /4 tbsps water. Cook on HIGH for 5 minutes.

4. Stir the courgettes, the broccoli and the beans into the carrots and cook on HIGH for 2 minutes.

5. Finally stir the peppers and spring onions into the vegetable mixture and cook on HIGH for 1 minute.

6. Season the vegetables to taste with the salt and pepper.

7. Drain the vegetables in a colander or with a slotted spoon and arrange them on a serving dish.

8. Sprinkle the topping over the vegetables, making sure that it is evenly spread.

9. Cook the gratin on MEDIUM for 4 minutes, or until the topping is melted and bubbling.

Cook's Notes

FREEZING: The vegetables in this recipe can be prepared, blanched and frozen in advance, then used as required.

SERVING IDEA: Serve with a hot tomato salad.

VEGETARIAN SUITABILITY: This recipe is suitable for lacto-vegetarians, but could be adapted for vegans by omitting the Cheddar cheese and using a vegetable margarine.

TIME: Preparation takes about 20 minutes, microwave cooking takes about 13 minutes.

WATERCRESS STUFFED POTATOES

SERVES 4

An unusual way of serving a favourite vegetable meal.

---

4 large baking potatoes
15ml /1 tbsp vinegar
4 eggs
15g /¹/₂oz butter or vegetable margarine
120g /4oz mushrooms, trimmed and sliced
1 shallot, finely chopped
45g /1¹/₂oz butter or vegetable margarine
30g /1oz plain flour
Pinch dry mustard
Pinch cayenne pepper
280ml /¹/₂ pint milk
60g /2oz vegetarian Cheddar cheese, grated
1 bunch watercress, chopped
Salt and freshly ground black pepper
140ml /¹/₄ pint milk
Watercress sprigs and grated cheese for garnish

---

1. Wash the potatoes and prick them several times with a fork.

2. Bake the potatoes on HIGH for 10-12 minutes. Remove the potatoes from the oven and wrap them completely in aluminium foil. Allow them to stand for at least 5 minutes.

3. Pour 1150ml /2 pints of hot water into a large, shallow dish. Add 15ml /1 tbsp vinegar and 5ml /1 tsp salt to the water. Heat for 5 minutes on HIGH, or until the water is boiling.

4. Break the eggs, one at a time, into a cup and slide them carefully into the vinegar water.

5. Prick the yolks of each egg once with a sharp knife or skewer to prevent them from bursting, and cook on MEDIUM for 3 minutes.

6. Fill a bowl with cold water and carefully remove each egg from the cooking liquid and stand them in the cold water until required.

7. Melt the 15g /¹/₂oz of butter in a shallow bowl for 30 seconds on HIGH.

8. Add the mushrooms and shallot to the butter and stir well. Cook on HIGH for 1 minute and set aside.

9. Melt the 45g /1¹/₂oz of butter in a bowl or jug for 30 seconds on HIGH.

10. Stir the flour, mustard and cayenne into the melted butter, mixing it well with a wooden spoon to form a roux.

11. Add the 280ml /¹/₂ pint of milk gradually to the flour mixture, cooking on HIGH for a total of 3 minutes, and stirring well between each addition to make a smooth, white sauce.

12. Stir the grated cheese into the sauce and cook for 1 minute to melt.

13. Cut a slice off the top of each potato.

14. Using a grapefruit knife or a spoon, carefully scoop the potato pulp out of each potato, taking care to leave a border inside each skin to form a firm shell.

15. Put equal amounts of the mushrooms and shallot mixture into the base of each potato shell, and top this with a well drained egg.

16. Spoon the cheese sauce over each egg.

17. Heat the 140ml /¹/₄ pint of milk. Finely chop the watercress and mash the potato pulp.

18. Beat together the watercress and mashed potato, then gradually whisk in the hot milk, until the potato mixture is well blended and light.

19. Pipe or spoon this mixture over the cheese sauce in the potato shells.

20. Sprinkle the top of each potato with a little extra cheese to garnish and cook each potato for 3 minutes on HIGH to melt the cheese and heat through.

21. Top each hot potato with a watercress sprig, and serve immediately.

WHOLEMEAL VEGETABLE QUICHE

SERVES 4

This wholesome lunch or supper dish is equally good served hot or cold.

90g /3oz wholemeal plain flour
15g /¹/₂oz bran
60g /2oz vegetable margarine
30ml /2 tbsps cold water
1 small red pepper, seeded and diced
120g /4oz courgettes, diced
2 spring onions, trimmed and sliced
1 tomato, skinned and chopped
2 eggs
15ml /1 tbsp milk
Salt and freshly ground black pepper

1. Put the flour and the bran into a bowl. Rub in the margarine with the fingertips until the mixture resembles fine breadcrumbs.

2. Add the water and mix well to form a soft dough.

3. Put the dough into a well greased 16cm /6¹/₂-inch, shallow flan dish.

4. Press out the dough with the fingertips to form a pie case.

Step 4 With lightly floured hands, carefully press the dough evenly into the base and sides of the prepared flan dish, to make a shallow pie case.

Step 9 Spread the cooked vegetables and the chopped tomato evenly over the base of the cooked pie case.

5. Cook the pie case, uncovered, on HIGH for 4 minutes, turning the case a quarter turn after each minute.

6. Put the diced pepper into a bowl. Cover the bowl with cling film, and pierce this several times with the tip of a sharp knife.

7. Cook the pepper on HIGH for 2 minutes.

8. Uncover the bowl and stir in the courgettes and onions. Re-cover and cook on HIGH for 3 minutes.

9. Spread the cooked vegetables over the base of the pastry case and top with the chopped tomato.

10. Put the eggs and the milk into a jug or bowl and beat together. Add some salt and pepper then pour over the vegetables in the pastry case.

11. Cook, uncovered, for 12-14 minutes on LOW, or until the egg mixture has completely set. Turn the dish once or twice during this cooking time.

Cook's Notes

 VARIATION: Use any combination of your favourite vegetables in this recipe.

 SERVING IDEA: Serve with a jacket potato and green salad.

TIME: Preparation takes about 20 minutes, microwave cooking takes about 23 minutes.

 VEGETARIAN SUITABILITY: This recipe is suitable for lacto-vegetarians only.

PANCAKES PROVENÇALE

SERVES 4

These more-ish pancakes are both quick and easy to make.

50g /2oz plain flour
Pinch salt
1 egg
140ml /¼ pint milk or water
2 medium-sized green peppers
1 large red pepper
1 Spanish onion, peeled and finely chopped
1 clove garlic, peeled and crushed
1 small courgette, diced
3 tomatoes, skinned, seeded and chopped
5ml /1 tsp fresh chopped basil
30ml /2 tbsps tomato purée
30g /1oz vegetarian Cheshire or Wensleydale
    cheese, crumbled
Salt and freshly ground black pepper
Parsley sprigs to garnish

1. Put the flour and salt into a bowl. Make a slight well in the centre and break in the egg.

2. Using a wooden spoon, gradually incorporate the flour into the egg. Gradually add the milk and beat well to form a smooth batter.

Step 4 Cut the cored and seeded peppers into small dice with a sharp knife.

Step 8 Using the back of a spoon, spread equal amounts of the vegetable mixture over each pancake, making sure that the filling does not come quite to the edge of each one.

3. Use this batter to make 8 thin pancakes, using a conventional frying pan.

4. Cut the peppers in half and remove the core, white pith, and all the seeds. Dice the peppers using a sharp knife.

5. Put the diced peppers, the onion and the garlic into a bowl. Cover the bowl with cling film and pierce this several times with the tip of a sharp knife.

6. Cook the peppers and onion on HIGH for 5 minutes, or until the peppers are soft.

7. Stir the courgette, chopped tomatoes, basil, tomato purée and cheese into the cooked pepper mixture. Re-cover and cook for 2 minutes on HIGH. Season to taste.

8. Divide the vegetable mixture equally between each pancake and spread it lightly with the back of a spoon.

9. Roll each filled pancake up Swiss roll fashion and arrange on a suitable serving dish.

10. Cook each serving on HIGH for 1 minute to re-heat, then serve, garnished with a sprig of parsley.

Cook's Notes

VARIATION: Omit the cheese from the filling and substitute halved pitta breads for the pancakes to make a vegan variation.

TIME: Preparation takes about 15 minutes plus time for cooking the pancakes. Microwave cooking takes 12-14 minutes.

VEGETARIAN SUITABILITY: This recipe is suitable for lacto-vegetarians only. See variations for vegans.

SPINACH AND PEPPER CASSEROLE

SERVES 4

This hearty, warm casserole makes a substantial lunch or supper, or could be used as an accompanying vegetable for up to 8 people.

450g /1lb spinach, washed, trimmed and roughly chopped
1 medium red pepper, seeded and cut into thin strips
1 medium green pepper, seeded and cut into thin strips
4 celery stalks, trimmed and thinly sliced
2 medium onions, peeled and finely chopped
30g /1oz sultanas
Pinch paprika
Pinch sugar
Pinch ground cinnamon
5ml /1 tsp salt
30ml /2 tbsps tomato purée
10ml /2 tsps cornflour
30g /1oz Cheddar cheese
30ml /2 tbsps fresh breadcrumbs

1. Shake any excess water off the spinach and place it into a roasting bag. Seal the top of the bag loosely with an elastic band.

2. Put the bag, upright, into the microwave and cook for 5-6 minutes on HIGH. Drain the spinach well, reserving the cooking liquid for the sauce.

3. Put the peppers, celery and onion into a shallow casserole dish and cover with cling film or with a tight fitting lid.

4. Cook for 15 minutes on HIGH, stirring the

Step 5 Stir the drained spinach into the cooked vegetables, mixing carefully to avoid breaking up the peppers.

vegetables several times during the cooking time.

5. Stir the drained spinach into the cooked pepper mixture and re-cover the casserole. Set aside.

6. Mix together the sultanas, paprika, sugar, cinnamon, salt, tomato purée, cornflour and reserved spinach cooking liquor in a jug or basin. Cook for 2-3 minutes on HIGH, stirring occasionally, until the sauce has thickened.

7. Stir the sauce into the cooked vegetables. Re-cover the casserole dish and cook on HIGH for 2 minutes.

8. Mix the cheese and the breadcrumbs together in a small bowl and sprinkle this mixture on to the cooked vegetables in the casserole dish.

9. Grill the topping under a conventional grill until the crumbs are golden brown.

Cook's Notes

FREEZING: The vegetables in this recipe can be prepared and frozen successfully for up to 3 months. Prepare and cook the topping just before the casserole is required.

VEGETARIAN SUITABILITY: This recipe is suitable for lacto-vegetarians, but can be adapted to suit vegans. See variations.

TIME: Preparation takes about 15 minutes, microwave cooking takes about 25 minutes.

RED LENTIL AND MUSHROOM LOAF

SERVES 4-6

*This delicious and highly nutricious vegetable loaf
is equally good served hot or cold.*

180/6oz red lentils
340ml/12oz vegetable stock or water
1 egg
30ml/2 tbsps double cream
90g/3oz mushrooms, trimmed and chopped
120g/4oz vegetarian curd or cream cheese
1 clove garlic, crushed
15ml/1 tbsp chopped fresh parsley
Salt and freshly ground black pepper
400g/14oz tin tomatoes, chopped
15ml/1 tbsp tomato purée
10ml/2 tsps dry tarragon
Pinch sugar
15ml/1 tbsp chopped fresh tarragon

1. Put the lentils into a large bowl and cover them with water. Cook on HIGH for 10 minutes then allow to stand for 1 hour.

2. Drain the lentils and discard the liquid. Return the lentils to the bowl and add the stock or water.

3. Cover the bowl with cling film and pierce this several times with the tip of a sharp knife. Cook the lentils on HIGH for 10-12 minutes, or until they are very soft and most of the cooking liquid is absorbed.

4. Allow the cooked lentils to stand for 5

Step 5 Using a potato masher, mash the lentils in the bowl to a thick purée.

Step 7 Press the lentil and mushroom mixture into a loaf dish, using a wooden spoon to smooth the top and press out any air pockets in the mixture.

minutes, or until any remaining cooking liquid has been completely absorbed.

5. Using a potato masher, mash the lentils to a thick purée.

6. Beat the egg and the cream together, stir this into the lentil purée along with the mushrooms, cream cheese, garlic, herbs and seasoning. Mix all the ingredients together thoroughly.

7. Lightly grease a microwave-proof loaf dish, and press the lentil and mushroom mixture into this, using a wooden spoon to smooth the top of the loaf and push out any air pockets in the mixture.

8. Cover the bowl with cling film and pierce this several times with the tip of a sharp knife.

9. Cook the loaf on MEDIUM for 7-8 minutes, or until the loaf is firm around the edges but is still soft in the middle. Allow to stand for 10 minutes to set.

10. Put all the remaining ingredients, except for the fresh tarragon, into a bowl and cook, uncovered, on HIGH for 8 minutes.

11. Pour the sauce mixture into a food processor or liquidiser and blend until smooth.

12. Season with salt and pepper and stir in the fresh tarragon before serving with the lentil and mushroom loaf.

RED BEAN CREOLE

SERVES 4

This bright and colourful dish is ideal served on its own or as part of a larger meal.

180g/6oz dried red kidney beans
1 bay leaf
Salt and freshly ground black pepper
180g/6oz long-grain brown or white rice
30g/1oz butter or vegetable margarine
1 green pepper, seeded and cut into thin strips
120g/4oz mushrooms, sliced
Pinch cayenne pepper
Pinch ground nutmeg
3-4 tomatoes, peeled, seeded and cut into strips
4 spring onions, trimmed and chopped
30ml/2 tbsps fresh, chopped parsley

Step 9 Add the strips of tomato and the chopped spring onions to the rice and bean mixture, stirring well to mix thoroughly.

1. Cover the beans with water in a large bowl, and microwave on HIGH for 10 minutes. Leave to stand for 1 hour then drain and discard the liquid.

2. Return the drained beans to the bowl, add the bay leaf, a little seasoning and enough fresh water to just cover.

3. Cover the bowl with cling film and pierce this several times with the tip of a sharp knife. Cook

Step 6 Stir the peppers and mushrooms into the melted butter, coating the vegetables as evenly as possible.

the beans on MEDIUM for 1 hour, then allow to stand for 10 minutes before draining completely.

4. Put the rice into another bowl with a little salt. Pour over 570ml/1 pint cold water. Cook the rice on HIGH for 10 minutes. Leave to stand for 5 minutes, then drain and rinse in cold water.

5. Put the butter into a bowl and melt on HIGH for 30 seconds.

6. Add the peppers and the mushrooms to the melted butter and stir well to coat them evenly before cooking on HIGH for 2 minutes.

7. Stir the peppers and mushrooms, then add the cayenne pepper, the nutmeg, cooked rice and the beans.

8. Mix well, then cook on HIGH for 3 minutes, stirring once during cooking time.

9. Add the tomatoes and spring onions to the bean and rice mixture and cook on HIGH for a further 1 minute before serving. Garnish with the chopped parsley.

Cook's Notes

TIME: Preparation takes about 20 minutes, microwave cooking time is about 1 hour 24 minutes, with 1 hour 10 minutes standing time.

VEGETARIAN SUITABILITY: This recipe is suitable for vegans if vegetarian margarine is used instead of butter.

PREPARATION: This recipe can be made in advance and then re-heated before serving for 6 minutes on HIGH.

BUTTER BEAN, LEMON AND FENNEL SALAD

SERVES 4

This interesting combination of textures and flavours
makes an unusual lunch or supper dish.

225g/8oz dried butter beans
1 large bulb fennel, thinly sliced
1 lemon
60ml/4 tbsps vegetable or soya oil
Pinch sugar
Salt and freshly ground black pepper
Lettuce and radicchio leaves, for serving

1. Put the beans into a bowl and cover them completely with cold water. Cook on HIGH for 10 minutes then allow to stand for 1 hour.

2. Drain the beans and discard the cooking liquid. Return the beans to the bowl and cover with fresh water.

3. Cook the beans on MEDIUM for 1 hour. Stand for 10 minutes before draining thoroughly.

4. Put 570ml/1 pint water into a bowl and bring to the boil on HIGH for 10 minutes.

5. Reserving the green tops of the fennel for

Step 2 Put the softened, drained beans back into the bowl and pour over enough fresh water to just cover them.

Using a fork or small whisk, briskly whisk the lemon juice, oil, sugar and seasoning together in a small bowl, until the dressing is thick.

decoration, blanch the fennel slices in the boiling water for 2 minutes on HIGH. Drain the fennel thoroughly.

6. Remove the rind from the lemon using a potato peeler. Make sure to remove any white pith from the rind.

7. Cut the rind into very thin strips.

8. Squeeze the juice from the lemon. Put the lemon juice, oil, sugar and seasoning into a small bowl and whisk them together with a fork or small whisk until the mixture is thick.

9. Chop the reserved fennel tops finely and add these to the dressing.

10. Mix the cooked beans and the fennel together in a large bowl.

11. Pour over the lemon dressing and mix well to coat all the ingredients thoroughly.

12. Serve on a bed of mixed lettuce and radicchio leaves.

Cook's Notes

 TIME: Preparation takes about 12 minutes, microwave cooking will take about 1 hour 25 minutes, plus 1 hour 10 minutes standing time.

VEGETARIAN SUITABILITY: This recipe is suitable for vegans.

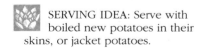 SERVING IDEA: Serve with boiled new potatoes in their skins, or jacket potatoes.

BLACK-EYED BEANS AND ORANGE SALAD

SERVES 4

*This colourful salad has a delightful, fresh taste which
is given 'bite' by the addition of watercress.*

225g/8oz dried black-eyed beans
1 bay leaf
1 slice onion
Juice and rind of 1 orange
75ml/5 tbsps olive or grapeseed oil
6 black olives, pitted and quartered
4 spring onions, chopped
30ml/2 tbsps fresh, chopped parsley
30ml/2 tbsps fresh, chopped basil leaves
Salt and freshly ground black pepper
4 whole oranges
1 large or two small bunches watercress

Step 7 Add the cooked, drained beans to the dressing in the bowl and mix thoroughly to coat the beans evenly with the dressing mixture.

1. Put the beans into a bowl and cover them with cold water.

2. Cook on HIGH for 10-12 minutes, allow to stand for 1 hour, then drain the beans and discard the cooking liquid.

3. Return the beans to the bowl and re-cover them with fresh water. Add the bay leaf and onion slice.

4. Cover the bowl with cling film and pierce this several times with the tip of a sharp knife. Cook on MEDIUM for 1 hour, then stand for 10 minutes before draining thoroughly.

5. Put the orange rind, the juice and the oil, into a large bowl and whisk with a fork.

6. Stir the olives, spring onions and chopped herbs into the orange and oil dressing.

7. Add the cooked, drained beans to the dressing mixture in the bowl, season with salt and pepper and mix thoroughly to coat the beans well.

8. Carefully peel the oranges, removing as much white pith as possible.

9. Cut the oranges into segments, removing the thin inner membrane and any remaining white pith from each segment.

10. Chop the segments of 2 of the oranges into 3-4 pieces each segment. Mix these chopped segments into the bean salad.

11. Arrange the watercress on 4 individual serving plates, and pile equal amounts of the bean and orange salad on to this.

12. Arrange the remaining orange slices on the plates for decoration and serve immediately.

Cook's Notes

 TIME: Preparation takes about 20 minutes, microwave cooking time is about 1 hour 22 minutes, plus 10 minutes standing time.

SERVING IDEA: Serve in split wholemeal pitta bread or in taco shells.

 VEGETARIAN SUITABILITY: This recipe is suitable for vegans.

PASTA, PEAS AND PEPPERS

SERVES 4

*This very colourful salad is simple, but is substantial
enough to be a meal in itself.*

225g /8oz plain and wholemeal pasta shells,
  mixed
Salt
225g /8oz frozen peas
1 green pepper, seeded and sliced
1 red pepper, seeded and sliced
1 yellow pepper, seeded and sliced
140ml /¼ pint vegetable or olive oil
60ml /4 tbsps white wine vinegar
15ml /1 tbsp Dijon or whole grain mustard
10ml /2 tsps poppy seeds
10ml /2 tsps fresh, chopped parsley
5ml /1 tsp fresh, chopped thyme
4 spring onions, shredded
120g /4oz vegetarian Cheddar cheese, finely
  grated

1. Put the pasta shells into a large bowl. Pour
over 570ml /1 pint cold water and add a pinch
of salt.

2. Cover the bowl with cling film, pierce this
several times with the tip of a sharp knife, and

Step 6 Using a
fork or small whisk,
vigorously whisk
the dressing
ingredients together
until they become
thick and pale
coloured.

Step 8 Pour the
dressing over the
pasta and
vegetables in the
bowl and mix
thoroughly to coat
the ingredients
evenly.

cook on HIGH for 6 minutes. Leave the pasta to
stand, still covered, for 10 minutes, before
draining completely.

3. Put the peas and the sliced peppers into
another bowl and add 30ml /2 tbsps water and a
pinch of salt.

4. Cover with cling film as before, and cook for
3 minutes on HIGH. Drain the vegetables and
allow to cool completely.

5. Put the oil, vinegar, mustard, poppy seeds,
herbs and a little seasoning into a small bowl.

6. Using a fork or small whisk, whisk the
dressing ingredients together vigorously, until
the dressing is thick and pale coloured.

7. Put the pasta into a large bowl and stir in the
cooked vegetables.

8. Pour the dressing over the pasta and
vegetables, and mix this in thoroughly to coat
the ingredients completely.

9. Chill the pasta in a refrigerator.

10. Stir the cheese and spring onions into the
salad and serve immediately.

Cook's Notes

VEGETARIAN SUITABILITY:
This recipe is suitable for
lacto-vegetarians, but could be
used by vegans if the cheese was
omitted.

TIME: Preparation takes about
20 minutes, microwave
cooking time is about 13 minutes,
plus 10 minutes standing time.

VARIATION: Use 60g /2oz
salted peanuts instead of the
cheese in this recipe.

RATATOUILLE

SERVES 4-6

This delicious, classic dish, is equally good served hot or cold.

1 large aubergine
30ml /2 tbsps olive oil
1 large onion, peeled and thinly sliced
1 clove garlic, crushed
450g /1lb courgettes, trimmed and thinly sliced
1 green pepper, seeded and thinly sliced
450g /1lb fresh tomatoes, skinned and chopped
5ml /1 tsp fresh chopped thyme
10ml /2 tsps fresh chopped basil
Salt and freshly ground black pepper

1. Cut the aubergine in half lengthways and score the cut surface in a diamond fashion with a sharp knife.

2. Sprinkle plenty of salt over the scored surface, rubbing it into the cuts. Allow to stand for at least 30 minutes to remove excess moisture.

3. Rinse the aubergine thoroughly to remove the saltiness and pat as dry as possible with absorbent kitchen paper.

4. Chop the aubergine into small slices.

5. Put the oil into a large bowl and heat on HIGH for 30 seconds.

Step 1 Score diagonal cuts into the cut surface of each aubergine half. Try to avoid cutting through the outer skins.

Step 2 Sprinkle salt over the scored surface of each aubergine half, rubbing it well into the cuts with the fingertips.

Step 7 Stir all the remaining ingredients into the onions.

6. Add the onion and garlic to the oil, stirring well to coat the vegetables thoroughly. Cook on HIGH for 2 minutes, or until the onion is softened but not coloured.

7. Stir all the remaining ingredients into the onions. Cover the bowl with cling film and pierce this several times with the tip of a sharp knife.

8. Cook on HIGH for 10-15 minutes, stirring after each 4-5 minutes, until the vegetables are completely cooked.

9. Adjust the seasoning if necessary.

Cook's Notes

 SERVING IDEA: Serve in pitta bread or with crusty wholemeal rolls.

 VARIATION: Serve as an accompaniment for 8 people, with another vegetarian meal.

TIME: Preparation takes about 45 minutes, microwave cooking time is about 17 minutes.

CURRIED VEGETABLES
SERVES 6-8

This wholesome vegetable curry includes an interesting combination of unusual vegetables, nuts and spices.

15ml /1 tbsp groundnut oil
1 large onion, peeled and chopped
1 green chilli pepper, seeded and very finely chopped
1 small piece fresh ginger, peeled and grated
2 cloves garlic, crushed
2.5ml /¹/₂ tsp ground coriander
2.5ml /¹/₂ tsp ground cumin
5ml /1 tsp ground turmeric
2 potatoes, peeled and diced
1 aubergine, cut into small cubes
390g /14oz canned tomatoes, drained
1 small cauliflower, washed and cut into florets
225g /8oz okra, trimmed and washed
140ml /¹/₄ pint vegetable stock
120g /4oz roasted, unsalted cashews
60g /4 tbsps desiccated coconut
60ml /4 tbsps natural yogurt, optional

1. Put the oil into a large bowl and heat on HIGH for 30 seconds.

2. Stir the onion, chilli pepper, ginger and garlic into the oil, mixing well to coat the ingredients thoroughly. Cook on HIGH for 1 minute.

3. Add the spices to the onion and chilli

Step 7 Mix the cashews and coconut into the vegetable curry, mixing them in well with a wooden spoon.

mixture. Cook on HIGH for a further minute.

4. Stir the potatoes, aubergine and tomatoes into the spice mixture. Mix well to blend evenly. Cover the bowl with cling film and pierce this several times with the tip of a sharp knife.

5. Cook on HIGH for 10 minutes, or until the potatoes and aubergines are almost tender.

6. Add the cauliflower, okra and stock to the potato mixture. Re-cover and continue cooking on HIGH for a further 4 minutes.

7. Mix the cashews and coconut into the vegetable curry and heat through for 2 minutes before serving, topped with the natural yogurt if desired.

Cook's Notes

PREPARATION: Great care must be taken when preparing chilli peppers. Do not get the juice into eyes or mouth. If this happens, rinse with plenty of cold water.

COOK'S TIP: Wear rubber or plastic gloves when preparing chilli peppers. This will prevent juice from getting on to fingers and from there into eyes or mouth.

FREEZING: This recipe freezes very well for up to 3 months. To serve, defrost and re-heat on HIGH for 6-10 minutes before serving. N.B. The flavour of spices is enhanced during the freezing process.

SERVING IDEA: Serve on its own with chapatis or boiled brown rice, or as part of a larger Indian meal.

TIME: Preparation takes about 30 minutes, microwave cooking time is about 18 minutes.

VEGETARIAN SUITABILITY: This recipe is suitable for lacto-vegetarians, and if the yogurt is omitted, vegans also.

MACARONI AND BLUE CHEESE

SERVES 4

The classic combination of apples and blue cheese sets this delicious variation of macaroni cheese apart from its humble origins.

340g /12oz wholemeal macaroni
5ml /1 tsp vegetable oil
570ml /1 pint milk
30g /1oz butter or margarine
30ml /2 tbsps wholemeal flour
30ml /2 tbsps arrowroot
5ml /1 tsp dried tarragon
2.5ml /$^1/_2$ tsp salt
225g /8oz vegetarian blue cheese, crumbled or grated
2 apples, quartered, cored and chopped
2 onions, peeled and chopped
1 clove garlic, crushed
15ml /1 tbsp vegetable oil

1. Put the macaroni into a large bowl along with 5ml /1 tsp vegetable oil, and enough water to cover. Cook for 10 minutes on HIGH, or until the pasta is just cooked.

2. Drain the pasta and rinse in cold water to prevent it from becoming soggy.

Step 7 Cover the bowl of apples and onions with cling film and pierce this several times with the tip of a sharp knife to allow steam to escape whilst the ingredients are cooking.

Step 9 Combine all the ingredients together in a bowl, mixing well to distribute the pasta evenly.

3. Combine the milk, butter, flour, arrowroot, tarragon and salt in a small bowl and mix well.

4. Cook on HIGH for 2 minutes. Stir very well then cook again for a further 2 minutes on HIGH.

5. Reserve 60g /2oz of the cheese for the topping. Stir the remaining cheese into the sauce mixture and cook for 1 minute on HIGH, to melt the cheese.

6. Put the apples, onions, garlic and oil into a large bowl and mix well to coat the ingredients thoroughly.

7. Cover the bowl with cling film and pierce this several times with the tip of a sharp knife.

8. Cook the apple and onion mixture for 3-4 minutes on HIGH, just to soften.

9. Mix the sauce into the apple and onion mixture and then stir in the drained pasta.

10. Transfer to a serving dish and sprinkle the reserved cheese over the top. Cook on HIGH for 4 minutes to heat through and melt the topping.

Cook's Notes

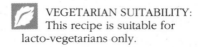 COOK'S TIP: Use a whisk when cooking the sauce mixture, to prevent lumps from forming.

VEGETARIAN SUITABILITY: This recipe is suitable for lacto-vegetarians only.

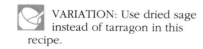 VARIATION: Use dried sage instead of tarragon in this recipe.

SPAGHETTI WITH PINE NUTS

SERVES 4

This crunchy, flavoursome combination, makes good use of convenience ingredients often found in the store cupboard.

340g /12oz spaghetti
15ml /1 tbsp vegetable oil
1 large onion, sliced
1 clove garlic, crushed
90ml /3fl.oz olive oil
30g /1oz fresh, chopped parsley
120g /4oz pine nuts
400g /14oz can artichoke hearts
60g /2oz vegetarian Cheddar cheese, grated,
  optional

1. Put 700ml /1¼ pints of hot water into a large bowl and heat for 2 minutes on HIGH until the water boils.

2. Carefully place the spaghetti into the boiling water, pressing it in gradually as it softens.

3. Stir in the vegetable oil, cover the bowl with cling film and pierce this several times with the tip of a sharp knife. Cook the pasta for 5 minutes on HIGH.

Step 7 Using a sharp knife, cut the drained artichoke hearts into bite sized pieces.

Step 10 Stir the onion and pine nut sauce into the drained spaghetti, mixing it well with a fork and spoon, to combine all the ingredients thoroughly.

4. If the pasta is not cooked after this time, stir it and continue cooking for a further 2 minutes, until it is soft. Allow the pasta to stand in the water for 5 minutes before draining.

5. Put the onion, garlic and the olive oil into a bowl and cook on HIGH for 2 minutes.

6. Stir in the parsley and pine nuts.

7. Drain the can of artichoke hearts and chop them into bite-sized pieces.

8. Stir the chopped artichoke hearts into the onion and pine nut mixture. Cook for 2 minutes on HIGH.

9. Drain the pasta and return the spaghetti to the large bowl.

10 Stir the pine nut sauce into the drained spaghetti, mixing well to combine all the ingredients thoroughly.

11. Just before serving, stir the grated cheese, if used, into the spaghetti.

12. Re-heat for 1 minute on HIGH before serving.

Cook's Notes

COOK'S TIP: If fresh pasta is used, reduce the cooking time to 2 minutes on HIGH after it has been added to the boiling water and vegetable oil.

TIME: Preparation takes about 10 minutes, microwave cooking time is about 10 minutes, with 5 minutes standing time for the spaghetti.

VEGETARIAN SUITABILITY: This recipe is suitable for lacto-vegetarians if the cheese is used and for vegans if it is omitted.

CAULIFLOWER AND CABBAGE IN WALNUT AND CHEESE SAUCE

SERVES 4

A delicious combination of flavours and textures lifts this recipe above its more usual classic counterpart, the humble cauliflower cheese.

1 cauliflower
1 small green cabbage
60g /2oz butter
60g /2oz wholemeal flour
570ml /1 pint milk
120g /4oz vegetarian Cheddar cheese, grated
90g /3oz shelled walnuts, chopped

1. Wash the cauliflower and break it into small florets.

2. Wash and thickly shred the cabbage.

3. Put the cauliflower and the cabbage into a large bowl along with 6 tbsps water. Cover the bowl with cling film and pierce this several times with the tip of a sharp knife.

4. Cook the vegetables on HIGH for 10 minutes, or until they are cooked, but still slightly crunchy.

5. Put the butter and flour into a bowl and mix together with a fork. Blend in the milk and cook

Step 1 Break the cauliflower into small florets and cut away any thick stalks or leaves.

Step 2 Thickly shred the cabbage using a sharp knife.

Step 7 Mix the cheese and walnuts into the sauce mixture and stir well to blend thoroughly.

for 2 minutes on HIGH.

6. Stir the sauce well and cook for a further 2 minutes on HIGH.

7. Add the cheese and walnuts to the sauce and mix well to blend thoroughly. Cook on HIGH for 2 minutes to melt the cheese.

8. Drain the vegetables well and transfer them to a serving dish. Pour the sauce over the vegetables, and cook on HIGH for a few minutes, before serving.

Cook's Notes

TIME: Preparation takes about 15 minutes, microwave cooking time is about 19 minutes, plus a few minutes standing time.

COOK'S TIP: Use a whisk when preparing the sauce mixture to prevent any lumps from forming.

VEGETARIAN SUITABILITY: This recipe is suitable for lacto-vegetarians only.

MIXED GRAINS AND SEEDS

SERVES 4-6

This recipe makes a simple supper dish on its own, or an excellent base for curries and tomato dishes.

120g /4oz brown rice
60g /2oz wheat grains
90g /3oz rye grains
90g /3oz barley or oat groats
90g /3oz sunflower seeds or pine nuts
90g /3oz sesame seeds
570ml /1 pint water or vegetable stock
120g /4oz vegetarian Cheddar cheese, grated
30g /1oz butter or vegetable margarine

1. Put the grains and seeds into a large casserole dish and rinse several times in cold water to remove any grit or chaff.

2. Pour over the vegetable stock or water and cook on MEDIUM for 20 minutes.

3. Allow the grains and seeds to stand for 10 minutes, until they are soft and most of the liquid is absorbed.

Step 3 After standing, most of the cooking liquid should have been absorbed by the grains and seeds.

Step 5 Stir the cheese and butter into the grains and seeds, mixing well to ensure that they are evenly combined.

Step 1 Rinse the grains and seeds in cold water before cooking to remove any grit or chaff.

4. Drain the grains and seeds and rinse in boiling water. Allow to drain completely before returning to the casserole.

5. Stir the cheese and butter into the grains, mixing well to ensure that they are evenly combined.

6. Re-heat for 1 minute on HIGH before serving.

Cook's Notes

TIME: Preparation takes about 5 minutes, microwave cooking time is about 21 minutes, with 10 minutes standing time.

VEGETARIAN SUITABILITY: This recipe is suitable for lacto-vegetarians only. For a vegan recipe, see variation.

VARIATION: Omit the cheese and butter and stir in 120g /4oz finely chopped spring onions, which have been gently cooked in 2 tbsps of olive or walnut oil for 1 minute.

FREEZING: The cooked grains and seeds can be frozen for up to 2 months, but the cheese or the onions should not be added until just before they are served

CORNMEAL PROVENÇAL

SERVES 4

*Cornmeal served with a delicious provençal sauce makes a warming,
substantial lunch or supper dish.*

225g /8oz cornmeal
1.1l /2 pints water
5ml /1 tsp salt
120g /4oz vegetarian Cheddar cheese, grated
450g /1lb courgettes, sliced
450g /1lb tomatoes, chopped
1 clove garlic, crushed
10ml /2 tsps dried basil
5ml /1 tsp dried oregano
2.5ml /½ tsp dried rosemary

1. Put the cornmeal into a large bowl along with the water and the salt.

Step 2 After cooking, stir the cornmeal very well to ensure that the mixture is smooth and any large lumps are removed.

Step 4 Stir the herbs into the bowl of courgettes, tomatoes and garlic, mixing them together well with a spoon.

2. Cook on HIGH for 5 minutes, then stir very well to beat out any lumps that may have formed.

3. Mix in the cheese and cook for a further minute on HIGH. Set aside until required.

4. Put the courgettes, tomatoes and garlic into a large bowl. Stir in the herbs, cover the bowl with cling film and pierce this several times with the tip of a sharp knife.

5. Cook the vegetables on HIGH for 5 minutes.

6. Divide the cooked cornmeal into 4 serving dishes, and arrange equal amounts of the vegetables over each serving.

Cook's Notes

 VARIATION: Substitute the sliced courgettes with green beans, or carrots.

 SERVING IDEA: Serve with a tomato, onion and basil salad.

VEGETARIAN SUITABILITY: This recipe is suitable for lacto-vegetarians only. For a vegan variation, omit the cheese, and stir 2 tbsps of tomato or mushroom purée into the cooked cornmeal.

TIME: Preparation takes about 15 minutes, microwave cooking time is about 11 minutes.

CHICKPEAS AND BULGUR WHEAT

SERVES 4

*High in protein and flavour, this colourful main dish
is sure to become a firm family favourite.*

15ml /1 tbsp vegetable oil
2 small onions, chopped
1 medium-sized red pepper, seeded and
    chopped
225g /8oz cooked chickpeas
120g /4oz bulgur wheat
120ml /8 tbsps tomato purée
480ml /16 fl.oz vegetable stock or water

1. Put the oil into a bowl and stir in the onions
and pepper.

2. Cook on HIGH for 2 minutes, or until the
vegetables are soft, but not coloured.

Step 4 Blend the
tomato purée with
a little of the stock
or water to thin it.

Step 5 Gradually
add the remaining
stock or water,
mixing well
between additions
until the purée is
evenly blended,
and a smooth stock
is formed.

3. Stir the chickpeas and bulgur wheat into the
onions and peppers.

4. Put the tomato purée into a jug and blend it
with a little of the stock or water.

5. Gradually add the remaining stock or water,
mixing well between additions until the purée is
evenly blended.

6. Stir the tomato stock into the vegetables and
bulgur wheat. Cover the bowl with cling film
and pierce this several times with the tip of a
sharp knife.

7. Cook for 8 minutes on HIGH, then allow to
stand for 5 minutes before serving.

Cook's Notes

 VARIATION: Use green
peppers in place of the red
peppers in this recipe, and add ½
tsp of chilli powder to the tomato
purée for a hot and spicy
variation.

 SERVING IDEA: Serve with a
crunchy carrot and peanut
coleslaw.

TIME: Preparation takes about
10 minutes, microwave
cooking time is about 10 minutes,
plus 5 minutes standing time.

VEGETARIAN SUITABILITY:
This recipe is suitable for
vegans.

COOK'S TIP: Care should be
taken to ensure that the
chickpeas are well cooked. They
should be boiled for at least 30
minutes. As an alternative, use
450g /1lb canned chickpeas,
which will require no pre-cooking.

SPANISH BARLEY

SERVES 4

*Paprika gives this dish its distinctive taste. Spanish barley makes a
colourful and tasty main dish which is equally good hot or cold.*

340g /12oz barley
570ml /1 pint water or vegetable stock
1 large Spanish onion, peeled and chopped
1 clove garlic, crushed
1 green pepper, seeded and chopped
15ml /1 tbsp olive or vegetable oil
5ml /1 tsp paprika pepper
5ml /1 tsp salt
400g /14oz can tomatoes, roughly chopped

1. Put the barley into a bowl along with the
water or stock. Cook for 20 minutes on HIGH.

2. Drain any excess water from the barley, and
set aside.

3. Put the onion, garlic and green pepper into a
bowl along with the oil. Cook on HIGH for 2
minutes.

4. Put the drained barley into a large bowl. Stir
the seasonings and the tomatoes into the cooked

Step 2 Transfer the
cooked barley to a
colander and allow
any excess water to
drain away.

Step 4 Stir the
seasoning and the
tomatoes into the
cooked barley. Stir
well to combine the
ingredients
thoroughly and
distribute the
seasoning evenly.

Step 6 Cover the
bowl with cling film
and pierce this
several times with
the tip of a sharp
knife to allow the
steam to escape
during cooking.

barley. Stir well to combine the ingredients
thoroughly and distribute the seasoning evenly.

5. Add the vegetables to the tomato and barley
mixture, stirring them all together well.

6. Cover the bowl with cling film and pierce this
several times with the tip of a sharp knife.

7. Cook for 4 minutes on HIGH, then allow the
dish to stand for 5 minutes before serving to give
the flavour of the paprika time to develop.

Cook's Notes

 FREEZING: This recipe
freezes successfully for up to
3 months. The flavour of the
paprika will be enhanced during
this time.

SERVING IDEA: Serve with a
tomato and basil salad.

 TIME: Preparation takes about
15 minutes, microwave
cooking time is about 26 minutes.

VEGETARIAN SUITABILITY:
This recipe is suitable for
vegans.

VARIATION: Add 90g /3oz
pitted and sliced black olives
and 120g /4oz cubed vegetarian
Wensleydale cheese for a
delicious, lacto-vegetarian
alternative.

PEASE PUDDING

SERVES 4

*This traditional English dish is delicious eaten as a light lunch
or supper, or as an accompaniment to a larger meal.*

225g /8oz dried peas or green split peas, soaked
  overnight
1 large carrot, peeled and finely chopped
1 large onion, peeled and finely chopped
1 egg, beaten
2.5ml /$\frac{1}{2}$ tsp marjoram
2.5ml /$\frac{1}{2}$ tsp savoury
5ml /1 tsp salt
Freshly ground black pepper to taste
140ml /$\frac{1}{4}$ pint milk
30g /1oz butter
15ml /1 tbsp arrowroot
Tomato slices to garnish

Step 9 Stand the individual dishes of pease pudding in a roasting dish half filled with hot water.

1. Put the soaked peas into a bowl and cover them with boiling water. Cover the bowl with cling film and pierce this several times with the tip of a sharp knife. Cook on HIGH for 10 minutes. Reduce the power to MEDIUM, and continue cooking for a further 1 hour, or until the peas are soft.

2. Drain the peas from the cooking liquid, reserving a small amount to blend with the peas to make a purée.

3. Put the peas and the reserved liquid into a blender or food processor and blend until smooth.

4. Put the pea purée into a large bowl and add the carrot, onion, egg, herbs and seasoning. Mix well to combine all ingredients thoroughly.

5. Put the milk, butter and arrowroot into a bowl and mix well until the arrowroot is completely blended.

6. Cook on HIGH for 1 minute. Remove the bowl from the microwave oven and stir to prevent lumps from forming. Return the bowl to the microwave oven and continue cooking on HIGH for a further 1 minute, or until the sauce has thickened.

7. Pour the sauce into the pea mixture and stir well.

8. Divide the mixture equally between four individual microwave-proof dishes or moulds. Cover each dish with cling film and pierce this several times with the tip of a sharp knife.

9. Half fill a microwave-proof roasting dish with hot water and stand the individual dishes in this.

10. Cook on MEDIUM for 15-20 minutes, or until each pudding is practically set. Allow to stand for 5 minutes before turning out and serving, garnished with the tomato slices.

Cook's Notes

COOK'S TIP: If you do not have a liquidiser or food processor, the pea purée can be made by pushing the cooked peas through the mesh of a wire sieve with a wooden spoon.

TIME: Preparation takes about 1 hour, plus the overnight soaking of the peas. Microwave cooking takes about 1$\frac{1}{2}$ hours, plus 5 minutes standing time.

VEGETARIAN SUITABILITY: This recipe is suitable for lacto-vegetarians only.

GARBURE

SERVES 4

This thick, tasty, French country stew makes a warming lunch or supper dish. It is also an excellent source of protein.

225g /8oz dried haricot beans, soaked overnight
1 large potato, scrubbed and diced
4 carrots, peeled and sliced
2 leeks, washed and chopped
850ml /1½ pints vegetable stock
5ml /1 tsp marjoram
5ml /1 tsp thyme
2.5ml /½ tsp paprika
Salt to taste
1 small cabbage, finely shredded

1. Put the soaked beans into a large bowl and cover with cold water.

2. Cook for 10 minutes on HIGH. Reduce the power setting to MEDIUM and continue cooking for a further 1 hour, or until the beans are soft. Drain the beans and set them aside until required.

3. Put the potato, carrot, leeks and cooked beans into a large bowl or casserole dish. Mix them together well.

Step 1 Put the soaked beans into a large bowl and pour over just enough water to cover them.

Step 3 Combine the diced potato, carrot, leeks and cooked beans together in a large bowl or casserole dish, stirring well to mix evenly.

Step 7 Spread an even layer of the shredded cabbage over the top of the cooked bean stew.

4. Pour over the stock and stir in the herbs and seasoning.

5. Cover the bowl with cling film and pierce this several times with the tip of a sharp knife.

6. Cook for 20 minutes on HIGH.

7. Remove the cling film and spread the shredded cabbage evenly over the top of the bean stew.

8. Continue cooking, uncovered, on HIGH for a further 3-4 minutes, or until the cabbage is soft.

Cook's Notes

SERVING IDEA: Serve ladled over thick slices of wholemeal bread.

VEGETARIAN SUITABILITY: This recipe is suitable for vegans.

TIME: Preparation takes about 1 hour, plus overnight soaking the beans. Microwave cooking time is about 1 hour 35 minutes.

PREPARATION: Great care must be taken when cooking any dried beans. They should be well soaked, and then thoroughly cooked before being eaten.

FRESH AND DRIED BEANS PROVENÇALE

SERVES 4

This colourful dish is full of flavour and is high in protein, too.

225g /8oz dried flageolet beans, soaked
   overnight then drained
450g /1lb fresh tomatoes, chopped
1 clove garlic, crushed
10ml /2 tsps dried basil
5ml /1 tsp dried oregano
2.5ml /$\frac{1}{2}$ tsp dried rosemary
450g /1lb fresh or frozen green beans

1. Put the soaked beans into a large bowl and pour over enough water to just cover. Cook on HIGH for 10 minutes.

2. Cover the bowl of beans with cling film and pierce this several times with the tip of a sharp knife. Continue cooking the beans on MEDIUM

Step 4 The tomatoes should be starting to soften and the juices beginning to flow before adding the beans.

Step 5 Mix the green beans and the cooked flageolet beans thoroughly into the tomato mixture in the casserole.

for a further 1 hour, or until they are soft and thoroughly cooked.

3. Drain the cooked beans and set aside.

4. Put the tomatoes, garlic and dried herbs into a large casserole dish or bowl. Cover with a lid or with cling film, pierced as before, and cook on HIGH for 5 minutes, or until the tomatoes soften and the juice begins to flow.

5. Add the green beans and the cooked flageolet beans to the tomato mixture in the casserole and mix thoroughly.

6. Cook, uncovered, for 2 minutes on HIGH, stir, and then continue cooking for a further 3 minutes, or until all the ingredients are heated through.

Cook's Notes

SERVING IDEA: Serve this casserole over cooked cornmeal or brown rice. Lacto-vegetarians can sprinkle grated vegetarian cheese over the top just before serving.

COOK'S TIP: Tinned flageolet beans are now easily available and require no pre-cooking. Use 450g /1lb of these in place of the dried beans.

PREPARATION: It is most important to cook dried beans thoroughly. Make sure the beans are completely soft before eating

BEANS WITH TREE EARS AND BAMBOO SHOOTS

SERVES 4

Tree ears are Chinese black fungi. These are usually sold dried and are available from most ethnic shops or delicatessens.

6 Chinese tree ears, broken into small pieces
340g /12oz green beans
2 whole pieces canned bamboo shoot
30ml /2 tbsps vegetable oil
30ml /2 tbsps soy sauce
10ml /2 tsps cornflour
60ml /4 tbsps light vegetable stock
Dash sesame oil
Salt and freshly ground black pepper

1. Put the tree ears into a bowl and pour over enough warm water to just cover. Leave to soak for 30 minutes.

2. Trim the tops and tails from the green beans and cut each bean into 5cm /2-inch diagonal pieces with a sharp knife.

3. Slice the bamboo shoots and cut them into thin triangular pieces with a sharp knife.

Step 2 Cut the trimmed green beans into 5cm /2-inch diagonal pieces with a sharp knife.

Step 3 Slice the bamboo shoots, and cut them into thin, triangular pieces with a sharp knife.

4. Heat a browning dish for 5 minutes on HIGH. Pour in the vegetable oil.

5. Add the beans and bamboo shoots to the oil in the dish, and cook, uncovered, on HIGH for 2 minutes.

6. Stir the beans and bamboo shoots then add the soaked tree ears. Cover the browning dish and leave to stand for about 3 minutes while preparing the sauce.

7. Put the soy sauce, cornflour and stock into a small bowl and stir until the cornflour is smoothly blended.

8. Cook on HIGH for 1 minute, stir and continue cooking on HIGH for a further 1 minute, or until the sauce has thickened.

9. Carefully stir the sauce into the bean and tree ear mixture along with the sesame oil. Mix well and season to taste before serving.

Cook's Notes

TIME: Preparation takes about 30 minutes, microwave cooking time is about 4 minutes, with 2-3 minutes standing time.

SERVING IDEA: Serve with boiled rice or a crusty wholemeal roll.

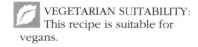

VEGETARIAN SUITABILITY: This recipe is suitable for vegans.

VEGETABLE PILAU

SERVES 4-6

*Lightly spiced and fragrant, this traditional Indian rice dish will serve 4
as a lunch or supper on its own, or 6 as part of a larger Indian meal.*

60g /2oz butter or vegetable oil
225g /8oz long grain rice
1 onion, peeled and finely sliced
1 small piece of cinnamon stick
1 bay leaf
4 cardamoms, husks removed and seeds crushed
4 cloves
2.5ml /$\frac{1}{2}$ tsp ground coriander
1.25ml /$\frac{1}{4}$ tsp ground turmeric
1.25ml /$\frac{1}{4}$ tsp garam masala
Salt and freshly ground black pepper
570ml /1 pint boiling vegetable stock or water
$\frac{1}{2}$ large aubergine
60g /2oz frozen cauliflower florets
120g /4oz frozen mixed vegetables

1. Put the butter or oil into a large, deep bowl along with the rice and onion. Cook, uncovered, for 2 minutes on HIGH.

Step 2 Stir the spices into the rice and onion, mixing them well to blend evenly.

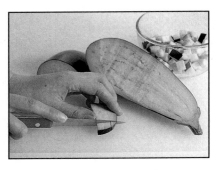

Step 4 Cut the aubergine into small cubes with a sharp knife.

2. Stir the spices into the rice and onion and continue cooking on HIGH for a further 2 minutes, or until the onion is beginning to soften.

3. Pour the stock or water on to the rice and spices, and stir well. Cover the bowl with cling film and pierce this several times with the tip of a sharp knife. Cook on HIGH for 7 minutes.

4. While the rice is cooking, cut the aubergine into small cubes with a sharp knife.

5. Put the aubergine, cauliflower and mixed vegetables into the rice and stock mixture and stir well.

6. Re-cover and continue cooking on HIGH for a further 7-10 minutes, or until the rice is soft and most of the cooking liquid is absorbed.

7. Allow the pilau rice to stand for 5 minutes to finish cooking. Stir to separate the grains of rice and serve.

Cook's Notes

 COOK'S TIP: Just before serving, sprinkle the pilau rice with freshly chopped coriander leaves to enhance the taste and give a superb fragrance to this dish.

FREEZING: This recipe will freeze well for up to 2 months.

SERVING IDEA: Serve with a cucumber raita or chutney.

 TIME: Preparation takes about 15 minutes. Microwave cooking time is about 18-21 minutes, plus 5 minutes standing time.

PASTA PRIMAVERA
SERVES 4

Primavera is Italian for springtime, and this recipe certainly tastes at its best when tender young spring vegetables and herbs are used.

450g /1lb pasta shapes
15ml /1 tbsp vegetable oil
225g /8oz fresh asparagus
120g /4oz French beans
2 medium-sized carrots
60g /2oz button mushrooms, trimmed and sliced
140ml /¼ pint double cream
Salt and freshly ground black pepper
3 tomatoes, peeled, seeded and cut into strips
6 spring onions
30ml /2 tbsps fresh chopped parsley
10ml /2 tsps fresh chopped tarragon

1. Put the pasta into a large bowl and cover with 1150ml /2 pints of hot water. Stir in a pinch of salt and 15ml /1 tbsp vegetable oil.

2. Cover the bowl with cling film and pierce this several times with the tip of a sharp knife. Cook the pasta on HIGH for 6 minutes, then allow to stand for 10 minutes before draining.

3. Trim any thick woody ends from the

Step 4 Slice the beans and carrots into thin diagonal slices using a sharp knife.

Step 8 Stir the cream carefully into the vegetable and pasta mixture, mixing well to blend thoroughly.

asparagus spears, then cut each spear diagonally into 2.5cm /1-inch pieces, leaving the actual tips whole.

4. Cut the beans and carrots into thin diagonal slices.

5. Put the carrots and the asparagus into a large bowl along with 2 tbsps of water. Cook on HIGH for 4 minutes.

6. Add the beans and mushrooms to the carrots and asparagus and cook on HIGH for a further 2 minutes. Drain the vegetables thoroughly.

7. Stir the cooked, drained vegetables into the well drained pasta.

8. Add the cream and seasoning to the vegetables and pasta mixture and stir well to coat thoroughly.

9. Cook for 1 minute on HIGH.

10. Stir the tomatoes, onions and herbs into the cream and pasta mixture then cook for a further 1 minute on HIGH to heat through before serving.

Cook's Notes

 TIME: Preparation takes about 20 minutes, microwave cooking time is about 14 minutes, plus 10 minutes standing time.

SERVING IDEA: Serve with garlic bread and a tomato salad.

 VARIATION: Use wild mushrooms in place of the button mushrooms.

VEGETARIAN MICROWAVE COOKING

CHAPTER ~ 4

· FAMILY · MEALS ·

VEGETABLE STIR FRY WITH TOFU

SERVES 4

The inclusion of tofu in this recipe makes it an excellent protein meal.

60ml /2 fl oz vegetable oil
30g /1oz blanched whole almonds
4 spears broccoli
120g /4oz baby corn on the cob
1 clove garlic, crushed
1 red pepper, seeded and thinly sliced
120g /4oz mange tout peas
60g /2oz water chestnuts, thinly sliced
60ml /2 fl oz soy sauce
5ml /1 tsp sesame oil
5ml /1 tsp sherry
140ml /¼ pint vegetable stock
10ml /2 tsps cornflour
120g /4oz fresh bean sprouts
4 spring onions, cut into thin diagonal slices
225g /8oz tofu, cut into small dice
Salt and freshly ground black pepper

---

1. Heat a browning dish on HIGH for 5 minutes.

2. Pour the vegetable oil on to the dish and add the almonds. Cook these on HIGH for 5 minutes, or until they are golden brown, stirring them after each 1 minute of cooking time.

3. Remove the almonds from the dish and set them aside.

4. Remove the florets from the broccoli and reserve these.

5. Trim the broccoli stems and cut them diagonally with a sharp knife.

6. Cut the corn cobs in half lengthways with a sharp knife.

Step 10 Stir the cornflour mixture into the vegetables, mixing well to blend evenly.

7. Add the sliced broccoli stalks and the corn cobs to the oil on the browning dish and cook on HIGH for 1 minute.

8. Stir in the garlic, red pepper, mange tout, water chestnuts and the broccoli florets. Cook on HIGH for 1 minute.

9. Mix the soy sauce, sesame oil, sherry, stock and cornflour together in a small bowl or jug, until it is smooth and well blended.

10. Pour the cornflour mixture over the vegetables on the browning dish, stirring well to mix evenly. Cook on HIGH for 1 minute.

11. Add the bean sprouts, browned almonds, spring onions and the tofu. Stir thoroughly once more and cook on HIGH for 30 seconds to heat through.

12. Season to taste with the salt and pepper and serve at once.

Cook's Notes

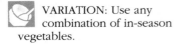 VARIATION: Use any combination of in-season vegetables.

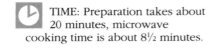 TIME: Preparation takes about 20 minutes, microwave cooking time is about 8½ minutes.

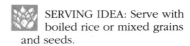 SERVING IDEA: Serve with boiled rice or mixed grains and seeds.

VEGETABLE CASSOULET

SERVES 4

This warming vegetable stew is an ideal recipe for using delicious autumn vegetables.

225g /8oz haricot beans, soaked overnight
30g /1oz vegetable margarine
60g /2oz dry wholemeal breadcrumbs
60ml /2 fl oz vegetable oil
2 cloves garlic, crushed
2 small leeks, washed and cut into 2.5cm /1-inch pieces
3 carrots, peeled and sliced
4 sticks celery, trimmed and cut into 2.5cm /1-inch pieces
2 parsnips, peeled and cut into 2.5cm /1-inch pieces
2 turnips, peeled and cut into 2.5cm /1-inch pieces
1 bay leaf
15ml /1 tbsp soy sauce
15ml /1 tbsp fresh marjoram, chopped
Salt and freshly ground black pepper
430ml /³⁄₄ pint vegetable stock

1. Drain the soaked beans and put them into a large microwave-proof bowl. Pour over just enough cold water to cover them.

2. Cover the bowl with cling film and pierce this several times with the tip of a sharp knife. Cook the beans for 5 minutes on HIGH. Reduce the power setting to MEDIUM, and cook for 1 hour, or until they are completely soft.

3. Drain the beans and rinse them thoroughly with cold water. Set them aside.

4. Heat a browning dish for 5 minutes on HIGH. Add the margarine and allow it to melt.

5. Stir the breadcrumbs into the melted margarine, mixing them well to coat evenly.

Step 5 Stir the breadcrumbs into the melted margarine on the browning dish, mixing them well to coat them thoroughly.

6. Cook on HIGH for 2-3 minutes, stirring frequently until the breadcrumbs are crisp and brown. Set them aside.

7. Put the oil on to the browning dish. Heat for 1 minute on HIGH.

8. Stir the prepared vegetables into the hot oil and cook for 2 minutes on HIGH, stirring them after 1 minute to ensure that they brown evenly.

9. Put the drained beans into a casserole dish along with the garlic, bay leaf, soy sauce, marjoram, salt and pepper. Add half of the stock and heat through for 5 minutes on HIGH.

10. Stir in the browned vegetables and enough of the remaining stock to make a sufficient amount of gravy. Cover the dish with a lid, or with cling film as described before and cook for 15-20 minutes on HIGH, adding more stock as required.

11. Allow the cassoulet to stand for 15 minutes.

12. Sprinkle the breadcrumbs evenly over the vegetables, and cook for 2 minutes on HIGH before serving.

Cook's Notes

 VEGETARIAN SUITABILITY: This recipe is suitable for vegans.

 VARIATION: Use any combination of vegetables, depending on the season.

 SERVING IDEA: Serve with jacket potatoes.

CHICKPEA AND PEPPER CASSEROLE

SERVES 4

*This colourful casserole can be made in advance
and re-heated before serving.*

225g /8oz dried chickpeas, soaked overnight
30ml /2 tbsps vegetable oil
1 large onion, sliced
1 green pepper, seeded and sliced
1 red pepper, seeded and sliced
1 clove garlic, crushed
2.5ml /½ tsp ground cumin
10ml /2 tsps chopped parsley
5ml /1 tsp chopped mint
4 large tomatoes, seeded and cut into strips
Salt and freshly ground black pepper

---

1. Drain the chickpeas and put them into a large microwave-proof bowl. Pour in just enough cold water to cover them.

Step 4 Stir the onions, garlic and cumin into the hot oil, mixing well to coat the ingredients thoroughly.

Step 6 Mix the chopped herbs, tomatoes and seasonings into the chickpea casserole.

2. Cover the bowl with cling film and pierce this several times with the tip of a sharp knife. Cook for 10 minutes on HIGH, then reduce the power setting to MEDIUM and cook for 1 hour, or until the chickpeas are soft.

3. Drain the chickpeas and reserve the liquid.

4. Put the oil into a large bowl and heat on HIGH for 30 seconds. Add the onions, peppers, garlic and cumin to the oil and stir well to coat thoroughly. Cook on HIGH for 1 minute.

5. Add the chickpeas to the onion and pepper mixture, along with half of the reserved cooking liquid. Cover the bowl as before and cook on HIGH for 5 minutes.

6. Uncover the bowl and stir in the parsley, mint, tomatoes and seasoning. Cook, uncovered, for 2 minutes on HIGH before serving.

Cook's Notes

TIME: Preparation takes about 20 minutes, plus overnight soaking of the chickpeas. Microwave cooking time is about 1 hour 6 minutes.

SERVING IDEA: Serve in warm wholemeal pitta bread, and, for lacto-vegetarians, top with a mixture of chopped cucumber and natural yogurt.

PREPARATION: Care must be taken when re-hydrating and cooking dries pulses. They must be soft and completely cooked before eating.

PASTA-STUFFED CABBAGE LEAVES

SERVES 4

*The nutty texture and flavour of the filled cabbage leaves is
ideally complemented by the mushroom and tomato sauce.*

120g /4oz soup pasta
1 head, large-leafed cabbage, white or green
Salt
15ml /1 tbsp walnut oil
1 small onion, peeled and finely chopped
1 green pepper, seeded and chopped
450g /1lb tinned tomatoes, roughly chopped
120g /4oz button mushrooms, washed and
    chopped
30ml /2 tbsps tomato purée
1 bay leaf
Pinch sugar
Black pepper
1 hard-boiled egg, finely chopped
60g /2oz shelled walnuts, roughly chopped
15ml /1 tbsp fresh chopped chives
30ml /2 tbsps fresh chopped parsley
5ml /1 tsp fresh chopped marjoram

1. Put the soup pasta into a large bowl and pour
over 570ml /1 pint lightly salted boiling water.
Cover the bowl with cling film and pierce this
several times with the tip of a sharp knife. Cook
for 5 minutes on HIGH then leave to stand, still
covered, for 10 minutes.

2. Carefully separate the cabbage leaves and put
about 8-12 of the largest into a roasting bag. Add
a pinch of salt and 30ml /2 tbsps cold water. Tie
up the roasting bag and cook for 4 minutes on
HIGH.

Step 9 Spread
equal amounts of
the pasta filling
over the thicker
stalk end of each
cabbage leaf,
leaving enough of a
border at each side
to fold over.

Step 10 Roll the
thinner tops of each
leaf over the filling
and folded sides of
the cabbage leaves,
tucking it
underneath to seal
completely.

3. Drain the cabbage leaves in a colander, then
lay them flat on absorbent kitchen paper to dry
slightly.

4. Put the oil into a bowl and cook on HIGH for
30 seconds.

5. Add the onions and pepper to the oil and stir
to coat thoroughly. Cook for 1 minute on HIGH.

6. Stir the tinned tomatoes, the mushrooms,
tomato purée, bay leaf and sugar into the
peppers and onions. Season to taste, and cook,
uncovered, for 8 minutes on HIGH, stirring the
mixture twice during the cooking time.

7. Drain the pasta thoroughly and put it into a
large bowl.

8. Stir in all the remaining ingredients and
season lightly.

9. Spread equal amounts of the pasta mixture
over the stalk end of each of the cabbage leaves,
leaving a border at the edges to fold over.

10. Fold the sides over the filling, then roll the
top of the leaf over the top of the filling and tuck
it under the stalk end, envelope fashion, to seal
the filling inside.

11. Arrange each filled cabbage leaf in a serving
dish.

12. Pour the sauce over the cabbage leaves and
cook, uncovered, on MEDIUM for 8-10 minutes,
or until completely heated through. Serve
immediately.

VEGETABLE MOUSSAKA

SERVES 4

This traditional Greek dish loses nothing by being made without meat.

---

1 large aubergine
Salt
2 medium potatoes, peeled and sliced
15ml /1 tbsp olive oil
1 medium onion, peeled and finely chopped
1 clove garlic, crushed
Salt and freshly ground black pepper
400g /14oz tinned tomatoes, roughly chopped
15ml /1 tbsp tomato purée
1.25ml /¼ tsp ground cinnamon
1.25ml /¼ tsp ground cumin
Pinch of sugar
30ml /2 tbsps vegetable oil
120g /4oz button mushrooms, peeled and sliced
1 green pepper, seeded and sliced
2 courgettes, sliced
4 fresh tomatoes, peeled and sliced
30g /1oz vegetable margarine
30g /1oz plain flour
Pinch ground nutmeg
280ml /½ pint milk
60g /2oz vegetarian Cheddar cheese, grated
1 egg, beaten

---

1. Cut the aubergine in half lengthways and lightly score the cut surface diagonally.

2. Sprinkle the aubergine with salt, rubbing it into the scored surface. Leave to stand for ½ hour.

3. Put the potatoes into a roasting bag. Seal and cook on HIGH for 10 minutes.

4. Put the tinned tomatoes, the tomato purée, cinnamon, cumin and sugar into a bowl along with the onions and garlic. Stir the ingredients together, and season with a little salt and pepper.

5. Put the tinned tomatoes, tomato purée, cinnamon, cumin and sugar into the bowl along with the onions and garlic. Stir the ingredients together thoroughly and season with a little salt and pepper.

6. Stirring the mixture twice during the cooking time, cook the tomato sauce for 6 minutes on HIGH, or until the vegetables are completely soft and it has thickened slightly.

7. Wash the aubergine thoroughly to remove the salt and slice thinly with a sharp knife.

8. Heat the vegetable oil in a large bowl and add the sliced aubergine. Mix well to coat each slice evenly with the hot oil then cover the bowl with cling film and pierce this several times with the tip of a sharp knife. Cook on HIGH for 2 minutes.

9. Remove the cooked aubergine from the bowl and set it aside. Add the green pepper, courgette and the tomatoes to the bowl and cook, uncovered, for 1 minute on HIGH.

10. Layer the vegetables in a serving dish, starting with the aubergines and ending with the potatoes. Spoon equal amounts of the tomato sauce over each layer, except the potato layer. Continue layering until all the vegetables and sauce are used up.

11. Put the margarine into a bowl and cook on HIGH for 30 seconds to melt.

12. Stir the flour, nutmeg and a little seasoning into the melted margarine, mixing it well to form a paste.

13. Add a little of the milk to the flour paste and cook on HIGH for 30 seconds. Stir well and add a little more milk.

14. Continue adding milk and stirring until all the milk has been incorporated and the sauce is smooth and thick.

15. Add the cheese and the egg to the white sauce and pour this evenly over the layered vegetables in the serving dish.

16. Cook the moussaka for 4 minutes on HIGH to heat through before serving.

SWEET AND SOUR PEANUTS

SERVES 4

This highly nutritious meal is very quick and simple to prepare.

90g /3oz muscovado sugar
75ml /5 tbsps wine vinegar
45ml /3 tbsps soy sauce
15ml /1 tbsp arrowroot
1 large red pepper
120g /4oz fresh bean sprouts
120g /4oz shelled, unsalted roasted peanuts
225g /8oz tinned bamboo shoots, drained

1. Put the sugar, vinegar and soy sauce into a bowl. Add the arrowroot and stir well until it has blended completely.

2. Cook the arrowroot mixture on HIGH for 30 seconds. Stir and cook for a further 30 seconds, or until the mixture has thickened and cleared.

3. Halve the red pepper and remove the seeds.

Step 1 Blend the sugar, vinegar, soy sauce and arrowroot together until they are smooth.

Step 4 Cut the seeded pepper into thin strips using a sharp knife.

Step 5 Put the vegetables and nuts into the sauce mixture, stirring well to coat all the ingredients thoroughly.

4. Cut the red flesh into thin strips 1cm x 5cm / ¼ inch x 2 inches, using a sharp knife.

5. Stir the pepper strips and all the remaining ingredients into the thickened sauce mixture.

6. Cook on HIGH for 3 minutes, or until the pepper strips are tender.

Cook's Notes

 VARIATION: Use cashew nuts instead of peanuts, and add 60g /2oz fresh, chopped pineapple.

 TIME: Preparation takes about 15 minutes, microwave cooking time is about 4 minutes.

 VEGETARIAN SUITABILITY: This recipe is suitable for vegans.

SAVOURY BREAD PUDDING
SERVES 4

This easy-to-prepare family meal is both filling and nutritious.

225g /8oz wholemeal bread
60g /2oz sunflower seeds
60g /2oz walnuts or hazelnuts, chopped
15ml /1 tbsp dried mixed herbs
1 large onion, peeled and chopped
1 clove garlic, crushed
430ml /¾ pint vegetable stock
Salt and freshly ground black pepper

---

1. Cut the bread into thick slices and then into cubes.

2. Put the cubed bread into a large bowl along with the sunflower seeds, nuts and herbs. Mix these ingredients together thoroughly, making sure that they are well distributed.

3. Put the onion and the garlic into another bowl or a jug and pour over 60ml /4 tbsps of the stock.

4. Cook on HIGH for 2 minutes, or until the onion has softened slightly.

Step 1 Cut the thick slices of bread into 2.5cm /1-inch cubes with a sharp knife.

Step 2 Put the cubes of bread, along with the sunflower seeds, nuts and herbs into a large bowl and mix them well to distribute the ingredients evenly.

Step 5 Mix the onion mixture and the stock into the dry bread, stirring well to moisten all the ingredients thoroughly.

5. Add the cooked onion mixture and the remaining stock to the bread, seeds, nuts and herbs in the first bowl. Season with the salt and pepper and stir well to mix thoroughly.

6. Cover the bowl with cling film and pierce this several times with the tip of a sharp knife. Cook on HIGH for 3 minutes.

7. Allow the bread mixture to stand for 2 minutes before serving.

Cook's Notes

VARIATION: For a lacto-vegetarian meal, add 120g /4oz grated vegetarian sage Derby cheese to the onion mixture and omit the dried herbs.

VEGETARIAN SUITABILITY: This recipe is suitable for vegans.

TIME: Preparation takes about 15 minutes, plus 2 minutes standing time.

CHEESE SANDWICH SOUFFLÉ
SERVES 4

*Unlike a true soufflé, there is no need to rush this dish to the table
as it will not sink and is equally delicious served either hot or cold.*

15ml /1 tbsp wholegrain mustard
8 slices of wholemeal bread
2 tomatoes
180g /6oz vegetarian Cheddar cheese
2 large eggs
570ml /1 pint milk
5ml /1 tsp dried basil
Salt and freshly ground black pepper

1. Spread equal amounts of the mustard over four slices of the bread.

2. Slice the tomatoes using a sharp knife and finely grate the cheese.

3. Arrange the tomato slices over the mustard-spread bread and sprinkle the cheese evenly over the tomatoes.

Step 3 Sprinkle the cheese evenly over the tomatoes on the mustard-spread slices of bread.

Step 7 After standing, the egg and milk mixture should have almost completely soaked into the cheese sandwiches.

4. Use the remaining four slices of bread to cover the tomatoes and cheese.

5. Place the cheese and tomato sandwiches into a dish which they will nearly fill.

6. Break the eggs into a jug or bowl and pour over the milk. Whisk these together along with the herbs and seasoning.

7. Pour the egg mixture over the cheese sandwiches in the dish and allow to stand for 30 minutes, or until the bread is completely soaked.

8. Cover the bowl with cling film and pierce this several times with the tip of a sharp knife.

9. Cook the soufflé on HIGH for 1 minute, then reduce the power setting to MEDIUM, and cook for a further 20 minutes, or until the egg and milk mixture has set.

10. Stand for 3 minutes before serving.

Cook's Notes

 COOK'S TIP: If a crispy brown top is preferred, brown under a conventional grill before serving.

SERVING IDEA: Serve with braised mushrooms or fennel.

TIME: Preparation takes about 20 minutes, microwave cooking time is about 21 minutes, plus approximately 33 minutes standing time.

VARIATION: Use slices of Spanish onion in place of the tomato, and vegetarian Stilton in place of the Cheddar cheese in this recipe.

HERB AND CHEESE COBBLER

SERVES 4

Although frozen vegetables are very convenient, fresh vegetables can be used in this warming winter dish if you prefer.

450g /1 lb frozen mixed vegetables
30g /1oz vegetable margarine
30g /1oz wholemeal flour
5ml /1 tsp arrowroot
5ml /1 tsp mixed dried herbs
280ml /½ pint strong vegetable stock
Salt
60g /2oz bran
60g /2oz plain flour
5ml /1 tsp baking powder
120g /4oz vegetarian Cheddar cheese, grated
60g /2oz solid vegetable fat
120ml /4 fl oz milk

1. Put the vegetables into a bowl and cook, uncovered, for 4 minutes on HIGH.

2. Put the margarine into a bowl along with the flour, arrowroot and herbs. Pour over the stock.

3. Cook the flour and stock for 2 minutes on HIGH, stir well and cook for a further 2 minutes on HIGH.

4. Mix the sauce thoroughly to remove any

Step 4 Mix the sauce thoroughly using a small whisk to remove any lumps.

Step 7 Rub the vegetable fat dice into the flour mixture using the fingertips, until it resembles breadcrumbs.

lumps and cook for a further minute on HIGH if it has not quite thickened.

5. Pour the sauce into the cooked vegetables and mix well to coat them evenly.

6. Put the bran, flour, baking powder and cheese into a mixing bowl. Add a pinch of salt.

7. Cut the vegetable fat into small dice and rub these into the flour mixture until it resembles breadcrumbs.

8. Pour the milk into the flour mixture and stir well until the ingredients form a soft dough.

9. Turn the dough out onto a lightly floured surface and roll it to 1.5cm /½-inch thick. Cut the dough into 8 rounds using a biscuit cutter.

10. Put the vegetables in the sauce into a serving dish and arrange the 8 rounds of dough over the top of these.

11. Bake the cobbler, uncovered, on HIGH for 10 minutes, or until the cheesy rounds are well risen and firm.

12. Stand for 3 minutes before serving.

Cook's Notes

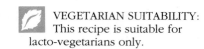

TIME: Preparation takes about 20 minutes, microwave cooking time is about 16 minutes, plus 3 minutes standing time.

VEGETARIAN SUITABILITY: This recipe is suitable for lacto-vegetarians only.

SERVING IDEA: Serve with jacket potatoes and grilled tomatoes.

VEGETARIAN TOMALE PIE

SERVES 4

This spicy vegetable pie has a definite South American flavour.

225g /8oz red lentils, soaked overnight
570ml /1 pint strong vegetable stock
15ml /1 tbsp corn oil
1 large onion, peeled and chopped
1 clove of garlic, crushed
450g /1lb fresh tomatoes, roughly chopped
225g /8oz frozen or tinned sweetcorn kernels
1 green pepper, seeded and chopped
45ml /3 tbsps tomato purée
15ml /1 tbsp chilli powder
Salt
180g /6oz cornmeal
570ml /1 pint milk
15g /½oz vegetable margarine
2 eggs, beaten
225g /8oz vegetarian Cheddar cheese, grated

---

1. Drain the lentils from the soaking liquid and put them into a large bowl. Pour over the vegetable stock. Cook, uncovered, for 15 minutes on HIGH, or until they are soft.

2. Put the oil into a microwave-proof casserole dish, along with the onions and garlic. Cook for 2 minutes on HIGH, or until the onion is soft but not browned.

3. Drain any liquid from the cooked lentils and reserve this.

4. Add the cooked lentils to the onions in the

Step 9 Stir the diced margarine into the milk and cornmeal mixture, mixing well to blend thoroughly.

Step 11 Spread the cornmeal batter over the lentils and tomatoes in the casserole dish, spreading it with the back of a spoon to make an even topping.

casserole and stir in the tomatoes, sweetcorn and green pepper.

5. Blend the tomato purée and the chilli powder with 280ml /½ pint of the reserved liquid from the lentils.

6. Pour the blended tomato purée into the lentil and vegetable mixture, mixing well to blend all ingredients thoroughly.

7. Cover the casserole dish with cling film and pierce this several times with the tip of a sharp knife. Cook for 3 minutes on HIGH.

8. Put the cornmeal into a large bowl and stir in the milk.

9. Cut the margarine into small dice and add these to the cornmeal and milk along with a little salt. Cook, uncovered, on MEDIUM for 5 minutes.

10. Add the eggs and half of the cheese to the part-cooked cornmeal mixture. Beat well with a wooden spoon.

11. Pour the cornmeal batter over the lentils and tomatoes in the casserole dish. Cover the casserole with cling film as before and bake on HIGH for 10 minutes.

12. Sprinkle the remaining cheese over the tomale pie, and cook, uncovered, for a further 2 minutes, or until the cheese has melted.

STIR-FRIED BEANS AND SPROUTS

SERVES 4

High in both protein and fibre, this stir-fry makes a flavoursome change for an easy meal.

225g /8oz dried adzuki beans, soaked overnight
   in water
1 large onion
1 large green pepper
15ml /1 tbsp soya oil
225g /8oz fresh bean sprouts
60ml /4 tbsps soy sauce

---

1. Drain the beans. Put the soaked beans into a large bowl and cover them with boiling water. Cover the bowl with cling film and pierce this several times with the tip of a sharp knife.

2. Cook the beans on HIGH for 10 minutes, reduce the power setting to MEDIUM and cook for a further 30 minutes, or until the beans are soft and completely cooked.

3. Drain the beans and rinse them in cold water.

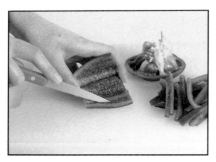

Step 5 Thinly slice the cored and seeded pepper halves with a sharp knife.

Step 8 Stir the bean sprouts thoroughly into the onions and peppers to coat them evenly with the hot oil.

Leave them in a colander to drain completely.

4. Peel the onion and cut it in half. Thickly slice each half and pull the slices apart.

5. Cut the pepper in half and remove the seeds. Cut the pepper flesh into thin strips.

6. Heat the oil in a large bowl for 1 minute on HIGH.

7. Put the onion and the pepper slices into the hot oil and stir well to coat evenly. Cook, uncovered, on HIGH for 2 minutes.

8. Add the bean sprouts to the onions and peppers in the bowl and stir them in well to mix thoroughly. Cook, uncovered, on HIGH for a further 1 minute.

9. Add the cooked beans and the soy sauce to the vegetables in the bowl, mix well and re-heat for 4 minutes on HIGH before serving.

Cook's Notes

TIME: Preparation takes about 10 minutes, microwave cooking time is about 50 minutes.

VEGETARIAN SUITABILITY: This recipe is suitable for vegans.

COOK'S TIP: Use drained, tinned beans in place of the dried beans in this recipe to cut down on the cooking time. Remember that dried beans re-hydrate to double their weight so use 450g /1lb of tinned beans.

PREPARATION: Great care must be taken when re-hydrating and cooking dried beans. The beans must be well soaked and completely cooked before being eaten.

CHILLI CORN PIE

SERVES 4

*Freshly made chilli sauce really enhances the flavour
of this Mexican-style dish.*

180g /6oz cornmeal
570ml /1 pint milk or water
Freshly ground sea salt
15g /½oz vegetable margarine, diced
2 large eggs, beaten
225g /8oz vegetarian Cheddar cheese, grated
450g /1lb tomatoes
1 large onion, peeled and chopped
60ml /2 fl oz wine vinegar
60g /2oz muscovado sugar
2.5ml /½ tsp ground cinnamon
2.5ml /½ tsp ground ginger
2.5ml /½ tsp ground mustard seeds
2.5ml /½ tsp chilli powder
350g /12oz cooked red kidney beans
225g /8oz frozen or tinned sweetcorn kernels

1. Put the cornmeal into a large bowl and gradually add the milk, a little at a time, beating well between additions until all the milk is incorporated.

2. Season with a little salt and stir in the margarine, eggs and half the cheese. Cook uncovered on MEDIUM for 5 minutes.

3. Remove the bowl from the microwave oven and beat well with a wooden spoon to remove any lumps that may have formed.

4. Roughly chop the tomatoes, remove the green stem and any hard core. Put the chopped tomatoes into a large bowl.

Step 4 Roughly chop the tomatoes, removing any green stem or core as you do so.

5. Stir the onions into the chopped tomatoes along with the vinegar, sugar, cinnamon, ginger, mustard seed and chilli. Season with a little salt and mix well.

6. Cover the bowl with cling film and pierce this several times with the tip of a sharp knife. Cook the tomato mixture for 5 minutes on HIGH.

7. Put the kidney beans and sweetcorn into the tomato sauce mixture and stir well to coat all ingredients thoroughly.

8. Transfer the chilli bean mixture to a serving dish and carefully spread the cornmeal and cheese topping over, using a metal spoon or round bladed knife to smooth the top.

9. Cook the chilli corn pie, uncovered, for 8 minutes on HIGH.

10. Sprinkle the remaining cheese over the top and cook for a further 2 minutes on HIGH to melt the cheese.

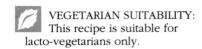

Cook's Notes

PREPARATION: If fresh tomatoes are too expensive, use a 400g /14oz tin of chopped tomatoes instead.

VEGETARIAN SUITABILITY: This recipe is suitable for lacto-vegetarians only.

TIME: Preparation takes about 10 minutes, microwave cooking time is about 20 minutes.

KIDNEY BEAN CURRY

SERVES 4

The kidney beans are wonderfully enhanced by the flavour
of the spices in this delicious curry.

1 large onion
30ml /2 tbsps vegetable oil
2 cloves garlic, crushed
1 x 2.5cm /1-inch piece of fresh root ginger
5ml /1 tsp ground chilli powder
5ml /1 tsp ground coriander
5ml /1 tsp ground cumin
5ml /1 tsp garam masala
1 cinnamon stick
2 fresh green chillies
425g /15oz canned tomatoes in their juice,
    chopped
1 bay leaf
450g /1lb canned red kidney beans, drained
Freshly ground sea salt
Few sprigs of fresh coriander leaf, chopped

1. Peel the onion and slice it thinly with a sharp knife.

2. Heat the oil in a large bowl or casserole for 30 seconds on HIGH. Add the onions and the garlic to the oil and stir well. Cook for 2 minutes on HIGH, until the onions have softened but have not coloured.

3. Carefully peel off the outer brown skin from the ginger. Using a fine grater, grate the fleshy root.

4. Stir the grated ginger into the onions and cook for a further 30 seconds.

Step 7 Mix the tomatoes, bay leaf, beans and salt thoroughly into the spice mixture to distribute the flavour evenly.

5. Stir the chilli powder, ground coriander, cumin, garam masala and the cinnamon, into the onion and ginger mixture and cook on HIGH for 1 minute to fry the spices.

6. Cut the chilli peppers in half lengthways and remove the white core and the seeds. Finely chop the flesh using a very sharp knife, and stir this into the onion and spice mixture. Cook on HIGH for 30 seconds.

7. Add the tomatoes, bay leaf, the kidney beans and some salt to the spice mixture. Stir well to mix thoroughly and cook, uncovered, on HIGH for 12 minutes.

8. Sprinkle the chopped coriander leaf over the top of the curry and stand for 5 minutes before serving.

Cook's Notes

PREPARATION: Great care must be taken when preparing fresh chillies. Wear rubber gloves to prevent the juice being left on fingers, and take precautions not to get any juice into the eyes or mouth. If this should happen, rinse with plenty of cold water.

TIME: Preparation takes about 15 minutes. Microwave cooking time is about 17 minutes, plus 5 minutes standing time.

VEGETARIAN SUITABILITY: This recipe is suitable for vegans.

SERVING IDEA: Serve with a cucumber raita if you are a lacto-vegetarian, or hot lime pickle if you are a vegan. Nan bread and chapatis are also excellent accompaniments.

NUT AND HERB BULGUR

SERVES 4

Bulgur wheat cooks in a similar way to rice and can be used as an interesting alternative to many rice dishes.

1 red pepper
1 onion
60g /2oz fresh hazelnuts
30g /1oz pine nuts
15ml /1 tbsp walnut oil
120g /4oz cucumber
15ml /1 tbsp fresh chopped coriander
15ml /1 tbsp fresh chopped mint
30ml /2 tbsps fresh chopped parsley
225g /8oz bulgur wheat
430ml /¾ pint strong vegetable stock

1. Cut the pepper in half and remove the white core and seeds. Slice the flesh thinly.

2. Peel the onion and chop it into small pieces.

3. Roughly chop the hazelnuts and mix them in a small bowl with the pine nuts.

Step 7 Stir the diced cucumber and the herbs into the nut mixture, mixing well to blend thoroughly.

Step 9 Cook the wheat in the stock until all the liquid has been absorbed.

4. Put the oil into a large bowl or casserole, and heat on HIGH for 30 seconds. Stir in the peppers, onions and mixed nuts.

5. Cover the dish with a lid or with cling film which has been punctured twice only with the tip of a knife.

6. Cook on HIGH for 3 minutes. Remove the cover and stir well.

7. Dice the cucumber and mix this, along with the coriander, mint and parsley, into the pepper and nut mixture.

8. Stir in the wheat, and pour over the stock. Re-cover the dish or bowl and cook on HIGH for 10 minutes, or until all the moisture has been absorbed. Stir the mixture twice during this cooking time.

9. Allow the wheat to stand for 5 minutes, then fluff up with a fork and serve.

Cook's Notes

VARIATION: Use brown rice instead of the bulgur wheat in this recipe.

SERVING IDEA: Serve with a mixed salad.

TIME: Preparation takes about 10 minutes, microwave cooking time is about 14 minutes, plus 5 minutes standing time.

VEGETARIAN SUITABILITY: This recipe is suitable for vegans.

CHEESE AND TOMATO PASTA

SERVES 4

This favourite Italian classic is perfect served as a lunch or supper dish.

15ml /1 tbsp vegetable oil
1 onion, peeled and chopped
120g /4oz button mushrooms, finely sliced
15ml /1 tbsp tomato purée
400g /14oz tinned tomatoes, chopped
30ml /2 tbsp dried mixed herbs
120g /4oz vegetarian Cheddar cheese, finely grated
225g /8oz tagliatelle verde

1. Put the oil into a large bowl and stir in the onions.

2. Cook, uncovered, for 2 minutes, on HIGH, or until the onion has softened but is not coloured.

3. Add the mushrooms, tomato purée, chopped tomatoes and the herbs to the onions and stir well to mix the ingredients thoroughly.

Step 3 Stir the mushrooms, tomato purée, the chopped tomatoes and the herbs into the onions, mixing well to combine all the ingredients thoroughly.

Step 7 Pour enough boiling water over the pasta to just cover.

4. Cook, uncovered, for 4-5 minutes on HIGH, or until the tomatoes are boiling.

5. Continue cooking on HIGH, stirring occasionally, until the sauce has reduced and has thickened slightly.

6. Stir the cheese into the tomato sauce, cover the bowl and keep warm.

7. Put the pasta into a large bowl and cover with the boiling water.

8. Cover the bowl with cling film and pierce this several times with the tip of a sharp knife. Cook on HIGH for 8-10 minutes, or until the pasta is soft.

9. Drain the pasta thoroughly and arrange it on a serving dish or bowl.

10. Re-heat the sauce on HIGH for 2 minutes if necessary, then pour the sauce over it and serve straight away.

Cook's Notes

TIME: Preparation takes about 10 minutes, microwave cooking time is about 23 minutes.

VEGETARIAN SUITABILITY: This recipe is suitable for lacto-vegetarians only.

COOK'S TIP: Fresh pasta is now easily available in many supermarkets and delicatessens; use this to cut down on the cooking time, it will only need about 5 minutes in a microwave.

SERVING IDEA: Serve with a mixed Italian salad and hot garlic bread.

VARIATION: Use any variety of pasta shapes in this recipe.

STUFFED AUBERGINES
SERVES 4

When filled with this delicious stuffing, these interesting vegetables make a substantial hot meal.

2 large aubergines
15g /½oz butter or 15ml /1 tbsp vegetable oil
1 clove garlic, crushed
1 onion, peeled and finely chopped
1 small green pepper, seeded and chopped
60g /2oz mushrooms, trimmed and roughly chopped
450g /1lb tinned tomatoes, chopped and juice reserved
15ml /1 tbsp tomato purée
10ml /2 tsps fresh chopped basil
Pinch sugar
Salt and freshly ground black pepper
30g /1oz dry wholemeal breadcrumbs
2.5ml /½ tsp dried oregano
30g /1oz lightly toasted walnuts, chopped
60g /2oz vegetarian Cheddar cheese, grated, optional

1. Cut the aubergines in half lengthways, and score the flesh lightly in a diamond fashion, taking care not to cut through to the outer skin.

2. Sprinkle the cut flesh with salt and leave to stand for 20-30 minutes.

3. Rinse the aubergine halves thoroughly in running water and pat dry.

4. Wrap each aubergine half in cling film and cook on HIGH for 7-9 minutes, or until the flesh has softened. Leave to stand whilst preparing the filling.

5. Put the butter or oil into a large bowl, along with the garlic and onion. Cook for 1 minute on HIGH. Stir the vegetables and continue cooking for a further 2 minutes on HIGH.

6. Add the green peppers and the mushrooms to the onion mixture. Stir well and cook on HIGH for 2-3 minutes, or until the pepper begins to soften.

Step 1 Score the cut surface of each aubergine half lightly in a diamond fashion, taking care not to pierce the outer skin with the knife.

7. Stir the drained tomatoes, the tomato purée, basil, sugar and seasoning into the onion and pepper mixture, mixing thoroughly with a wooden spoon.

8. Cover the bowl with cling film and pierce this several times with the tip of a sharp knife. Cook for 6-8 minutes then set aside to stand.

9. Unwrap the aubergines. Scoop out the scored flesh, leaving a 5mm /¼-inch lining inside the skin of each half to form a shell.

10. Chop the flesh roughly and add this to the tomato mixture along with a little of the reserved tomato juice if the mixture looks too dry.

11. Fill each aubergine shell with equal amounts of the tomato filling, pressing it well into each half to form a good shape.

12. Cook the stuffed aubergines for 3 minutes on HIGH.

13. In a small bowl, mix together the breadcrumbs, oregano, nuts and cheese if used. Sprinkle each filled aubergine half lightly with this mixture and cook on LOW for 2-3 minutes to heat through before serving.

GLAZED VEGETABLES

SERVES 4

*Using everyday vegetables, this delicious way of preparing
vegetable casserole makes an interesting change.*

30g /1oz vegetable margarine
15ml /1 tbsp unrefined brown sugar or molasses
15-30ml /1-2 tbsps water or vegetable stock
2 carrots, peeled and cut into strips
2 salsify, peeled and cut into rounds
2 turnips, peeled and cut into wedges
180g /6oz pickling onions or shallots, peeled and
   left whole
120g /4oz large mushrooms, quartered
5ml /1 tsp fresh rosemary or thyme
Salt and freshly ground black pepper
10ml /2 tsps Dijon mustard

1. Put the margarine into a large microwave-proof casserole dish and melt it on HIGH for 30 seconds.

2. Stir the brown sugar into the melted margarine along with the stock or water. Heat

Step 4 Add the onions to the vegetables in the casserole dish, stirring well to coat them evenly with the sugar glaze.

Step 7 The vegetables are cooked when the tip of a sharp knife will pierce the turnips easily.

for a further 30 seconds on HIGH, then stir to dissolve the sugar.

3. Put the carrots, salsify and turnips into the bowl with the sugar mixture. Stir well to coat the vegetables, then cook on HIGH for 2 minutes.

4. Add the onions to the glazed vegetables and stir them in well to coat them with the glaze. Cook on HIGH for a further 2 minutes, or until the onions and vegetables are beginning to soften.

5. Add the mushrooms to the glazed vegetables, sprinkle over the herbs and the salt and pepper. Stir in the mustard and mix well.

6. Cover the casserole with a lid or with cling film which should be punctured twice only to allow a little steam to escape.

7. Cook the casserole on HIGH for 6 minutes, or until the vegetables are completely tender.

8. Allow the casserole to stand for 2 minutes before uncovering and serving.

Cook's Notes

TIME: Preparation takes about 20 minutes, microwave cooking time is about 12 minutes, plus 2 minutes standing time.

VARIATION: Change the combination of fresh vegetables to suit the season or personal taste.

SERVING IDEA: Serve with wholemeal bread or jacket potatoes.

Vegetarian
Microwave
Cooking

CHAPTER ~ 5

· Entertaining ·

TRI-COLOURED TAGLIATELLE AND VEGETABLES

SERVES 4

A delicious Italian dish which is ideal for an informal supper party.

225g /8oz tagliatelle (mixture of red, green and white)
60g /2oz vegetable margarine
225g /8oz broccoli florets
1 large onion, peeled and thinly sliced
2 red peppers, seeded and thinly sliced
2 cloves garlic, crushed
10ml /2 tsps fresh chopped rosemary, thick stalks removed
Salt and freshly ground black pepper
90g /3oz vegetarian Cheddar cheese, finely grated

1. Put the pasta into a large bowl and pour over just enough boiling water to cover.

2. Cover the bowl with cling film and pierce this several times with the tip of a sharp knife. Cook the pasta on HIGH for 20 minutes. Allow to stand for 5 minutes.

3. Put half of the margarine into a large bowl and cook on HIGH for 30 seconds to melt.

4. Stir the broccoli, onion and pepper into the melted margarine and stir well to coat evenly. Cover the bowl with cling film as before, and

Step 6 Toss the pasta and the vegetables together in a large bowl.

Step 8 Carefully strain the flavoured margarine through a small sieve onto the pasta and vegetables.

Step 1 Put the pasta into a large bowl and pour over just enough boiling water to cover.

cook on HIGH for 2 minutes.

5. Drain the pasta and rinse it in hot water.

6. Put the pasta into a large bowl and toss in the cooked vegetables.

7. Put the remaining margarine into a bowl along with the garlic and rosemary. Cook on HIGH for 1 minute to release the flavours.

8. Strain the melted margarine through a small sieve onto the pasta in the bowl.

9. Season the pasta with a little salt and pepper and sprinkle over the cheese.

10. Mix together the pasta, margarine, seasoning and cheese thoroughly before serving.

Cook's Notes

COOK'S TIP: Use fresh pasta in this recipe and reduce the cooking time by half.

VARIATION: Use other combinations of vegetables in this recipe.

VEGETARIAN SUITABILITY: This recipe is suitable for lacto-vegetarians only.

SESAME STIR-FRY
SERVES 2

This recipe can be prepared in advance and cooked quickly for a romantic Oriental meal for two.

30ml /2 tbsps vegetable oil
2.5ml /^{1}/$_2$ tsp finely chopped, fresh ginger root
15g /^{1}/$_2$oz sesame seeds
60g /2oz mange tout
1 stick celery, sliced
2 ears baby corn, halved lengthways
60g /2oz water chestnuts, thinly sliced diagonally
30g /1oz button mushrooms, thinly sliced
1 spring onion, diagonally sliced
1 small red pepper, seeded and thinly sliced
120g /4oz Chinese leaves, shredded
120g /4oz fresh bean sprouts
15g /^{1}/$_2$oz cornflour
30ml /2tbsps soy sauce
15ml /1 tbsp sherry
2.5ml /^{1}/$_2$ tsp sesame oil
60ml /4 tbsps water

1. Heat a browning dish for 5 minutes on HIGH.

2. Put the oil onto the browning dish, and add the ginger and the sesame seeds. Cook on HIGH for 30 seconds. Stir well.

Step 3 Stir the mange tout, celery, corn, chestnuts, mushrooms and onions into the hot oil and pepper, mixing well with a spoon or spatula to coat all of them evenly.

Step 7 Stir the thickened sauce into the vegetables in the browning dish, mixing well to coat them all evenly.

3. Add the mange tout, celery, corn, chestnuts, mushrooms, onions and pepper. Stir well to coat with the oil then cook for 4 minutes on HIGH, stirring well after each minute to brown the vegetables evenly.

4. Toss in the Chinese leaves and the bean sprouts. Stir well and cook for a further 1 minute on HIGH.

5. In a small bowl, combine the cornflour with the soy sauce, the sherry, sesame oil and water to form a smooth liquid.

6. Cover the bowl with cling film and pierce this several times with the tip of a sharp knife. Cook the sauce on HIGH for 1-2 minutes, or until it is smooth and clear.

7. Pour this sauce over the vegetables in the browning dish and stir well to coat them all evenly.

8. Heat through for 1 minute on HIGH for if necessary before serving.

Cook's Notes

 TIME: Preparation takes about 15 minutes, microwave cooking time is about 7 minutes.

 VEGETARIAN SUITABILITY: This recipe is suitable for vegans.

 VARIATION: Use any combination of vegetables in this recipe.

VEGETABLES MORNAY

SERVES 4

This simple but elegant dish will add a touch of class to your entertaining.

225g /8oz new potatoes, scrubbed but not
   peeled
2-3 carrots, peeled and cut into thin strips
2 parsnips, peeled and cut into thin strips
225g /8oz shallots or pickling onions
90g /3oz vegetable margarine
5ml /1 tsp brown sugar or molasses
120g /4oz mange tout
120g /4oz small button mushrooms
45g /1½oz plain flour
5ml /1 tsp dry mustard
Pinch cayenne pepper
570ml /1 pint milk
120g /4oz vegetarian Cheddar cheese, finely
   grated
Salt and freshly ground black pepper
Grated nutmeg for garnish

1. Put the new potatoes into a bowl along with 4 tablespoons of water and a pinch of salt. Cover the bowl with cling film and pierce this several times with the tip of a sharp knife.

2. Cook the potatoes on HIGH for 8-10 minutes then leave them to stand, still covered, for a further 5 minutes.

3. Put the carrots and parsnips into another bowl, along with 4 tbsps of water. Cover as before and cook for 6 minutes on HIGH. Allow to stand as before.

4. Put the onions, 15g/½oz of the margarine and the sugar into a bowl. Cover as before and cook for 7 minutes on HIGH, stirring twice during the cooking time and replacing the covering each time.

5. Melt a further 30g /1oz of the margarine in another bowl for 30 seconds on HIGH. Stir the mange tout and the mushrooms into the melted margarine, mixing well to coat evenly.

Step 9 Stir the flour, mustard, cayenne and a little seasoning into the melted butter, blending until the mixture forms a smooth roux.

6. Cover this bowl as before and cook for 2 minutes on HIGH.

7. Keep all the cooked vegetables warm whilst preparing the mornay sauce.

8. Melt the remaining margarine for 1 minute on HIGH, in a bowl or measuring jug.

9. Stir in the flour, mustard, cayenne and a little seasoning, mixing the ingredients together thoroughly to form a roux.

10. Gradually add the milk to the roux, whisking it in well and cooking for 30 seconds on HIGH after each addition.

11. Whisk the sauce well after the final addition of milk to remove any lumps.

12. Continue cooking the sauce on HIGH until it has thickened. Stir the cheese into the sauce and cook for a further 30 seconds to melt the cheese.

13. Arrange the cooked vegetables attractively on a warmed serving platter, keeping each vegetable in a different pile. Spoon a little of the sauce over the vegetables and sprinkle with nutmeg.

14. Serve the remaining sauce separately.

BEANS BOURGUIGNONNE

SERVES 4

*Rich and flavoursome, this vegetarian adaptation of the traditional
French dish makes a luxurious main course when entertaining.*

225g /8oz borlotti or red kidney beans, soaked
   overnight
1 bay leaf
Freshly ground sea salt
4 medium carrots
225g /8oz small onions or shallots
225g /8oz small button mushrooms, or larger
   ones, quartered
45ml /3 tbsps olive or groundnut oil
4 slices wholemeal bread
45g /3 tbsps vegetable margarine
140ml /$\frac{1}{4}$ pint vegetable stock
280ml /$\frac{1}{2}$ pint red wine
5ml /1 tsp fresh chopped thyme
10ml /2 tsps fresh chopped parsley

Step 14 Cook the bread triangles in the melted margarine until they are nicely brown on both sides.

1. Drain the beans from the soaking water. Put the beans into a large bowl along with the bay leaf and a pinch of salt. Pour over just enough cold water to cover them.

2. Cover the bowl with cling film and pierce this several times with the tip of a sharp knife.

3. Cook the beans on HIGH for 10 minutes, then reduce the power setting to MEDIUM and cook for a further 45 minutes, or until the beans are completely soft.

4. Allow the beans to stand for 5 minutes, then drain and rinse in cold water. Set the beans to one side.

5. Heat a browning dish on HIGH for 5 minutes.

6. Whilst the dish is heating up, peel the carrots and cut them into 2.5cm /1-inch diagonal slices with a sharp knife.

7. Peel the onions and leave them whole.

8. Wash the mushrooms and pat them dry with absorbent kitchen paper.

9. Pour the oil onto the browning dish and stir in the vegetables. Cook on HIGH for 3 minutes, stirring them frequently to brown evenly.

10. Remove the vegetables from the dish and set them aside.

11. Remove the crusts from the slices of bread and cut each slice into 4 triangles.

12. Put the margarine onto the browning dish and cook for 1 minute on HIGH, or until it has melted.

13. Put the bread triangles onto the browning dish, turning each piece over to coat it evenly with the melted margarine.

14. Cook the bread triangles on HIGH for 1 minute on each side, or until the bread has browned nicely. Remove the triangles from the dish and set aside to drain on absorbent kitchen paper.

15. Put the drained beans into a large casserole dish and pour over the stock and the red wine. Cover the casserole with a lid, or with cling film as previously described, and cook on HIGH for 15 minutes.

16. Stir the prepared carrots, onions and mushrooms into the beans and wine, along with the thyme and the parsley. Stir well to mix all ingredients thoroughly.

17. Re-cover the casserole, and cook for a further 15-20 minutes on HIGH, or until the vegetables are completely tender.

18. Allow the casserole to stand for 15 minutes before arranging the bread triangles around the edge of the dish and serving.

CHINESE BLACK BEAN CASSEROLE

SERVES 4

Black beans are a traditional Chinese delicacy. They are easily available at ethnic shops or delicatessens.

450g /1lb Chinese black beans, soaked overnight
1 small piece of fresh root ginger, grated
1 piece star anise
1 clove garlic, crushed
10ml /2 tsps five-spice powder
6-8 sticks celery
90ml /3 fl oz sherry
15ml /1 tbsp soy sauce
5ml /1 tsp sesame seed oil
1 small can of water chestnuts
120g /4oz bean sprouts
4 spring onions, shredded

1. Drain the beans and put them into a large bowl. Add the root ginger, star anise, garlic and five-spice powder.

2. Pour over enough cold water to just cover the beans.

3. Cover the bowl with cling film and pierce this several times with the tip of a sharp knife.

Step 1 Add the ginger, star anise, five-spice powder and garlic to the beans.

Step 6 After cooking, most of the cooking liquid should have been absorbed to produce a thick sauce.

4. Cook the beans on HIGH for 10 minutes, then reduce the power setting to MEDIUM and continue cooking for a further 1 hour, or until the beans are completely soft.

5. Cut the celery into thin slices and add this to the beans. Re-cover the bowl and cook for a further 15 minutes on HIGH.

6. Stir the sherry, soy sauce and sesame oil into the beans and celery and cook for a further 5 minutes, uncovered, on HIGH. If after this time a lot of cooking liquid remains, continue cooking on HIGH, stirring occasionally, until most of it has been absorbed.

7. Drain the can of water chestnuts. Using a sharp knife, slice each water chestnut into thin diagonal slices and add these to the bean casserole. Stir well and heat through for 1 minute on HIGH.

8. Mix together the bean sprouts and spring onions, and sprinkle these over the top of the casserole just before serving.

Cook's Notes

 TIME: Preparation takes about 20 minutes, plus overnight standing time. Microwave cooking time is about 1 hour 35 minutes.

SERVING IDEA: Serve with vegetable fried rice or boiled brown rice.

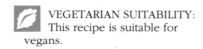 VEGETARIAN SUITABILITY: This recipe is suitable for vegans.

CURRIED LENTILS

SERVES 4

A classic curry which does take a while to prepare,
but is worth the extra effort.

225g /8oz brown lentils, soaked overnight
60ml /4 tbsps vegetable oil
1 large onion, peeled and finely chopped
1 clove garlic, crushed
1 red or green chilli pepper, seeded and finely
  chopped
5ml /1 tsp ground cumin
5ml /1 tsp ground coriander
5ml /1 tsp ground turmeric
2.5ml /½ tsp ground cinnamon
2.5ml /½ tsp ground nutmeg
570ml /1 pint vegetable stock
60g /2oz whole, blanched almonds
Salt and freshly ground black pepper
30g /1oz vegetable margarine
2 slightly under-ripe bananas, peeled and sliced
15ml / 1 tbsp soft brown sugar
30ml /2 tbsps lemon juice
Pinch each of cinnamon, nutmeg, and garam
  masala
2 dessert apples, core removed and flesh
  chopped
60g /2oz raisins
120g /4oz cucumber, finely chopped
60ml /4 tbsps mango chutney
2 large fresh tomatoes, skinned and chopped
1 small green pepper, seeded and finely
  chopped
10ml /2 tsps walnut oil
Pinch cayenne pepper
15ml /1 tbsp desiccated coconut
Fresh coriander leaves

1. Drain the lentils and rinse in cold water. Set aside.

2. Put the oil into a large bowl and heat on HIGH for 1 minute.

3. Add the onion, garlic, chilli pepper, cumin, coriander, turmeric, cinnamon and nutmeg to the oil and mix well to coat these ingredients thoroughly.

4. Cover the bowl with cling film and pierce this several times with the tip of a sharp knife. Cook the onion and the spice mixture on HIGH for 1 minute, then reduce the power setting to MEDIUM and cook for a further 3 minutes.

5. Add the drained lentils and vegetable stock to the onion and the spice mixture. Mix well to incorporate all the ingredients thoroughly.

6. Cook the lentils on HIGH for 30 minutes, or until they are completely soft and most of the liquid has been absorbed. Continue cooking on HIGH if there is any liquid left.

7. Allow the lentils to stand for 5 minutes, then stir in the almonds and transfer the curry to a serving dish.

8. Heat a browning dish on HIGH for 5 minutes. Put the margarine onto the dish and allow it to melt.

9. Add the sliced banana and cook on HIGH for 30 seconds on each side.

10. Sprinkle with the sugar, 15ml /1 tbsp of lemon juice, the nutmeg, cinnamon and garam masala. Stir well and arrange on a small accompaniments dish.

11. Put the apple into a small bowl along with the raisins, cucumber and chutney. Mix these ingredients together thoroughly and arrange them in another small dish for accompaniment.

12. Mix together the tomatoes, green pepper, spring onions, remaining lemon juice, walnut oil and cayenne pepper. Season with salt and arrange in a third dish.

13. Re-heat the lentil curry on HIGH for 3 minutes, if necessary. Sprinkle with the desiccated coconut and arrange the fresh coriander leaves on the top as a garnish.

14. Serve surrounded by the accompaniments.

MUSHROOM CROQUETTES WITH GREEN PEPPERCORN SAUCE

SERVES 4

This is an elegant way of serving a favourite vegetable and is sure to win praise when you entertain.

45g /1½oz vegetable margarine
2 shallots, finely chopped
120g /4oz mushrooms, finely chopped
45g /1½oz plain flour
140ml /¼ pint milk
90g /3oz fresh breadcrumbs
5ml /1 tsp fresh chopped parsley
5ml /1 tsp fresh chopped thyme
1 egg, beaten
Salt and freshly ground black pepper
Dry breadcrumbs, for coating
60ml /4 tbsps vegetable oil, for frying
30ml /2 tbsps dry vermouth or white wine
280ml /½ pint double cream
30ml /2 tbsps bottled green peppercorns,
   drained
1 small red pepper, diced

Step 7 Shape each of the 16 squares into small oval croquettes with lightly floured hands.

1. Put 30g /1oz of the margarine into a large bowl and cook it for 1 minute on HIGH to melt.

2. Stir one of the chopped shallots and the mushrooms into the margarine and stir well to coat completely. Cook for 1 minute on HIGH.

3. Add 30g /1oz of the flour to the shallot mixture and stir well to blend thoroughly.

4. Gradually add the milk, a little at a time, and cook for a total of 2 minutes on HIGH, removing the bowl from the microwave and adding more milk after each 30 seconds cooking time. Beat the mixture well between additions, to avoid lumps forming.

5. Stir the breadcrumbs, parsley, thyme and half the beaten egg into the mushroom mixture. Mix well to form a thick paste. Season to taste.

6. Spread the mushroom paste into a lightly greased square pan and chill in a refrigerator until it is firm.

7. Cut the chilled mixture into 16 equal sized pieces, and shape each piece into small ovals, with lightly floured hands.

8. Dip each oval into the remaining beaten egg, using a pastry brush to coat each side evenly.

9. Coat the croquettes with the dry breadcrumbs, pressing them to form an even, firm coating. Shake off any loose breadcrumbs, before frying.

10. Heat a browning dish on HIGH for 5 minutes. Pour on the oil and heat for 30 seconds on HIGH.

11. Put the croquettes into the hot fat and cook on HIGH for 2 minutes on each side. Remove the croquettes from the browning dish and drain them on absorbent kitchen paper. Set aside to keep them warm.

12. Put the remaining margarine into a small deep bowl and melt on HIGH for 30 seconds.

13. Add the remaining shallot to the margarine and stir well. Cook on HIGH for 30 seconds.

14. Stir the remaining flour into the shallot mixture, mixing it well to blend.

15. Whisk in the vermouth and the cream. Season to taste and cook on HIGH for 3 minutes, stirring frequently, until the sauce has thickened slightly.

16. Add the peppercorns to the sauce along with the red pepper and cook for a further 1 minute, before serving with the warm croquettes.

183

HAZELNUT ESCALOPES WITH PEAR BRANDY SAUCE

SERVES 4

These delicious escalopes, complemented perfectly by the flavour of the pear brandy sauce, create real style when entertaining.

30g /1oz vegetable margarine
1 shallot, finely chopped
30g /1oz plain flour
140ml /¼ pint milk
120g /4oz lightly toasted, ground hazelnuts
60g /2oz fresh breadcrumbs
5ml /1 tsp fresh chopped parsley
5ml /1 tsp fresh chopped thyme
Salt and freshly ground black pepper
1 egg, beaten
Dry breadcrumbs for coating
60ml /4 tbsps vegetable oil, for frying
280ml /½ pint double cream
15ml /1 tbsp pear brandy
60g /2oz vegetarian Cheddar cheese, grated
4 small, ripe, unpeeled pears, halved and cored
Lemon juice
8 fresh sage leaves

1. Put the margarine into a bowl and cook on HIGH for 1 minute to melt.

2. Stir the shallot into the margarine, mixing well to coat evenly. Cook for 30 seconds on HIGH.

3. Add the flour to the shallot mixture and stir well to blend thoroughly.

4. Gradually add the milk, a little at a time, cooking for 2 minutes on HIGH and whisking thoroughly after each 30 seconds to remove any lumps.

5. Stir the hazelnuts, breadcrumbs, parsley, thyme, seasoning and half the beaten egg into the shallot mixture, mixing well to form a firm paste.

6. Spread the paste evenly into a lightly greased square dish and chill in a refrigerator until it has set.

7. Cut the chilled mixture into 8 even sized pieces and shape each piece into a rounded, thin pattie, with lightly floured hands.

8. Brush each pattie on both sides with the remaining beaten egg.

9. Press dry breadcrumbs on to each egg-coated pattie, shaking off any excess crumbs after a good coating has been pressed on.

10. Heat a browning dish on HIGH for 5 minutes. Add the oil and cook for 30 seconds on HIGH.

11. Put the escalopes into the hot oil and cook on HIGH for 2 minutes on each side.

12. Remove the escalopes from the browning dish, and drain on absorbent kitchen paper. Set aside and keep warm.

13. Put the cream and the brandy into a small deep bowl or jug and cook on HIGH for 6 minutes.

14. Stir in the cheese and season to taste. Heat on HIGH for 30 seconds to melt the cheese.

15. Place a spoonful of the sauce on to each of 4 serving plates. Brush the cut side of the pears with a little lemon juice to prevent them from browning and arrange the pears on the sauce with the sage leaves.

16. Put 2 escalopes onto each plate and spoon a little more sauce over them. Serve any remaining sauce separately.

Cook's Notes

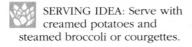 SERVING IDEA: Serve with creamed potatoes and steamed broccoli or courgettes.

VEGETARIAN SUITABILITY: This recipe is suitable for lacto-vegetarians only.

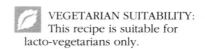 TIME: Preparation takes about 25 minutes, microwave cooking time is about 20 minutes.

WALNUT CUTLETS WITH THREE PEPPER SALPICON

SERVES 4

This colourful dish combines style with high nutritional value and is ideal for any type of entertaining.

60g /2oz vegetable margarine
1 shallot, finely chopped
45g /1½oz plain flour
140ml /¼ pint milk
120g /4oz walnuts, finely chopped or ground
60g /2oz fresh breadcrumbs
5ml /1 tsp fresh chopped parsley
5ml /1 tsp fresh chopped thyme
1 egg, beaten
Dry breadcrumbs for coating
60ml /4 tbsps vegetable oil, for frying
1 onion, peeled and sliced
Juice of 1 lemon
90ml /6 tbsps vegetable stock
2 green peppers, seeded and sliced
2 red peppers, seeded and sliced
2 yellow peppers, seeded and sliced
10ml /2 tsps capers
Pinch cayenne pepper
Salt and freshly ground black pepper

1. Melt 30g /1oz of the margarine in a large bowl on HIGH for 1 minute. Stir in the shallot and cook on HIGH for a further 30 seconds.

2. Stir 30g /1oz of the flour into the shallot mixture, mixing well to form a soft paste.

3. Gradually add the milk and cook for 2 minutes on HIGH, stirring after every 30 seconds to prevent lumps from forming.

4. Add the nuts, fresh breadcrumbs, herbs and half of the egg to the shallot mixture and mix thoroughly to form a firm but spreadable paste.

5. Spread the walnut mixture evenly into a square, lightly greased dish, and chill in a refrigerator until it has completely set.

6. Cut the set nut mixture into 8 equal portions and shape each portion into a cutlet, with lightly floured hands.

Step 7 Using a pastry brush, coat each side of the walnut cutlets with a layer of the remaining beaten egg.

7. Brush each side of the cutlets with the remaining beaten egg.

8. Press an even coating of the dried breadcrumbs onto each egg-coated cutlet, shaking off any excess breadcrumbs before frying.

9. Heat a browning dish on HIGH for 5 minutes. Add the oil and cook for 30 seconds on HIGH.

10. Put the cutlets on to the browning dish and cook on HIGH for 2 minutes on each side. Remove the cutlets from the dish and drain on absorbent kitchen paper. Set aside and keep warm.

11. Heat the remaining margarine in a large bowl or casserole for 30 seconds on HIGH.

12. Add the sliced onion to the melted margarine, stir well and cook for 30 seconds on HIGH.

13. Carefully blend in the remaining flour, the lemon juice and the stock. Cook for 1 minute on HIGH, stirring after 30 seconds to prevent lumps from forming.

14. Add the sliced peppers and the capers to the onion and stock sauce and mix well to coat thoroughly. Cook on HIGH for 3 minutes.

15. Stir in the cayenne pepper and seasoning and arrange the pepper salpicon on 4 serving plates along with the cutlets.

187

AUBERGINE ROLLS

SERVES 4

*This colourful and flavoursome dish is ideal
when entertaining informally.*

2 large aubergines
Salt
1 x 450g /1lb can of tomatoes
30ml /2 tbsps tomato purée
1 onion, peeled and finely chopped
Pinch sugar
Pinch dried oregano
1 bay leaf
2 stalks fresh parsley
Freshly ground black pepper
45ml /3 tbsps olive oil
225g /8oz vegetarian Cheshire cheese
120g /4oz black olives, pitted and chopped
180g /6oz vegetarian Cheddar cheese, grated
60g /2oz pine nuts
15ml /1 tbsp dry white wine
1 clove garlic, crushed
5ml /1 tsp each fresh chopped parsley and basil
Pinch nutmeg

1. Slice the aubergines, then lightly score the cut surfaces of each slice diagonally with a sharp knife.

2. Rub salt into the diagonal scoring on both sides and leave the slices to stand for 30 minutes on absorbent kitchen paper to degorge.

3. Put the tomatoes, tomato purée, onion, sugar, oregano, bay leaf, parsley sprigs and some salt and pepper into a bowl. Cook, uncovered, on HIGH for 8 minutes, stirring twice during this cooking time.

4. Remove the bay leaf and parsley from the sauce, discard these and blend the sauce thoroughly in a liquidiser or food processor.

5. Push the puréed sauce through a metal sieve into a bowl to remove the tomato seeds.

6. Thoroughly rinse the aubergine slices in cold water and pat them dry with kitchen paper.

Step 13 Fold the unfilled half of each aubergine slice over the Cheshire cheese filling to form a roll.

7. Heat a browning dish on HIGH for 5 minutes, then add the oil. Cook on HIGH for 30 seconds.

8. Add the aubergine slices to the browning dish and cook for 1 minute on each side.

9. Remove the slices from the dish and drain on absorbent kitchen paper.

10. Put the Cheshire cheese, the olives, 60g/2oz of the Cheddar cheese, the pine nuts, white wine, parsley, basil, nutmeg, and a little seasoning, into the bowl and mix thoroughly to combine the ingredients.

11. Put half of the tomato sauce into the base of a shallow serving dish.

12. Put equal amounts of the Cheshire cheese filling on to one half of each aubergine slice.

13. Fold the other half of each slice over the filling and arrange the filled rolls on the sauce in the serving dish.

14. Spoon the remaining sauce over the filled aubergine roll, cover the dish with cling film, and pierce this several times with the tip of a sharp knife.

15. Cook for 3 minutes on HIGH, then remove the cling film and sprinkle over the remaining Cheddar cheese. Cook, uncovered, for a further 3 minutes before serving.

SWEET AND SOUR NUGGETS

SERVES 4

*Almond nuggets, with the crunchy texture of water chestnuts,
are accompanied by sweet and sour sauce to create a
dish which tastes as good as it looks.*

30g /1oz vegetable margarine
1 shallot, peeled and finely chopped
30g /1oz plain flour
140ml /¼ pint milk
60g /2oz ground almonds
60g /2oz water chestnuts, finely chopped
5ml /1 tsp fresh chopped parsley
5ml /1 tsp ground ginger
1 egg, beaten
Salt and freshly ground black pepper
Dry breadcrumbs, for coating
Sesame seeds, for coating
60ml /4 tbsps groundnut oil, for frying
60g /2oz soft brown sugar
60ml /4 tbsps vinegar
30ml /2 tbsps tomato ketchup
30ml /2 tbsps soy sauce
1 x 225g /8oz tin pineapple chunks
30g /1oz cornflour
1 green pepper, seeded and sliced
2 spring onions, trimmed and cut into thin
    diagonal slices
1 small tin bamboo shoots
225g /8oz fresh bean sprouts

1. Put the margarine into a large bowl and cook on HIGH for 1 minute to melt.

2. Add the shallot and stir well to coat evenly. Cook for 30 seconds on HIGH to soften.

3. Stir the flour into the shallot mixture, blending it well with a wooden spoon to form a paste.

4. Gradually add the milk, beating well and cooking for 30 seconds between additions, until the sauce is thick and smooth.

5. Stir the almonds, water chestnuts, parsley, ginger, half the beaten egg and some seasoning into the shallot sauce, mixing well to form a firm paste.

6. Spread the almond paste onto a square dish and chill in a refrigerator until firm.

7. Divide the chilled mixture into 16 evenly sized balls.

8. Put the breadcrumbs and the sesame seeds into a dish and mix together thoroughly.

9. Brush each almond nugget with the remaining beaten egg and then coat them in the breadcrumbs and sesame seed mixture, pressing this onto the surface firmly to form a good coating.

10. Heat a browning dish on HIGH for 5 minutes. Pour on the oil and heat for 30 seconds.

11. Fry the coated almond nuggets in the hot oil for 3-4 minutes, stirring them frequently to brown evenly.

12. Put the almond nuggets onto absorbent kitchen paper to drain, and keep warm whilst preparing the sauce.

13. Mix together the sugar, vinegar, ketchup and soy sauce in a deep-sided bowl or jug.

14. Drain the juice from the pineapple and stir this into the vinegar mixture. Reserve the chunks.

15. Blend the cornflour into the sauce liquid, whisking until it is smooth. Cook the sauce on HIGH for 2-3 minutes, or until it has thickened and cleared.

16. Add the peppers, sliced onions, and bamboo shoots to the sauce.

17. Chop the pineapple chunks into convenient sized pieces and stir these into the sauce, mixing all the ingredients together thoroughly.

18. Heat the sauce through for 1 minute.

19. Arrange the bean sprouts on to a serving dish and put the nuggets on top of these. Heat through for 1 minute. Pour a little of the sauce over the nuggets, and serve any remaining sauce separately.

JAPANESE STEAMER
SERVES 4

*The Japanese are renowned for their elegant cuisine,
and this recipe is no exception. For a meal with a feel
for the Orient, this recipe is ideal.*

120g /4oz buckwheat noodles
16 dried black mushrooms, soaked overnight
120g /4oz small button mushrooms
8 baby corn on the cob
1 small piece fresh ginger root, finely grated
140ml /¼ pint soy sauce
60ml /4 tbsps vegetable stock
15ml /1 tbsp sherry
5ml /1 tsp cornflour
1 packet dried sea spinach, soaked for 1 hour
3 packages tofu, drained
1 small daikon (mooli) radish, sliced
1 small bunch fresh chives
1 lemon, thinly sliced

1. Carefully arrange the noodles in a bowl containing 570ml /1 pint boiling water. Add a pinch of salt.

2. Cover the bowl with cling film and pierce this several times with the tip of a sharp knife. Cook the noodles on HIGH for 6 minutes. Leave the noodles to stand, still covered, for 10 minutes.

3. Remove the stems from the black mushrooms and discard these.

4. Return the mushroom caps to the soaking liquor and heat in the microwave on HIGH for 5 minutes. Set aside until required.

5. Put the button mushrooms and the cobs of

Step 1 Carefully arrange the noodles into the boiling water, pressing them down gently as they soften.

Step 7 After cooking, the sauce should have cleared and thickened slightly.

Step 9 Using a sharp knife, cut the drained tofu into 1.25cm /½-inch slices.

baby corn cobs into a small bowl with 15ml /1 tbsp of water. Cover the bowl with cling film and puncture as before. Cook for 2 minutes on HIGH and set aside.

6. Put the ginger, soy sauce, stock, sherry and cornflour into a small bowl, and whisk until the cornflour is blended.

7. Cook the sauce on HIGH for 3 minutes, or until it has thickened and cleared.

8. Drain the sea spinach, mushrooms and noodles.

9. Slice the tofu into 1.25cm /½-inch slices with a sharp knife.

10. Arrange all the prepared ingredients on 4 separate serving dishes and pour a little of the sauce over them.

11. Heat each dish for 1 minute on HIGH, then garnish with the radish, chives and lemon slices.

12. Serve the remaining sauce separately.

MUSHROOMS FLORENTINE

SERVES 4

This delicious way of serving large mushrooms is suitable for informal entertaining or for a substantial supper or lunch dish.

900g /2lb fresh spinach, stalks removed and washed
105g /5½ oz vegetable margarine
450g /1lb open cap mushrooms
2 shallots, finely chopped
4 tomatoes, peeled, seeded and chopped
Salt and freshly ground black pepper
Pinch nutmeg
45g /1½oz plain flour
2.5ml /½ tsp dry mustard
Pinch cayenne pepper
570ml /1 pint milk
225g /8oz vegetarian Cheddar cheese, finely grated
Paprika, for garnish

---

1. Put the spinach into a large bowl with a pinch of salt. Cover the bowl with cling film and pierce this several times with the tip of a sharp knife.

2. Cook the spinach for 4 minutes on HIGH. Leave to stand until required.

3. Put 60g /2oz of the margarine into a large bowl, cook on HIGH for 30 seconds to melt.

4. Wash the mushrooms. Peel off any tough outer skin and trim the stalk with a sharp knife.

5. Add the mushrooms to the melted margarine and stir well to coat them evenly. Cook for 3 minutes on HIGH, stirring after each minute of cooking time.

6. Remove the mushrooms from the bowl with a slotted spoon, draining off as much cooking liquid as possible before setting them to one side on a plate.

7. Stir the shallots into the mushroom juices and cook on HIGH for 2 minutes, stirring once during this cooking time.

8. Drain the spinach and shred it roughly.

9. Add the shredded spinach to the cooked shallots along with the tomato, seasoning and nutmeg. Stir well to mix evenly.

10. Spread the spinach mixture evenly over the base of a large casserole dish. Arrange the cooked mushrooms over the top.

11. Melt the remaining margarine in a deep bowl or jug on HIGH for 1 minute.

12. Stir in the flour, mustard, seasoning and cayenne pepper, blending thoroughly with a wooden spoon to form a roux.

13. Gradually add the milk to the flour paste, beating thoroughly and cooking, uncovered, for 30 seconds between additions.

14. Whisk the sauce until it is smooth, then stir in 180g /6oz of the cheese. Heat on HIGH for 1 minute to melt the cheese.

15. Pour the sauce over the mushrooms and sprinkle the remaining cheese and the paprika evenly over the top.

16. Cook for 3 minutes on HIGH to heat through before serving.

Cook's Notes

VARIATION: Wild mushrooms are now easily available and make a sophisticated alternative to the cap mushrooms in this recipe.

PREPARATION: If the sauce does have lumps in it, push it through a wire sieve with a wooden spoon to remove them.

TIME: Preparation takes about 20 minutes, microwave cooking time is about 18 minutes.

PASTA SPIRALS WITH WALNUTS AND STILTON

SERVES 4

This classic combination creates an unusual;
but delicious, Italian style recipe.

450g /1lb pasta spirals
15ml /1 tbsp vegetable oil
280ml /½ pint double cream
450g /1lb vegetarian Stilton cheese
120g /4oz shelled walnut halves
Ground black pepper
4 sprigs fresh thyme
2 ripe figs

1. Put the pasta spirals into a large bowl and pour over 1150ml /2 pints of boiling water. Stir in a pinch of salt and 15ml /1 tbsp vegetable oil.

2. Cover the bowl with cling film and pierce this several times with the tip of a sharp knife. Cook the pasta on HIGH for 10 minutes and allow to stand, still covered, for a further 10 minutes.

3. Meanwhile prepare the sauce. Put the cream into a large bowl or jug.

Step 6 Add the walnut halves to the cheese and cream, stirring thoroughly with a metal spoon.

Step 7 Pour boiling water over the pasta spirals in a colander to rinse thoroughly.

4. Grate or crumble the Stilton cheese into the cream and stir well.

5. Cook the cream and the cheese for 4 minutes on HIGH, or until the cheese is completely melted. Stir the mixture once or twice during the cooking to blend the ingredients thoroughly.

6. Stir the walnut halves into the cream and cheese mixture. Season with the black pepper.

7. Drain the pasta spirals and rinse them thoroughly with boiling water.

8. Stir the pasta into the cheese and cream mixture, stirring the ingredients together thoroughly to coat the pasta completely.

9. Divide the pasta in sauce between 4 warmed serving plates and garnish each dish with a sprig of thyme and half a fresh fig before serving.

Cook's Notes

VARIATION: Use hazelnuts and vegetarian Cheshire cheese, or peanuts and vegetarian Cheddar cheese, for 2 interesting variations.

COOK'S TIP: The nutty sauce, or either of the variations, makes a superb fondue sauce into which can be dipped crusty bread or fresh vegetables.

TIME: Preparation takes about 15 minutes, microwave cooking time is about 12 minutes, plus 10 minutes standing time.

CURRIED CASHEW NUTS
SERVES 4

The semi-sweet flavour of cashew nuts, coupled with the spicy curry sauce, produces a curry which has a most interesting flavour and is highly nutritious as well.

1 medium onion
1 green pepper
15ml /1 tbsp soya oil
15ml /1 tbsp white mustard seeds
5ml /1 tsp ground cumin
5ml /1 tsp ground coriander
5ml /1 tsp garam masala
120g /4oz cashew nuts, chopped
225g /8oz fresh bean sprouts
60g /2oz raisins
480ml /16 fl oz tomato juice
Cucumber slices and coriander leaves for garnish

1. Peel the onion and chop it finely with a sharp knife.

2. Cut the pepper in half, lengthways, and remove the white pith and seeds.

3. Slice the pepper into thin strips.

Step 2 Remove the white pith and the small seeds from the halved pepper.

Step 8 Stir the nuts, bean sprouts, raisins and tomato juice thoroughly into the fried spices, mixing them well to blend completely.

4. Put the oil into a large bowl and cook on HIGH for 30 seconds. Stir in the mustard seeds and spices.

5. Cover the bowl with cling film and pierce this several times with the tip of a sharp knife.

6. Cook the spices on HIGH for 1 minute, or until they are lightly browned and the mustard seeds have popped.

7. Stir in the onion and pepper. Re-cover the bowl as before, and cook on HIGH for 2 minutes.

8. Uncover the bowl and stir in the nuts, bean sprouts, raisins and tomato juice. Stir well to incorporate the spices thoroughly into the sauce and cook on HIGH for 5 minutes, or until the sauce has thickened.

9. Garnish the curry with the cucumber slices and coriander leaves when served.

Cook's Notes

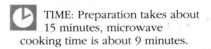 TIME: Preparation takes about 15 minutes, microwave cooking time is about 9 minutes.

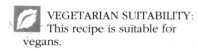 VEGETARIAN SUITABILITY: This recipe is suitable for vegans.

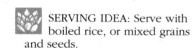 SERVING IDEA: Serve with boiled rice, or mixed grains and seeds.

199

VEGETABLE COUSCOUS

SERVES 4

Couscous is a popular dish in North Africa, where it is normally cooked by steaming over an accompanying stew.

225g /8oz chickpeas, soaked overnight
3 cloves garlic, crushed
2 onions, peeled and thickly sliced
1 large potato, peeled and diced
4 carrots, peeled and sliced
2 small turnips, peeled and diced
1 green pepper, seeded and sliced
570ml /1 pint vegetable stock or water
225g /8oz courgettes, sliced
60g /2oz raisins or sultanas
60g /2oz dried apricots, chopped
5ml /1 tsp each, ground coriander, cumin,
  turmeric and chilli powder
450g /1lb couscous
850ml /1½ pints water
5ml /1 tsp salt

1. Drain the chickpeas and put them into a bowl with enough cold water to just cover them.

2. Cover the bowl with cling film and pierce this several times with the tip of a sharp knife. Cook on HIGH for 10 minutes, then reduce the power setting to MEDIUM and cook for a further 45 minutes, or until the chickpeas are completely soft.

Step 6 Blend the spices to a smooth paste with 30ml /2 tbsps of cold water.

Step 9 Leave the couscous to stand in the water until it has swollen and absorbed most of the liquid.

3. Put the garlic, onions, potato, carrots, turnips and green pepper into a large bowl with the vegetable stock. Cook, uncovered, for 5 minutes on HIGH.

4. Add the courgettes, raisins and apricots and stir well.

5. Drain the chickpeas and add these to the vegetable casserole.

6. Put the spices into a small cup or bowl and blend to a smooth paste with 30ml /2 tbsps of cold water.

7. Blend this paste into the vegetable casserole, seasoning with a little salt if required.

8. Cook the casserole for 15 minutes on HIGH, then set aside for 10 minutes whilst you prepare the couscous.

9. Put the couscous into a large bowl along with the water and salt. Leave to stand for 5 minutes, or until the couscous has swollen and absorbed most of the liquid.

10. Cover the bowl with cling film as before and cook on HIGH for 5 minutes.

11. Uncover the bowl and fluff up the couscous with a fork.

12. Pile the couscous on to a serving plate and serve the vegetable casserole over the top.

Cook's Notes

TIME: Preparation takes about 25 minutes, microwave cooking time is about 30 minutes.

VEGETARIAN SUITABILITY: This recipe is suitable for vegans.

SERVING IDEA: Serve with natural yogurt for a lacto-vegetarian meal.

TEN VARIETIES OF BEAUTY

SERVES 4

*The ten varieties refers to the selection of vegetables in this exotic
Chinese dish, which is simplicity itself when using a microwave oven.*

10 Chinese dried mushrooms
2 carrots, peeled
60ml /4 tbsps vegetable oil
3 sticks celery, diagonally sliced
90g /3oz mange tout
1 red pepper, seeded and sliced
8 ears of baby corn
4 spring onions, diagonally sliced
60g /2oz fresh bean sprouts
10 water chestnuts, sliced
½ small can sliced bamboo shoots
280ml /½ pint vegetable stock
30ml /2 tbsps cornflour
45ml /3 tbsps light soy sauce
5ml /1 tsp sesame oil

Step 10 Stir the cooked sauce carefully into the vegetables, taking care not to break them up.

1. Put the mushrooms into a bowl and pour over just enough boiling water to cover. Leave to stand for 30 minutes.

2. Drain the mushrooms from the water, remove and discard the tough stalks.

3. Cut the carrots into ribbons with a potato peeler, slicing the vegetables into thin strips.

4. Heat a browning dish on HIGH for 5 minutes. Pour on the oil and heat for 30 seconds on HIGH.

5. Add the carrots and celery to the oil and stir well. Cook for 1 minute on HIGH. Remove the vegetables with a slotted spoon and set aside.

6. Add the mange tout, red pepper and the corn to the browning dish, stir well and cook for 1 minute on HIGH. Set these vegetables to one side with the carrot and celery.

7. Cook the onions, bean sprouts, water chestnuts and bamboo shoots in the browning dish for 1 minute on HIGH, adding the Chinese mushroom caps after 30 seconds and stirring these well into the other vegetables before continuing the cooking.

8. Combine all the vegetables together and set aside.

9. Put all the remaining ingredients into a jug or deep-sided bowl. Cook for 2-3 minutes on HIGH, or until the sauce has thickened and cleared.

10. Pour the sauce over the vegetables and stir carefully so that they do not begin to break up.

11. Re-heat the vegetables for 1-2 minutes on HIGH before serving.

Cook's Notes

COOK'S TIP: If there are any lumps in the sauce after cooking, strain it onto the vegetables through a nylon sieve.

SERVING IDEA: Serve with boiled rice.

PREPARATION: If you do not have a browning dish, this recipe can be prepared in a bowl. This will not require any pre-warming but the vegetables will not brown as they would on a browning dish. The cooking times should remain the same.

TIME: Preparation takes about 30 minutes, microwave cooking time is about 6-8 minutes.

VEGETARIAN SUITABILITY: This recipe is suitable for vegans.

VEGETABLE NIRAMISH

SERVES 4

*This highly fragrant curry is both quick and
simple to make in a microwave oven.*

1 small aubergine
Salt
45ml /3 tbsps vegetable oil
1 onion, peeled and sliced
5ml /1 tsp cumin seed
1 large potato, peeled and cut into chunks
120g /4oz cauliflower florets
1 small green pepper, seeded and sliced
2 small carrots, peeled and cut into thick slices
5ml /1 tsp each ground coriander, turmeric and
    chilli powder
90ml /6 tbsps vegetable stock
5ml /1 tsp fresh chopped coriander leaves
1 green chilli, seeded and very finely chopped
Juice of 1 lime
Lime slices and coriander leaves to garnish

1. Cut the aubergine into chunks and sprinkle
liberally with salt.

2. Leave the aubergine to stand for at least 30
minutes to degorge. Rinse the chunks thoroughly
after this time and drain them well.

3. Put the oil into a large bowl and heat for 30
seconds on HIGH.

4. Stir the onion and cumin seeds into the hot
oil and cook on HIGH for 1 minute to soften the
onion.

5. Add the potato to the onion mixture, stirring
it well to coat with the oil. Cover the bowl with

Step 1 Mix liberal
amounts of salt into
the chopped
aubergine, stirring
the pieces well to
make sure that they
are coated evenly.

Step 5 Stir the
potato into the oil
and onion mixture,
making sure that
each piece is well
coated in the oil
before cooking.

Step 8 Carefully
stir the blended
spices into the
mixed vegetables,
mixing well to
distribute the spices
evenly.

cling film and pierce this several times with the
tip of a sharp knife.

6. Cook for 5 minutes on HIGH.

7. Stir the drained aubergine into the potato
mixture along with the cauliflower, green pepper
and carrot.

8. Blend the spices with the stock, and 5ml /1
tsp of salt. Carefully stir this mixture into the
vegetables, mixing well to distribute the spices
evenly.

9. Re-cover the bowl with cling film, as before,
and cook for 10 minutes on HIGH.

10. Add the coriander leaves and chilli to the
cooked vegetables, and season with the lime
juice and more salt if required. Allow to stand,
still covered, for 5 minutes before serving,
garnished with the coriander leaves and lime
slices.

VEGETARIAN
MICROWAVE
COOKING

CHAPTER ~ 6
· SIDE · DISHES ·

LEEKS PROVENÇALE

SERVES 4

*This classic method of preparing vegetables is exceptionally well
suited to leeks, as this recipe will demonstrate.*

6 leeks
4 tomatoes
15ml /1 tbsp olive oil
2 cloves garlic, crushed
5ml /1 tsp dried thyme
30ml /2 tbsps fresh chopped parsley
60ml /4 tbsps dry white wine
Salt and freshly ground black pepper

1. Cut away the roots and tough outer leaves
from the leeks.

2. Slit each leek lengthways down one side and
wash thoroughly under cold running water.

3. Using a sharp knife, cut the leeks into 5cm /
2-inch pieces.

4. Put 480ml /1 pint of hot water into a bowl
and cook on HIGH for 4-5 minutes or until it is
boiling.

5. Whilst the water is heating, carefully cut a
shallow cross into the skins of each tomato.

6. Plunge the tomatoes into the boiling water

Step 5 Cut a small
cross into the skin
of each tomato to
make it easier to
peel them after they
have been plunged
in the hot water.

Step 15 Mix the
chopped tomatoes
into the cooked
leeks, making sure
that they are evenly
distributed.

and allow them to stand for 1 minute.

7. Remove the tomatoes from the water and
carefully peel away and discard the skins.

8. Chop the tomatoes roughly, discarding the
woody green cores, and set aside.

9. Put the oil into a large bowl and cook on
HIGH for 30 seconds.

10. Add the leeks and garlic to the oil, stirring
them well to coat evenly.

11. Cook, uncovered, on HIGH for 3-4 minutes,
or until the leeks are beginning to soften.

12. Add the herbs, wine and seasoning to the
partially cooked leeks and stir well to mix in
thoroughly.

13. Cover the bowl with cling film and pierce
this several times with the tip of a sharp knife.

14. Cook the leeks and herbs for 5 minutes on
HIGH.

15. Remove the covering and stir in the
chopped tomato flesh.

16. Mix well and cook, uncovered, for 1 minute
on HIGH before serving.

Cook's Notes

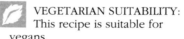

TIME: Preparation takes about
10 minutes, microwave
cooking time is about 8-10
minutes.

VEGETARIAN SUITABILITY:
This recipe is suitable for
vegans.

SERVING IDEA: Serve with
any vegetarian meal.

COURGETTE ROLLS

SERVES 4

*These artistic little rolls of vegetables are an impressive way of
serving an accompaniment to a sophisticated meal.*

2 large courgettes
Juice of 1 lemon
2 carrots
2 green peppers
4 spring onions
5ml /1 tsp fresh chopped basil or thyme
Salt and freshly ground black pepper
Bunch of fresh chives
30g /1oz vegetable margarine

1. Trim the ends from the courgettes and carefully cut each one lengthways in very thin slices.

2. Arrange the courgette slices evenly over the bottom of a large casserole dish and sprinkle with the lemon juice.

3. Cover the dish with cling film and pierce this several times with the tip of a sharp knife. Cook on HIGH for 1½ minutes, to just soften.

4. Remove the courgette slices with a slotted spoon or fish slice and set them aside until required.

5. Peel the carrots and cut them into very thin 'julienne' strips, about 8cm /3 inches long, with a sharp knife.

6. Put the carrot strips into the casserole with the courgette juices, re-cover and cook on HIGH for 4 minutes.

7. Cut the peppers in half lengthways and remove the white pith and the seeds.

8. Cut the pepper flesh into strips roughly the same size as the carrot.

9. Add the pepper strips to the carrots, cover

Step 12 Arrange the carrots, peppers and onions evenly across the strips of courgette, laying them horizontal to the courgette in small bundles.

again and cook for a further 2 minutes on HIGH.

10. Trim the spring onions, cutting away any tough, dark green outer leaves. Shred the onions lengthways into very fine strips using a sharp knife.

11. Sprinkle the onion strips and the herbs over the carrots and peppers in the casserole dish and cook, uncovered, for 1 minute to just soften the onion.

12. Lay out the courgette strips on an even surface and arrange bundles of the carrot, pepper, onion and herb mixture evenly, in piles, across them.

13. Carefully roll up the courgette strips around the vegetables, securing them by tying at each end with a few strips of the chives.

14. Return the bundles of vegetables to the casserole dish and dot them with the margarine.

15. Cover the dish as before and cook the vegetables for 2 minutes on HIGH to heat through before serving.

Cook's Notes

PREPARATION: The bundles of vegetables can be prepared a day in advance, but must then be re-heated for 4 minutes on HIGH before serving.

VARIATION: Use bundles of fresh green beans and red peppers in place of the carrots and green peppers in this recipe, for a summery variation.

TIME: Preparation takes about 20 minutes, microwave cooking time is about 11 minutes.

BROCCOLI AND CAULIFLOWER MOULD WITH SALSA

SERVES 4-6

Although this dish takes a little while to prepare, it will make a spectacular addition to your dinner table.

1 small head of cauliflower
225g /8oz broccoli or calabrese
45ml /3 tbsps walnut oil
15ml /1 tbsp white wine vinegar
5ml /1 tsp dry English mustard
½ clove garlic, crushed
Salt and freshly ground black pepper
4-5 tomatoes, depending on size
1 green pepper, seeded and finely chopped
15ml /1 tbsp olive oil
1 green chilli pepper, seeded and very finely chopped
5ml /1 tsp ground cumin seeds
4 spring onions, finely chopped

1. Divide the cauliflower into florets and trim down any long, thick stalks.

2. Trim the broccoli stalks to within 5cm / 2-inches of the florets and put these and the cauliflower into a large, deep bowl.

3. Pour over 30ml /2 tbsps cold water, cover the bowl with cling film and pierce this several times with the tip of a sharp knife. Cook on HIGH for 3 minutes.

4. Put the walnut oil, vinegar, mustard, garlic and some salt and pepper into a small bowl and whisk together well with a fork or small whisk.

5. Drain the cauliflower and broccoli from any cooking liquor that may have formed and pour over the walnut oil dressing while the vegetables are still warm.

6. Stir the dressing into the warm vegetables thoroughly so that they are coated evenly, but taking care not to break the vegetables at all.

Step 7 Arrange the cauliflower and broccoli in alternate layers in the pudding bowl, pressing them lightly to push the vegetables together and form an inverted dome shape.

7. Carefully arrange the cauliflower and broccoli into a deep-sided 570ml /1-pint bowl, alternating the 2 vegetables and pressing them together lightly to push them firmly into the bowl shape.

8. Leave the vegetables to cool, before refrigerating them ready for serving.

9. Cut a small cross into the skins of the tomatoes and plunge them into boiling water for 30 seconds.

10. Carefully peel away the skins from the tomatoes. Roughly chop the flesh, removing any hard green core.

11. Put the chopped tomatoes and the peppers into the bowl with the olive oil and cook on HIGH for 1 minute.

12. Stir well then add the chilli pepper, cumin seed and spring onions. Season with salt and pepper and cook on HIGH for 3 minutes.

13. Allow the tomato salsa to cool and then refrigerate well before serving.

14. To serve, carefully turn out the cauliflower mould on to an inverted serving plate and spoon the salsa sauce around the base.

BRUSSELS SPROUTS WITH HAZELNUTS

SERVES 4

*This is a delicious variation to Brussels sprouts with chestnuts,
but is one which will soon become a firm favourite.*

60g /2oz shelled hazelnuts
30g /1oz vegetable margarine
450g /1lb Brussels sprouts
Salt

1. Put the hazelnuts into a small bowl and pour over just enough boiling water to cover them.

2. Cook the nuts on HIGH for 3 minutes, then allow to stand for 10 minutes.

3. Drain the nuts and rub off the brown outer skins. Leave the nuts to dry completely on absorbent kitchen paper.

4. Heat a browning dish on HIGH for 5 minutes.

5. Put the margarine into the browning dish and allow it to melt.

Step 6 Stir the nuts frequently on the browning dish to ensure that they are evenly toasted.

Step 7 Trim the base stems of the Brussels sprouts and remove any tough outer leaves using a sharp knife.

6. Add the nuts to the melted butter and cook for 5 minutes on HIGH, stirring after every 30 seconds to ensure that they brown evenly.

7. Trim the Brussels sprouts, and put them into a large bowl along with 30ml /2 tbsps water and a little salt. Cover the bowl with cling film and pierce this several times with the tip of a sharp knife.

8. Cook the Brussels sprouts for 7-8 minutes on HIGH, or until they are completely tender.

9. Drain the Brussels sprouts and return them to the bowl along with the toasted hazelnuts and melted margarine.

10. Mix the sprouts and nuts together thoroughly before transferring to a serving dish.

Cook's Notes

 TIME: Preparation takes about 20 minutes, microwave cooking time is about 21 minutes.

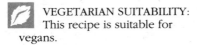 VEGETARIAN SUITABILITY: This recipe is suitable for vegans.

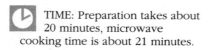 VARIATION: Use chestnuts, almonds or peanuts instead of the hazelnuts in this recipe.

 SERVING IDEA: Serve with grills, salads and roasts.

PREPARATION: If you do not have a browning dish, the hazelnuts can be cooked in a bowl, but this will not require pre-heating, nor will the hazelnuts brown.

215

POMMES NOISETTES

SERVES 4-6

These delicious, cheesy potato balls will complement any meal, either sophisticated or homely, and are also an excellent source of additional protein.

450g /1lb potatoes, scrubbed but not peeled
30ml /2 tbsps water
30g /1oz vegetable margarine
Salt and freshly ground black pepper
60g /2oz vegetarian Gruyere or Edam cheese, finely grated
60g /2oz ground toasted hazelnuts
Fresh chopped parsley, or watercress sprigs for garnish

1. Prick the potato skins with a fork and put them into a large bowl along with the water.

2. Cover the bowl with cling film and pierce this several times with the tip of a sharp knife. Cook the potatoes on HIGH for 12 minutes, or until they are completely tender when pierced with a knife.

3. Drain the potatoes and cut them in half.

Step 4 Carefully scoop the potato pulp out of the skins using a small spoon.

Step 7 Shape spoonfuls of the refrigerated mashed potato into balls approximately 2.5cm /1 inch in diameter.

4. Carefully scoop out the potato pulp and put this into a bowl along with the margarine.

5. Mash the potato pulp and the margarine together until they are smooth, then fork in the seasonings and cheese.

6. Refrigerate the mashed potatoes until they are completely cold.

7. Shape spoonfuls of the mashed potato into 2.5cm /1-inch round balls.

8. Spread the nuts on a plate and roll the potato balls into the nuts, making sure that they are evenly coated.

9. Arrange the coated potato balls in a circle on a baking dish and cook for 2-3 minutes on HIGH to heat through.

10. Serve garnished with parsley or sprigs of watercress.

Cook's Notes

 VARIATION: Use peanuts instead of the hazelnuts in this recipe.

 SERVING IDEA: Serve with grills, salads and roasts.

 PREPARATION: The noisettes can be prepared well in advance and stored in a refrigerator for up to 24 hours before the final cooking.

 TIME: Preparation takes about 15 minutes, plus refrigeration time. Microwave cooking time is about 15 minutes.

SWEET AND SOUR RED CABBAGE WITH APPLE

SERVES 4

A traditional way of serving red cabbage, made very quick and easy in the microwave oven.

30g /1oz vegetable margarine
1 medium-sized red cabbage
1 small onion, peeled and finely chopped
1 cooking apple, cored and chopped
30g /1oz soft brown sugar
30ml /2 tbsps red wine vinegar
140ml /¼ pint water
Pinch cinnamon
Salt and freshly ground black pepper
15ml /1 tbsp walnut oil
1 dessert apple, cored and chopped
10ml /2 tsps fresh chopped parsley

---

1. Put the margarine into a large bowl and melt it on HIGH for 30 seconds.

2. Using a sharp knife, carefully shred the cabbage into thin strips approximately 0.75cm /¼ inch thick.

3. Put the shredded cabbage, onion and the apple into the bowl along with the melted margarine and stir well to coat the ingredients evenly.

4. Cook on HIGH for 2 minutes.

5. Mix together the sugar, vinegar and water in a small bowl. Heat on HIGH for 1 minute, stirring after 30 seconds to dissolve the sugar.

6. Pour the sugar mixture into the cabbage and

Step 2 Carefully shred the cabbage into thin strips with a sharp knife.

Step 5 Dissolve the sugar with the vinegar and water in a small bowl.

Step 11 Stir the chopped parsley into the partially cooked apple, mixing well to distribute evenly.

apples along with the cinnamon and seasonings. Mix well to combine ingredients thoroughly.

7. Cover the bowl with cling film and pierce this several times with the tip of a sharp knife.

8. Cook the cabbage mixture on HIGH for 8 minutes, or until the cabbage is soft. Stir the mixture twice during the cooking time, re-covering each time.

9. Allow the cabbage to stand for 5 minutes.

10. Put the oil into a small bowl and heat on HIGH for 30 seconds.

11. Stir in the apple and cook uncovered on HIGH for 1 minute to partially soften. Stir in the parsley.

12. Transfer the cabbage to a serving dish and garnish with the apple and parsley mixture before serving.

SPINACH WITH BLUE CHEESE AND WALNUTS

SERVES 4

This hot salad is an ideal accompaniment to a rich meal.

900g /2lb fresh spinach
30g /1oz vegetable margarine
Pinch nutmeg
Salt and freshly ground black pepper
120g /4oz roughly chopped walnuts
120g /4oz vegetarian blue cheese, crumbled

1. Wash the spinach and trim away any tough stalks.

2. Put the spinach into a large bowl. Cover the bowl with cling film and pierce this several times with the tip of a sharp knife.

Step 1 Trim away the tough stalks from the spinach leaves using a sharp knife.

Step 7 Toss the walnuts and cheese quickly into the spinach, without allowing the cheese to melt too much.

3. Cook the spinach on HIGH for 4 minutes. Drain the spinach in a colander.

4. Put the spinach on to a large plate and firmly press another plate on top of it to remove all the excess moisture.

5. Put the margarine into a large bowl and melt it on HIGH for 30 seconds.

6. Add the spinach to the melted margarine along with the nutmeg and seasoning. Stir well to coat evenly.

7. Quickly stir in the walnuts and the cheese, tossing the ingredients together lightly. Serve before the cheese melts too much.

Cook's Notes

PREPARATION: The spinach can be cooked and drained in advance and then re-heated beforeadding the remaining ingredients.

SERVING IDEA: Serve with nut roasts, vegetable cutlets or pâtés.

VEGETARIAN SUITABILITY: This recipe is suitable for lacto-vegetarians only. See variation for vegan alternative.

VARIATION: Use diced tofu instead of the cheese in this recipe for a vegan alternative.

TIME: Preparation takes about 15 minutes. Microwave cooking takes about 4-5 minutes.

BRAISED FENNEL

SERVES 4

The aromatic, aniseed flavour of fennel makes it an ideal accompaniment to many richer casseroles and vegetable bakes.

2 x 225g /8oz bulbs of fennel
10ml /2 tsps fresh chopped lovage
60ml /4 tbsps hot vegetable stock
30ml /2 tbsps sherry
2.5ml ½ tsp celery seeds

1. Using a sharp knife, cut away the thick root end from the fennel bulbs.

2. Trim the upper stalks and fern like leaf parts to within 2.5cm /1 inch of the top of the oval bulb.

3. Carefully shred the fennel bulb, crosswise, into narrow strips approximately 0.75cm /¼ inch width, separating the strips from each other as you cut.

4. Put the shredded fennel into a large bowl along with the lovage.

5. Pour over the stock and sherry and mix well to coat the fennel evenly.

6. Cover the bowl with cling film and pierce this several times with the tip of a sharp knife.

Step 1 Using a sharp knife, trim away any thick root from the fennel bulbs.

Step 2 Trim away the stalk and any leafy parts to within 2.5cm /1 inch of the fennel bulbs.

Step 3 Shred the fennel bulbs into narrow strips, approximately 0.75cm /¼ inch wide, separating the strips from each other as they are cut.

7. Cook the fennel on HIGH for 5-7 minutes, or until it is just tender. Stir the fennel once or twice during this cooking time and re-cover each time.

8. Drain the fennel in a colander to remove any cooking liquid and transfer it to a warmed serving dish.

9. Sprinkle the celery seeds over the fennel just before serving.

Cook's Notes

VARIATION: Add 1 peeled, cored and thinly sliced cooking apple to the fennel for a delicious variation.

COOK'S TIP: If lovage is not available, use some of the leafy trimmings from the fennel in its place.

TIME: Preparation takes about 5 minutes, microwave cooking time is about 5-7 minutes.

GREEN BEANS WITH MUSTARD SAUCE

SERVES 4

An unusual way of serving these delicious vegetables, this recipe is best prepared when the beans are freshly picked. Do not use wholemeal flour in this recipe as this will discolour the sauce.

450g /1lb fresh green beans
140ml /¼ pint hot vegetable stock
Freshly ground sea salt
Approximately 140ml /¼ pint milk
30g /1oz vegetable margarine
30g /1oz plain flour
15ml /1 tbsp dry English mustard
Ground white pepper

1. Trim off the stalks and tips of each bean. Cut them into 5cm /2-inch lengths using a sharp knife.

2. Put the beans into a microwave-proof casserole dish or large bowl and season them lightly with the salt.

3. Add the vegetable stock, and cover the dish or bowl. Cook on HIGH for 6-8 minutes, or until the beans are tender.

4. Drain the beans through a colander, reserving the cooking liquid.

5. Arrange the beans on a warmed serving dish, cover them and set aside, keeping them warm until required.

6. Pour the reserved cooking liquor into a measuring jug, and make it up to 280ml /½ pint with the milk.

Step 4 Drain the cooked beans through a colander, which has been placed over a bowl in which the cooking liquid can be reserved.

Step 8 Stir the flour, mustard powder and pepper into the melted margarine, mixing it well to form a roux.

7. Put the margarine into a bowl and cook on HIGH for 30 seconds, or until it has melted.

8. Stir in the flour, mustard powder and the pepper and mix well to form a roux.

9. Cook the roux, uncovered, on HIGH for 45 seconds.

10. Gradually add the milk in four stages, mixing it in well and cooking it for 30 seconds between additions.

11. Continue cooking the sauce for a further 1-2 minutes after all the milk has been added to thicken it slightly. Whisk the sauce every 30 seconds during this time.

12. Pour the sauce over the beans and serve hot.

Step 1 Cut the trimmed beans into 5cm /2-inch lengths using a sharp knife.

RED HOT SLAW

SERVES 4

*Hot and spicy, this warm variation of a coleslaw will make
an interesting accompaniment to highly flavoured foods.*

450g /1lb red cabbage
2 red onions
1 small white daikon (mooli) radish
60ml /4 tbsps mayonnaise
60ml /4 tbsps natural yogurt
10ml /2 tsps grated horseradish
2.5ml /½ tsp aniseed
2.5ml /½ tsp chilli powder

Step 8 Mix the hot vegetables thoroughly into the mayonnaise mixture, making sure that they are evenly coated with the sauce.

1. Pull away any damaged outer leaves from the cabbage and shred the firm inner leaves into strips, approximately 0.75cm /¼ inch thick, using a very sharp knife.

2. Peel the onions and slice them, keeping the rings as intact as possible.

Step 3 Grate the peeled radish on the coarse side of a kitchen grater.

3. Peel the mooli radish and grate this on the coarse side of a grater.

4. Put the cabbage, onions and radish into a large bowl, cover it with cling film and pierce this several times with the tip of a sharp knife.

5. Cook the cabbage mixture on HIGH for 4-5 minutes, or until the vegetables are warmed through, but not cooked or softened.

6. Uncover the bowl and drain off any cooking juices which may have appeared.

7. Mix together the remaining ingredients in a large bowl.

8. Add the hot vegetables to the mayonnaise mixture and stir well to coat evenly.

9. Heat through for 1 minute, if necessary, before serving.

Cook's Notes

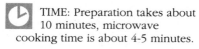

TIME: Preparation takes about 10 minutes, microwave cooking time is about 4-5 minutes.

VEGETARIAN SUITABILITY: This recipe is suitable for lacto-vegetarians only.

COOK'S TIP: Mooli radishes are long white Asian radishes, and can be bought from delicatessen or ethnic supermarkets if not available at local stores.

VARIATION: Grate a large, unpeeled cooking apple into this slaw for a slightly sweetened variation.

WILD RICE PILAU
SERVES 4

*Wild rice is now easily available at most delicatessens
or even at the supermarket, and its flavour and texture set it
apart from more traditional rice types.*

180g /6oz long grain brown or white rice
60g /2oz wild rice
15ml /1 tbsp vegetable oil
1 piece cassia bark
4 black cardamom pods, crushed with the seeds
8 cloves
4 black peppercorns
1 piece star anise
570ml /1 pint vegetable stock
60ml /4 tbsps dry white wine
60g /2oz flaked almonds
60g /2oz raisins

1. Put the rices into a fine-meshed sieve and wash them thoroughly under cold running water. Drain them completely.

2. Put the oil and spices into a large bowl and cook on HIGH for 30 seconds.

3. Stir in the rice and cook for 1 minute. Stir the rice after 30 seconds to coat it evenly in the oil.

4. Pour the stock and the wine into the rice and cook, uncovered, on HIGH for 10 minutes.

Step 1 Rinse the mixed rices under cold running water to remove any dust or particles of grit from the grains.

Step 3 Stir the rice into the hot oil, making sure that the grains are evenly coated as it is cooked.

Step 7 Fluff the cooked rice with a fork to separate the grains before serving.

5. Add the nuts and raisins to the partially cooked rice and continue cooking for a further 2-5 minutes, stirring after each minute, until most, if not all, of the cooking liquid has been absorbed.

6. Cover the rice with a tight-fitting lid or stretch a piece of cling film over the bowl, sealing it well. Allow the rice to stand for 5 minutes before removing the lid.

7. Fluff the rice up with a fork before serving.

Cook's Notes

 VARIATION: Add some chopped mixed vegetables to the rice instead of the nuts and raisins.

VEGETARIAN SUITABILITY: This recipe is suitable for vegans.

 SERVING IDEA: Serve with curries, casseroles or salads.

STUFFED TOMATOES

SERVES 4

These delicious filled tomatoes are excellent as a vegetable accompaniment, but would also make an interesting starter, garnished with a little salad.

4 large, ripe tomatoes (beefsteak are best)
30g /1oz vegetable margarine
1 shallot, peeled and finely chopped
225g /8oz button mushrooms, trimmed and finely chopped
15ml /1 tbsp dry white wine
1 clove garlic, crushed
45g /1½oz fresh white breadcrumbs
5ml /1 tsp Dijon mustard
5ml /1 tsp fresh chopped parsley
5ml /1 tsp fresh chopped oregano
1.25ml /¼ tsp fresh chopped thyme
Salt and freshly ground black pepper

Step 11 Arrange the hollowed out tomatoes, 'core' end down, in a circle on a shallow, microwave-proof dish.

1. Put 570ml /1 pint water into a large bowl. Cover the bowl with cling film and pierce this several times with the tip of a sharp knife. Heat the water on HIGH for 5-6 minutes, or until well boiling.

2. Cut a shallow cross into the skin of each tomato with a sharp knife, taking care not to cut into the flesh too deeply.

3. Plunge the tomatoes, two at a time, into the boiling water and allow to stand for 1-1½ minutes.

4. Remove the tomatoes from the boiling water and hold them under cold water for a few seconds.

5. Carefully peel away the skins from the tomatoes.

6. Stand the peeled fruit in a bowl of cold water while repeating this process with the remaining two tomatoes. Re-cover and re-heat the boiling water if necessary.

7. Drain the peeled tomatoes and carefully remove the green cores using a sharp knife.

8. Carefully slice off the rounded tops and reserve these for the lids.

9. Scoop out the tomato seeds and pulp using a sharp knife and a teaspoon.

10. Put the seeds and pulp into a small sieve over a bowl and reserve as much of the juice as possible.

11. Stand the hollowed out tomatoes, 'core' end down, in a circle on a shallow microwave-proof baking dish.

12. Put the margarine into a small bowl and melt on HIGH for 30 seconds.

13. Stir in the shallot and cook, uncovered, for a further 1 minute, or until the shallot is softened, but not browned.

14. Stir in the mushrooms, wine and the garlic and continue cooking, uncovered, on HIGH, for a further 2 minutes.

15. Add the breadcrumbs, mustard, herbs and seasoning to the shallot mixture and stir in any tomato juice collected from the strained seeds and pulp. Mix well.

16. Carefully fill each hollowed out tomato shell with equal amounts of the shallot and mushroom stuffing mixture.

17. Place the reserved lids over the filled tomatoes, arranging them at a slight angle.

18. Cook the filled tomatoes on HIGH for 1-2 minutes, or until the filling is heated through completely, and the tomato flesh has softened. Serve hot, garnished with parsley if desired.

Vegetarian Microwave Cooking

Chapter ~ 7

· Puddings and ·
· Desserts ·

CHOCOLATE ORANGE CHEESECAKE

SERVES 8-10

Chocolate and oranges are a traditional combination which is used to full advantage in this moreish cheesecake.

360g /12oz wholemeal chocolate biscuits
60g /2oz vegetable margarine
90g /3oz plain chocolate
45ml /3 tbsps water
450g /1lb cream or curd cheese
150g /5oz caster sugar
90ml /3fl oz natural yogurt
4 eggs
Grated rind and juice of 1 orange
2 oranges, peeled and segmented

Step 12 Carefully marble the chocolate through the cheese mixture, swirling it evenly with a skewer to form an attractive pattern.

1. Finely crush the biscuits using a blender or food processor.

2. Put the margarine into a small bowl and melt it on HIGH for 30 seconds.

3. Pour the melted margarine into the crushed biscuits and mix thoroughly to bind the crumbs together.

4. Lightly grease and base line a 20cm /8-inch round microwave-proof cake dish, preferably one with a removable base.

5. Spread the biscuit mixture as evenly as possible over the base of the dish, drawing it up slightly around the sides.

6. Cook the biscuit crust on HIGH for 1 minute, then set aside until required.

7. Put 60g /2oz of the chocolate into a small bowl along with 30ml /2 tbsps of the water.

8. Melt the chocolate on MEDIUM for 30 seconds, stirring it into the water to form a smooth cream.

9. Put the cheese, sugar, yogurt, eggs, orange rind and juice into a large bowl and beat them well together until they are smooth.

10. Cook the cheese mixture on HIGH for 2 minutes, stir the mixture well and continue cooking for a further 2 minutes.

11. Pour one third of the cheese mixture onto the biscuit base. Carefully drizzle one third of the chocolate evenly over this.

12. Carefully marble the chocolate through the cheese mixture, using a skewer or a knife, swirling it evenly to create and attractive pattern.

13. Continue with half the remaining cheese mixture and melted chocolate and finish with the third layer.

14. Cook the cheesecake for 10 minutes on MEDIUM, or until the cake is softly set in the centre.

15. Chill the cheesecake until it is quite firm, then remove the cake dish and slide the cheesecake from the base onto a serving plate.

16. Put the remaining chocolate and the remaining water into a small bowl and melt on MEDIUM for 30 seconds. Stir until they form a smooth cream.

17. Arrange the orange slices around the edge of the cheesecake and drizzle the chocolate cream over the oranges in an attractive pattern for decoration.

RASPBERRY MERINGUES

SERVES 2

Light, pale pink meringues form the basis of this delightful summer dessert.

1 egg white
120g /4oz icing sugar
2.5ml /½ tsp raspberry flavouring
2 drops red food colouring
120g /4oz fresh raspberries
30ml /2 tbsps raspberry liqueur
Caster sugar to taste
Icing sugar and cocoa powder for decoration

1. Put the egg white into a bowl and stir with a fork to break it up to a light froth.

2. Stir in the icing sugar, adding just enough to form a firm, pliable dough. Add the flavouring and colouring, and mix well to colour evenly.

3. Roll out the paste on a board lightly sprinkled with icing sugar, until it is 1.5cm /½-inch thick. Cut it into 4 5cm /2-inch heart shapes, or rounds, with a biscuit cutter.

4. Arrange the shapes 10cm /4 inches apart on a baking sheet which has been lined with silicone paper. If making heart shapes, arrange them so that the points are facing to the middle.

Step 1 Stir the egg white with a fork until it has broken up and forms a light froth.

Step 2 Mix the icing sugar, flavouring and colouring into the egg white to make an evenly coloured paste.

Step 3 Roll out the paste on a board sprinkled with icing sugar and cut the paste into 4 5cm / 2-inch heart shapes.

5. Cook the meringues for 1 minute on HIGH, or until they are firm and dry. Allow to stand for a couple of minutes, then stand on a wire rack to cool completely.

6. Put the raspberries into a bowl and stir in the liqueur, and sugar if required.

7. When the meringues are cooled, sandwich 2 of them together with the cream and a few of the liqueur-soaked raspberries.

8. Sprinkle the tops with the icing sugar and cocoa powder and serve any remaining raspberries separately.

Cook's Notes

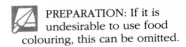

TIME: Preparation takes about 15 minutes, microwave cooking time is about 1 minute.

PREPARATION: If it is undesirable to use food colouring, this can be omitted.

SERVING IDEA: Serve with extra fruit salad if a more substantial dessert is required.

HALVA OF CARROTS AND CASHEWS

SERVES 4-6

Halva is a traditional Indian dessert made from carrots and cream. Do not let the use of vegetable in a dessert put you off trying this rather special recipe, as the results are really delicious.

1kg /2lbs carrots
280ml /½ pint double cream
180g /6oz dark brown sugar
30ml /2 tbsps clear honey
10ml /2 tsps ground coriander
5ml /1 tsp ground cinnamon
Pinch of saffron
60g /2oz vegetable margarine
60g /2oz raisins
120g /4oz chopped, unsalted cashew nuts

1. Peel and trim the carrots, then grate them using the coarse edge of a cheese grater.

2. Put the grated carrots into a large mixing bowl along with the cream, sugar, honey and

Step 2 Mix the cream, sugar, honey and spices thoroughly into the grated carrots.

Step 5 Stir the cooked carrots vigorously until the mixture is thick and the carrots are well broken down.

spices. Mix these ingredients together thoroughly.

3. Cook the carrot mixture, uncovered, on HIGH for 15 minutes, or until the carrots are soft. Stir the mixture frequently during this cooking time.

4. Add the margarine, raisins and nuts, and stir well to incorporate completely.

5. Continue cooking on HIGH for a further 5 minutes, stirring the mixture twice during this time, until the mixture has thickened and the carrots are well broken down.

6. Pile the carrot halva onto serving dishes and decorate with the candied violets, silver balls or desiccated coconut.

Cook's Notes

 COOK'S TIP: If you have one, use the grater attachment on a mixer or food processor to speed up the preparation time.

SERVING IDEA: Serve with spiced poached apples.

TIME: Preparation takes about 15 minutes, microwave cooking time is about 20 minutes.

VEGETARIAN SUITABILITY: This recipe is suitable for lacto-vegetarians only.

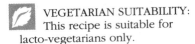 PREPARATION: If the mixture does not thicken in the specified cooking time, continue cooking on HIGH until it does.

WHITE COFFEE CREAMS
SERVES 6-8

An unusual combination of light coffee flavoured cream and tangy summer fruits, this dessert is a sure way to create an impressive finalé to any meal.

8 coffee beans
280ml /½ pint milk
3 eggs
60g /2oz caster sugar
140ml /¼ pint single cream
225g /8oz blackberries, blackcurrants or raspberries
15ml /1 tbsp lemon juice
Icing sugar to taste

1. Put the coffee beans and the milk into a small bowl and cook on HIGH for 3 minutes. Allow to stand for 30 minutes to infuse the flavour of the beans into the milk.

2. Whisk the eggs and the caster sugar together until they are thick, creamy and pale in colour.

3. Strain the flavoured milk onto the egg and sugar mixture through a fine sieve.

4. Stir the cream into the egg mixture and whisk well to blend thoroughly.

5. Pour equal amounts of the egg custard into 6-8 lightly greased individual ramekin dishes or small bowls.

6. Arrange the ramekins in a circle in a shallow dish.

7. Pour enough hot water around the ramekins to come halfway up the sides of the dishes.

8. Cook the custard creams on LOW for 7-8 minutes, or until they are set. Remove the dishes from the water bath and chill them completely before serving.

Step 7 Pour enough hot water around the circle of ramekins in the shallow dish to come halfway up the sides of each dish.

9. Reserving a few well shaped fruits for decoration, put most of the berries, the lemon juice and enough icing sugar to your own taste, into the goblet of a blender or food processor.

10. Process the fruit and sugar together until the berries are well broken down and the juice has run.

11. Strain the fruit purée through a fine mesh sieve to remove any seeds, pressing the pulp through with the back of a wooden spoon if necessary.

12. Carefully loosen the sides of the chilled creams with a round-bladed knife.

13. Invert a small serving plate over the top of each ramekin and turn the cream out, shaking them gently to loosen them if necessary.

14. Pour a little of the sauce around and partially cover each of the creams and decorate them with the reserved berries.

15. Serve any remaining sauce separately.

Cook's Notes

TIME: Preparation takes about 20 minutes, plus chilling time. Microwave cooking time is about 11 minutes, plus 30 minutes standing time.

VEGETARIAN SUITABILITY: This recipe is suitable for lacto-vegetarians only.

VARIATION: Use a vanilla pod instead of the coffee beans in this recipe.

COFFEE RASPBERRY ROULADES

SERVES 6

Light, fluffy rolls of soft coffee meringues filled with cream and raspberries create a luxurious and unusual dessert.

15g /½oz butter or vegetable margarine
6 egg whites
340g /12oz caster sugar
5ml /1 tsp vinegar
10ml /½ tsp instant coffee, dissolved in 5ml/ 2 tsps hot water
10ml /2 tsps cornflour
5ml /1 tsp cream of tartar
60g /2oz flaked almonds
280ml /½ pint double cream, whipped
225g /8oz fresh raspberries
Extra icing sugar and decorative coffee beans for decoration

1. Put the butter into a small bowl and melt on HIGH for 30 seconds.

2. Line 2 microwave-proof baking sheets with silicone paper and brush this with the melted butter or margarine.

3. Put the egg whites into a large bowl and whisk them vigorously until they are stiff and form soft peaks.

4. Add the sugar to the egg whites, a spoonful at a time, whisking well between additions.

5. Mix together the vinegar and the coffee. Fold this into the egg whites along with the cornflour and the cream of tartar.

6. Spoon the meringue into 12 equal-sized portions, well apart, on the baking sheets.

7. Smooth each spoonful out into even-sized rectangles approximately 1.25cm /½ inch thick,

Step 7 Carefully spread the piles of meringue into even sized rectangles approximately 1.25cm /½-inch thick. Make sure that there is plenty of space between each rectangle on the baking sheet.

Step 11 Carefully peel away the cooking paper from the cooked meringue rectangles, leaving them almond side down on the fresh, sugared paper.

Step 13 Roll up each cream covered, soft meringue, starting from a narrow end, as you would a Swiss roll.

ensuring that there is a good gap between each rectangle.

8. Sprinkle the almonds evenly over each of the rectangles.

9. Cook each batch of meringues for 3 minutes on HIGH, then leave to cool slightly.

10. Lay a clean piece of silicone paper on a flat surface and dust it liberally with icing sugar.

11. Turn the sheets of cooked meringue, almond side down onto the sugared paper, and carefully peel away the paper on which they were cooked.

12. Spread the upturned side of each meringue with a little of the whipped cream and scatter on a few of the raspberries, reserving about half of these for decoration.

13. Carefully roll up each cream-covered soft meringue, starting from a narrow end as with a Swiss roll.

14. Put 2 roulades onto each of 6 serving plates and decorate with any remaining whipped cream, the reserved raspberries and the decorative coffee beans.

CRANBERRY CRISP
SERVES 2

Cranberries are often overlooked as being a fruity accompaniment to savoury dishes. However, their bittersweet flavour is complemented perfectly by the honey in this recipe to produce an interesting dessert which you will want to try over and over again.

140ml /¼ pint orange juice
120g /4oz fresh cranberries
10ml /2 tsps caster sugar
10ml /2 tsps cornflour
1.25ml /¼ tsp cinnamon
15g /½oz plain flour
225g /8oz crunchy oatmeal cereal
30g /1oz vegetable margarine
30ml /2 tbsps clear honey

Step 10 Carefully drizzle the honey over the partially cooked topping, making sure that it is distributed as evenly as possible.

1. Put the orange juice, cranberries and caster sugar into a small bowl, cover with cling film and pierce this several times with the tip of a sharp knife.

2. Cook the cranberries on HIGH for 3 minutes, or until they begin to split and soften.

3. Blend the cornflour with a little water and stir this and the cinnamon into the cranberries.

Step 4 After cooking, the cranberry mixture should have thickened and cleared slightly.

4. Cook the cranberry mixture, uncovered, for 2 minutes on HIGH, or until the mixture thickens.

5. Stir the cranberry mixture well, then pour it into the base of a serving dish.

6. Put the flour into a bowl and mix in the cereal.

7. Put the margarine into a small bowl and melt it on HIGH for 45 seconds.

8. Stir the melted margarine into the flour and cereal mixture and mix well to incorporate thoroughly.

9. Spread this topping over the cranberries in the serving dish and cook on HIGH for 4 minutes.

10. Drizzle the honey over the partially cooked topping, trying to distribute it as evenly as possible.

11. Cook the cranberry crunch for a further 4 minutes on HIGH before serving.

Cook's Notes

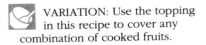 VARIATION: Use the topping in this recipe to cover any combination of cooked fruits.

 TIME: Preparation takes about 10 minutes, microwave cooking time is about 15 minutes.

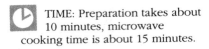 SERVING IDEA: Serve with fresh cream or a fruit purée.

CREME CARAMEL
SERVES 4-6

This classic dessert can be made in half the time when using a microwave oven.

120ml /4fl oz water
120g /4oz granulated sugar
3 eggs
60g /2oz caster sugar
5ml /1 tsp vanilla essence
Pinch salt
180ml /6fl oz single cream
180ml /6fl oz milk

1. Put the water and the granulated sugar into a deep bowl or glass measure and stir well. Cook on HIGH for 10-12 minutes, stirring occasionally during this cooking time, until the sugar has dissolved and the syrup has turned golden brown.

2. Pour the syrup into a warmed 17.5cm /7-inch souffle dish or glass bowl, tilting and turning the dish to swirl the caramel syrup around the base and sides.

3. Allow the caramel to cool and set.

4. Put the eggs, caster sugar, vanilla and salt into a bowl and beat them together until they become pale and fluffy.

5. Put the cream and the milk into a glass jug or bowl and heat on HIGH for 4 minutes.

6. Gradually add the scalded milk and cream to the egg mixture, whisking all the time until it is well incorporated.

7. Carefully strain the egg and cream mixture on to the set caramel through a sieve to remove any stringy bits that may have formed from the eggs.

Step 7 Strain the egg and cream mixture onto the caramel through a sieve to remove any lumps that may have formed.

8. Cover the bowl with cling film and pierce this several times with the tip of a sharp knife.

9. Stand the covered bowl in a microwave-proof roasting dish and pour in enough water to come 5cm /2-inches up the outside of the bowl.

10. Cook the custard on LOW for 10-13 minutes, turning the dish by a quarter turn after each 3 minutes.

11. Continue cooking the custard until it has set and a knife comes out clean when inserted into the centre of the dish.

12. Allow the custard to cool completely before chilling in a refrigerator.

13. To turn the custard out, gently loosen the sides of the set custard with a round bladed knife.

14. Invert a serving plate over the top of the bowl and carefully turn both of them over, shaking the creme caramel gently until it drops out onto the serving plate.

Cook's Notes

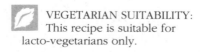 TIME: Preparation takes about 15 minutes, microwave cooking time is about 25-30 minutes.

VEGETARIAN SUITABILITY: This recipe is suitable for lacto-vegetarians only.

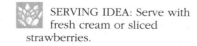 SERVING IDEA: Serve with fresh cream or sliced strawberries.

RUM BABAS

MAKES: 10-12

Easily cooked in the microwave oven, these delectable dessert cakes will always be a firm favourite.

180ml /6fl oz milk
10ml /2 tsps caster sugar
15ml /1 tbsp dry active baking yeast
450g /1lb plain flour
Pinch salt
150g /5oz vegetable margarine
4 eggs
60g /2oz currants
140ml /¼ pint clear honey
90ml /6 tbsps water
45ml /3 tbsps brandy or rum

1. Put the milk into a large jug or pudding bowl and cook on HIGH for 30 seconds. Mix in the sugar and yeast.

2. Sift the flour and salt into a large bowl and make a well in the centre.

3. Pour the yeast mixture into this well and carefully sprinkle a little flour over the top.

4. Leave the flour and yeast in a warm place for about 30 minutes, or until the yeast has become very frothy.

5. Carefully mix the flour, yeast and salt together to form a batter, mixing from the centre and incorporating only a little flour at a time from the edges.

6. Put the margarine into a bowl and soften it on HIGH for 30 seconds.

7. Beat the margarine into the yeast and flour batter along with the eggs, mixing well until it is shiny and elastic, but still very soft.

Step 7 Beat the margarine and eggs into the flour and yeast until the batter becomes shiny and elastic, but still very soft.

8. Stir the currants into the dough.

9. Thoroughly grease 10-12 individual ramekins or baba moulds and spoon in the baba mixture to about half way up the sides of each mould.

10. Lightly cover the dishes with floured cling film and leave them in a warm place for 30-40 minutes, or until the mixture has almost doubled in volume.

11. Cook the babas for 5 minutes on HIGH, or until the tops have set and look dry.

12. Leave to stand for 1 minute before turning onto a wire rack to cool completely.

13. When cooled, stand the babas in a shallow dish, ready to be soaked in the syrup.

14. Put the honey and the water into a deep bowl and heat on HIGH for 7 minutes.

15. Stir in the brandy or rum, and carefully spoon equal amounts of the syrup over the babas. Allow the syrup to soak into the babas completely before serving.

Cook's Notes

COOK'S TIP: If your microwave oven is not big enough to cook all the babas at once, cook them in two batches for 3-4 minutes on HIGH for each batch.

PREPARATION: If you have a mixer or food processor, this can be used to beat the margarine and eggs into the flour and yeast to make the baba batter.

TIME: Preparation takes about 1 hour, microwave cooking time is about 5 minutes, plus standing and proving time.

RHUBARB, ORANGE AND STRAWBERRY COMFORT

SERVES 4

*Delicious, easy to prepare and only 60 calories per serving,
what more could anyone ask of a scrumptious dessert?*

450g /1lb canned rhubarb in natural juice
1.25ml /¼ tsp ground ginger
298g /10½oz tin mandarin segments in natural juice
Liquid sweetener, to taste
30ml /2 tbsps low fat natural yogurt
180g /6oz fresh strawberries, hulled and rinsed
30ml /2 tbsps crunchy muesli

1. Put the rhubarb into a large bowl with the ginger.

2. Strain the juice from the mandarins and add this to the rhubarb, reserving the segments in a separate bowl.

3. Cook the rhubarb mixture on HIGH for 10-12 minutes, stirring occasionally during this cooking time, until the rhubarb is mushy.

Step 4 Beat the rhubarb mixture briskly until the fruit breaks up and the purée thickens slightly.

Step 8 Thinly slice all but 4 of the strawberries with a very sharp knife.

4. Beat the rhubarb mixture briskly until the fruit breaks up and the mixture becomes thicker.

5. Mix in the sweetener to taste.

6. Stir the yogurt into the rhubarb mixture along with the mandarin segments, taking care not to break them up too much.

7. Cover the rhubarb and oranges with cling film and leave to cool completely.

8. Reserve 4 of the best shaped strawberries for decoration and thinly slice the remainder with a sharp knife.

9. Mix the strawberry slices into the cooled rhubarb mixture and pour equal amounts into 4 individual serving goblets.

10. Just before serving, sprinkle the muesli over the top of each serving and decorate with a whole strawberry.

Cook's Notes

VEGETARIAN SUITABILITY: This recipe is suitable for lacto-vegetarians only. Vegans could substitute the yogurt with a vegetable cream substitute, but it would not then be so low in calories.

VARIATION: Use tinned apricots in place of the rhubarb, and a tin of pitted cherries in place of the mandarins in this recipe.

PREPARATION: If you have a blender or food processor, you could use this to break up the rhubarb instead of doing it by hand.

HOT FRUIT SALAD CUPS

SERVES 4

These attractive cups of warm fresh fruit make a delightful ending to any meal.

2 large oranges
30g /1oz caster sugar
5ml /1 tsp rum
1 small dessert apple
1 slice fresh pineapple
1 banana
8g /¹⁄₄oz shelled pistachio nuts, skins removed

1. Halve the oranges and stand the halves in a shallow dish, cut sides downwards.

2. Cook in the microwave oven, uncovered, for 2 minutes on HIGH to release the juices.

3. Gently squeeze out the juice using a lemon squeezer and put this into a bowl.

4. Using a grapefruit knife or serrated spoon, carefully remove any flesh and membranes from inside the orange skins, leaving just the white pith and outer zest to form a shell. Set them aside whilst preparing the filling.

5. Stir the sugar into the reserved juice and cook, uncovered, for 1-1½ minutes on HIGH, or

Step 7 Cut the quartered and cored apple pieces into bite-sized cubes with a sharp knife.

Step 8 Cut away the skin and any brown 'eyes' from the pineapple slices before chopping into small wedges.

until the juice is boiling. Stir the mixture twice during this cooking time to dissolve the sugar.

6. Remove the juice from the microwave oven and stir to ensure that the sugar has completely dissolved, then mix in the rum.

7. Cut the apple into quarters, but do not peel it. Remove the core and cut each quarter into bite-sized cubes with a sharp knife.

8. Remove the skin from the pineapple slice and cut out any brown eyes. Cut the pineapple flesh into small wedges.

9. Peel the banana and cut it into slices.

10. Mix the prepared fruits into the sweetened orange juice and cook, uncovered, for 30 seconds on HIGH. Stir the fruit once and cook again for a further 30 seconds on HIGH.

11. Divide the fruit equally between the orange shells and pour the syrup over.

12. Decorate with the pistachio nuts before serving.

Cook's Notes

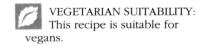

VARIATION: Use any combination of your favourite fruit for filling the orange shells in this recipe.

TIME: Preparation takes about 10 minutes, microwave cooking takes about 7 minutes.

VEGETARIAN SUITABILITY: This recipe is suitable for vegans.

BAKED BANANAS SAUCE À LA POIRE

SERVES 4

*Baked bananas are an established favourite for dessert,
and this recipe sets them apart with the inclusion of a delightful
fruity sauce to really enhance their flavour.*

1 large orange
2 ripe pears
Liquid sweetener to taste
4 bananas

1. Very carefully, so as not to remove any of the white pith, thinly pare the rind from the orange with a potato peeler.

2. Cut the pared rind into very thin strips with a sharp knife.

3. Put the orange strips into a small bowl and pour over just enough boiling water to cover them. Cook on HIGH for 1 minute to blanch.

4. Strain off the blanching liquid, and set the orange rind strips to one side to drain completely on absorbent kitchen paper.

5. Cut the orange in half and remove the peel and pith from one of the halves.

Step 8 Roughly chop the peeled, quartered and cored pears.

Step 11 Spread the pear purée evenly over the partially cooked bananas.

6. Carefully remove the orange segments from the peeled half and set them to one side.

7. Squeeze the juice from the remaining half and put this into the goblet of a liquidiser or food processor.

8. Peel, quarter and core the pears. Roughly chop the flesh and add this to the orange juice. Purée the pears and orange juice until smooth, adding the liquid sweetener to taste.

9. Peel the bananas and put them whole into a serving dish. Cook on HIGH for 2 minutes.

10. Carefully re-position the bananas in the serving dish so that even cooking is ensured.

11. Pour the pear purée over the bananas, spreading it evenly and cook, uncovered, for a further 2 minutes on HIGH.

12. Decorate the cooked bananas with the reserved orange segments and the strips of blanched orange rind. Serve hot.

Cook's Notes

VARIATION: Use pineapple instead of pears in this recipe, and sprinkle 15ml /1 tbsp flaked coconut over the finished dish as an added decoration.

PREPARATION: This recipe should be prepared no more than 1 hour before serving, otherwise the bananas will discolour.

SERVING IDEA: Serve with coconut biscuit, and some cream, if liked.

255

ALMOND SAVARIN

SERVES 6-8

*Savarins make ideal centre pieces for cold tables or buffets,
and this recipe is ideal for such an occasion as it can be made
well in advance and frozen until required.*

60g /2oz flaked almonds
225g /8oz strong plain flour
5ml /1 tsp salt
120ml /4 fl oz milk
10g /2 tsps fresh yeast, crumbled
10g /2 tsps sugar
3 eggs, beaten
90g /3oz butter or vegetable margarine
140ml /¼ pint water
90ml /6 tbsps amaretto
150g /5oz sugar
Fresh fruit and whipped cream to decorate

1. Put the almonds into a baking dish and cook on HIGH for 6 minutes, stirring occasionally until they begin to brown, and then stirring more frequently.

2. Take great care not to over-brown the almond flakes – they should be pale gold in colour and not too burnt.

3. Sift the flour and the salt into a large bowl and warm it on HIGH for 30 seconds.

4. Pour the milk into a glass jug and warm on HIGH for 30 seconds. Gradually blend in the yeast and the sugar until they have dissolved.

5. Gradually beat the eggs into the yeast mixture.

6. Make a well in the centre of the flour and pour in the yeast and egg mixture.

7. Begin to mix the liquid by stirring from the centre of the well and gradually drawing in the flour from the outside. Continue to slowly mix in all the flour in this way until the batter becomes a very sticky, elastic dough.

8. Cover the bowl with lightly floured cling film and warm for 10-15 seconds on HIGH to start the yeast working. Leave the bowl of dough to stand in a warm place until the yeast mixture has doubled in size.

9. Melt the butter or margarine on HIGH for 1 minute, then allow it to cool slightly. Beat the melted butter into the risen yeast mixture with a wooden spoon, until it is well incorporated.

10. Stir the almonds into the enriched dough.

11. Thoroughly grease a microwave-proof ring mould and spoon in the savarin dough. Lightly cover the mould with cling film and warm this on HIGH for 10-15 seconds.

12. Stand the savarin in a warm place until it has once again doubled in size.

13. Cook the savarin on HIGH for 5-6 minutes, or until it is firm to touch and the top appears only slightly moist. Allow it to stand for 10 minutes in the dish before turning it out onto a wire rack to cool completely.

14. Put the water, amaretto and sugar into a bowl and stir well. Bring to the boil on HIGH for 5 minutes, then stir to completely dissolve the sugar. Continue cooking on HIGH for a further 2 minutes, or until the mixture becomes syrupy.

15. Stand the cooled savarin in a shallow dish and prick it all over with a skewer.

16. Pour the syrup evenly over the savarin and allow it to soak in completely before transferring it to a serving dish and decorating it with fresh fruit and whipped cream.

Cook's Notes

PREPARATION: If you have an electric mixer, the dough can be beaten with this instead of by hand.

FREEZING: The savarin can be frozen for up to 2 months after the syrup has been soaked into it.

SERVING IDEA: To serve more people, serve the savarin with a bowl of fresh fruit salad.

BOMBE AUX ABRICOTS

SERVES 6-8

A delicious home made dessert, made easy by using convenience foods. No one will ever know that you didn't spend hours freezing and beating this luxurious ice cream!

120g /4oz dried apricots
30ml /2 tbsps brandy
850ml /1½ pints vanilla ice cream
60g /2oz toasted hazelnuts, finely chopped

1. Put a 1150ml /2-pint bombe mould or decorative mould into the freezer for 2 hours to chill.

2. Roughly chop the apricots and put them into a small bowl. Pour over the brandy and cover the bowl with cling film, puncturing this twice only with the tip of a sharp knife.

3. Cook the apricots on HIGH for 1 minute, then set aside, still covered, to cool completely.

4. Put 570ml /1 pint of the ice cream into a bowl and soften it slightly for 1 minute on HIGH.

5. Beat the softened ice cream until it is smooth, but not too soft.

6. Stir in the chopped hazelnuts, mixing well to incorporate them evenly.

7. If the ice cream has become too soft, re-freeze until it is of a spreading consistency.

8. Carefully coat the base and the sides of the chilled mould with the hazelnut ice cream, leaving a well in the middle and keeping the ice cream layer as even as possible.

Step 8 Carefully coat the base and sides of the mould with an even layer of the semi-frozen hazelnut ice cream, leaving a well in the centre of the bombe.

Step 13 Beat the re-frozen apricot ice cream with a fork until it becomes a thick, even slush.

9. Return the bombe mould to the freezer and freeze the ice cream layer until it is solid.

10. Put the remaining vanilla ice cream into a bowl and heat on HIGH for 1 minute, until it is a soft cream.

11. Stir in the brandied apricots and any juice that may have formed, mixing well to blend thoroughly.

12. Freeze the apricot ice cream in the freezer until it is becoming set around the edges and slushy in the middle.

13. Beat the apricot ice cream until it becomes evenly slushy. Chill it further if it once again becomes very soft.

14. Pour the apricot ice into the centre well left in the hazelnut ice and pack it down well with the back of a spoon to remove any air pockets.

15. Freeze the bombe completely.

16. Thirty minutes before serving, heat the mould in the microwave oven on HIGH for 30 seconds.

17. Invert a serving plate over the top of the mould, and carefully turn both the plate and the mould over, shaking the bombe gently until it drops out on to the plate.

18. Leave the bombe in the refrigerator to soften slightly for 30 minutes before serving.

CHOCOLATE BRANDY CAKE
SERVES 8

This sumptuous chocolate cake will make an impressive ending to a meal.

340g /12oz plain chocolate
120g /4oz vegetable margarine
2 eggs, beaten
60ml /4 tbsps brandy
225g /8oz digestive sweetmeal biscuits, coarsely
  crushed
60g /2oz blanched almonds, chopped
280ml /½ pint double cream, whipped
Candied rose petals, toasted almonds and slivers
  of angelica to decorate

1. Put the chocolate and the margarine into a bowl and cook on MEDIUM for 5 minutes to melt.

2. Stir the chocolate mixture several times during this cooking time to form a smooth cream.

3. Beat the eggs into the chocolate mixture, and cook for a further 2 minutes on MEDIUM to thicken. Stir twice during this cooking time.

4. Allow the mixture to cool slightly, then beat in the brandy, biscuits and chopped almonds.

Step 2 Stir the melted chocolate and the margarine together carefully to form a smooth cream.

Step 5 Lightly grease and base line with silicone paper, a loose bottomed or springform cake tin.

Step 6 Spread the chocolate mixture evenly into the cake tin with a round bladed palette knife.

5. Lightly grease and base line a 17.5cm /7 inch, springform or loose-based cake tin.

6. Carefully pour the chocolate cake mixture into the tin, spreading it evenly with a round bladed knife.

7. Chill the cake overnight in a refrigerator to set.

8. Loosen the sides of the cake with a warmed knife, then remove the sides of the cake tin.

9. Carefully slide the cake off the bottom of the tin onto a serving plate.

10. Pipe swirls of whipped cream around the edge of the cake and decorate with the rose petals, almonds and angelica.

Cook's Notes

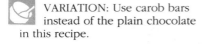 VARIATION: Use carob bars instead of the plain chocolate in this recipe.

 VEGETARIAN SUITABILITY: This recipe is suitable for lacto-vegetarians only.

 SERVING IDEA: Serve with strong black coffee for a rich dessert.

BURGUNDY GRANITA

SERVES 4-6

*Although it doesn't seem relevant to include a water ice in a book
on microwave cookery, the use of a microwave oven certainly does speed
up the preparation of this delicious dessert.*

90g /3oz caster sugar
Juice of ½ a lime
Juice of ½ an orange
15ml /1 tbsp water
½ bottle Burgundy
Finely grated orange rind or a few blackcurrants
    for decoration

1. Put the sugar, lime, orange juice and the water into a deep bowl. Cook on HIGH for 2 minutes, then stir the mixture to dissolve the sugar.

2. Continue cooking on HIGH for a further 2 minutes, then allow to cool.

Step 4 Freeze the burgundy mixture until it becomes fairly solid, but still soft enough to break up with a fork.

Step 5 Whisk the broken ice with an electric mixer until it forms a smooth slush.

3. Stir in the wine and pour the mixture into a shallow freezer container.

4. Freeze the Burgundy mixture until it is beginning to form a firm slush.

5. Break up the ice with a fork, then whisk with an electric mixer, or in a food processor until it forms a smooth slush.

6. Return the mixture to the ice tray and re-freeze until it is solid.

7. Just before serving, heat the granita on HIGH for 15-20 seconds to soften slightly. Stir the mixture until it becomes crumbly, and spoon into serving dishes.

8. Decorate with orange peel or the blackcurrants.

Cook's Notes

TIME: Preparation takes about 15 minutes plus freezing, microwave cooking takes about 4 minutes.

VEGETARIAN SUITABILITY: This recipe is suitable for vegans.

COOK'S TIP: If you do not have an electric whisk or food processor, the ice can be broken up with a hand whisk or fork, but you may have to re-freeze and re-beat one extra time to achieve the same crumbly finished texture.

SERVING IDEA: Serve as a refresher between dinner courses, in small port or sherry glasses.

ST. CLEMENT'S SORBET

SERVES 4-6

St. Clement's is possibly the most popular type of sorbet and this recipe has been made doubly quick and easy by using the microwave oven.

250g /10oz caster sugar
225ml /8fl oz water
4-5 lemons, depending on size
4-5 oranges, depending on size
60ml /4 tbsps orange liqueur
Thinly pared citrus peel and mint leaves to
    decorate

1. Put the sugar and the water into a large bowl, mix well then cook on HIGH for 5 minutes.

2. Stir the liquid again to completely dissolve the sugar, then cook for a further 1-2 minutes, or until it is boiling. Set the syrup to one side until it is completely cooled.

3. Finely grate the rind from one of the lemons and one of the oranges. Stir this into the sugar syrup.

Step 6 Break the frozen ice crystals with a fork, so that the frozen fruit ice can be removed easily from the container.

Step 7 Blend the ice crystals until they form a smooth slush.

4. Squeeze the juice from all the oranges and lemons and strain this into the cooled sugar syrup through a fine-mesh sieve to remove any pips or membranes.

5. Stir the orange liqueur into the fruit syrup and pour it into a freezer dish.

6. Put the dish into the coldest part of the freezer and freeze until it is virtually solid, but still soft enough to be broken up with a fork. Break up the ice crystals with a fork.

7. Spoon the broken ice into a bowl or goblet of a food processor and blend until a slush is formed.

8. Return the slush to the freezer and freeze until solid.

9. Just before serving, soften the sorbet on HIGH for 15-20 seconds and serve decorated with the citrus peel and the mint leaves.

Cook's Notes

VARIATION: Use all lemons or all oranges instead of the mixed fruit in this recipe.

SERVING IDEA: Spoon the smooth slush (Step 7) into hollowed out lemon or orange shells for an attractive way of serving.

TIME: Preparation takes about 20 minutes plus freezing, microwave cooking takes about 15 minutes.

VEGETARIAN SUITABILITY: This recipe is suitable for vegans.

PREPARATION: If you do not have an electric whisk or food processor, the ice crystals can be broken down with a hand whisk or fork, but the mixture may require re-freezing and re-whisking to produce the final smooth texture.

CREPES SUZETTE

SERVES 4-6

Although the pancakes in this recipe are made in the conventional way, the sauce is made quickly and easily in the microwave oven.

120g /4oz plain flour
Pinch salt
1 egg
280ml /½ pint milk
15ml / 1 tbsp vegetable oil
90g /3oz butter or vegetable margarine
60g /2oz caster sugar
Grated rind and juice of 1 orange
Grated rind and juice of ½ lemon
60ml /2 tbsps brandy or orange liqueur
Thin orange slices to decorate

1. Sift the flour into a bowl along with the salt. Make a well in the centre and break in the egg and half of the milk.

2. Begin to mix the batter from the centre, drawing the flour from the sides of the bowl into the egg and milk. Continue beating until all the flour has been mixed in.

3. Gradually add the remaining milk and the oil, whisking or beating well between additions to prevent lumps from forming.

4. Use the batter to make 12-15 small pancakes, conventionally, in a small, lightly greased crepê pan, frying them until they are golden brown on each side.

Step 5 Fold each pancake in half then in half again to form triangles.

5. Fold each pancake in half and then in half again to make a triangle shape. Arrange the folded pancakes in a shallow, microwave-proof serving dish.

6. Put the butter into a small bowl and melt it on DEFROST for 5 minutes.

7. Beat in the sugar and continue stirring the mixture until the sugar dissolves.

8. Add the orange and lemon juice and rinds and stir in the liqueur.

9. Cook the sauce on HIGH for 2 minutes, then pour over the folded pancakes in the serving dish.

10. Re-heat for 2-3 minutes on HIGH before serving, and decorate with the orange slices.

Cook's Notes

FREEZING: The pancakes can be covered with the sauce and then frozen for up to 2 weeks before use. To thaw, cook on HIGH for 5 minutes, then re-heat for a further 2-3 minutes if necessary.

SERVING IDEA: Serve, flambéed with a little warmed brandy for a spectacular dessert.

VEGETARIAN SUITABILITY: This recipe is suitable for lacto-vegetarians only.

TIME: Preparation takes about 25 minutes, microwave cooking takes about 10 minutes. Conventional cooking time for frying the pancakes takes about 15 minutes.

PARFAIT AU CASSIS
SERVES 6

Cassis is a liqueur flavoured with blackcurrant leaves and its slightly musky flavour is complemented superbly by the sharp flavour of the blackcurrant fruit itself.

340g /¾lb fresh blackcurrants
30ml /2 tbsps creme de cassis
3 egg yolks
120g /4oz soft brown sugar
280ml /½ pint single cream
280ml /½ pint double cream
Whole blackcurrants and mint leaves to decorate

1. Purée the blackcurrants in a blender or food processor and press them through a wire sieve with a wooden spoon to remove the skins and pips.

2. Add the cassis to the fruit purée and freeze until it becomes slushy, stirring occasionally to prevent any large ice lumps from forming.

3. Whisk the egg yolks and the sugar together until they become thick and mousse-like.

4. Put the single cream into a jug and heat on HIGH for 2 minutes.

5. Gradually add the scalded cream to the egg mixture, stirring constantly to keep a smooth consistency.

6. Stand the bowl of cream, eggs and sugar in another dish of hot water, making sure the water

Step 3 Whisk the egg yolks and the sugar together until they become thick and mousse-like.

Step 6 Stand the bowl of cream mixture in a dish of warm water, making sure that the water comes up to the same level as the cream in the bowl.

is at the same level as the cream and eggs inside the smaller bowl.

7. Cook the cream and eggs on LOW for 10 minutes, stirring frequently.

8. Cool the mixture quickly after this time, by standing it on a bed of ice cubes.

9. Whip the double cream until it is softly stiff and fold this into the cooled egg and cream mixture.

10. Freeze the cream mixture until it is almost solid, then break it up with a fork and put it into the goblet of a blender or food processor. Blend for a few seconds until the mixture forms a smooth slush.

11. Break up the blackcurrant ice with a fork, or with an electric whisk, and carefully fold this into the cream mixture to produce an attractive marbly effect.

12. Divide the mixture evenly between 6 freezer /microwave-proof serving dishes and freeze until required.

13. Just before serving, soften the parfait on HIGH for 10-20 seconds and decorate with the blackcurrants and the mint leaves.

PLUM AND GINGER CRISP
SERVES 4-6

*Plums and ginger biscuits complement each other beautifully
in this simple dish.*

450g /1lb dessert plums
90g /3oz raw cane sugar
75g /2½oz butter or vegetable margarine
225g /8oz ginger biscuits, crushed
60g /2oz flaked almonds

1. Wash the plums, then halve them and remove the stones.

2. Put the plum halves into a microwave-proof baking dish and sprinkle over the sugar.

3. Cover the dish with cling film and pierce this several times with the tip of a sharp knife.

4. Cook the plums on HIGH for 10 minutes, stirring them once during the cooking time and replacing the covering after this.

5. Put the butter into a large bowl and cook on MEDIUM for 2 minutes, or until it has melted completely.

Step 1 Halve the washed plums and remove the stones with a sharp knife.

Step 6 Stir the crushed biscuits and the flaked almonds into the melted butter, mixing them well to coat the crumbs evenly.

Step 8 Spoon the biscuit topping evenly over the cooked plums.

6. Stir the crushed biscuits and the flaked almonds into the butter, mixing well to coat all the crumbs.

7. Cook the biscuit topping on HIGH for 1 minute. Stir the mixture well then continue cooking for a further 1 minute.

8. Carefully spoon the biscuit crumb evenly over the cooked plums. Cook on HIGH for 3-5 minutes before serving.

Cook's Notes

 VARIATION: Use apricots instead of the plums and use wholemeal digestive biscuits instead of the ginger biscuits.

SERVING IDEA: Serve with custard sauce, cream or a vegan alternative.

VEGETARIAN SUITABILITY: This recipe is suitable for vegans if vegetable margarine is used, and care is taken to buy ginger biscuits that are prepared for vegetarians.

FREEZING: The finished dessert can be frozen when fully prepared, then served by defrosting on LOW for 10 minutes, and then re-heating on HIGH for 5 minutes.

PINEAPPLE UPSIDE-DOWN CAKE

SERVES 6

This cake is always a certain success at any table.

150g /5oz butter, or vegetable margarine
200g /7oz soft light brown sugar
90g /3oz walnut halves
6-8 maraschino, or glacé cherries
225g /8oz tinned pineapple slices, well drained
2 eggs, beaten
120g /4oz self-raising flour
5ml /1 tsp baking powder
60g /2oz digestive biscuits, finely crushed

1. Put 30g /1oz of the margarine or butter into a small bowl and melt for 30 seconds on HIGH.

2. Stir in 90g /3oz of the sugar and cook for a further 1 minute on HIGH, or until the sugar has partially dissolved.

3. Spread the butter syrup over the base of a lightly greased 20cm /8-inch round cake dish.

4. Arrange 4-5 whole walnut halves in a circle in the middle of the dish.

5. Cut the cherries in half and arrange a circle of cherry halves around the walnuts.

6. Cut the pineapple rings in half and place half circles, cut side outermost, around the walnuts and cherries.

Step 6 Place the halved pineapple rings around the edge of the dish, with cut sides outermost, to form a pinwheel arrangement around the walnuts and cherries.

Step 13 Drop the cake onto the inverted serving plate and remove the dish in which it was cooked.

7. Put the remaining margarine or butter, and the remaining sugar into a bowl and cream together until they are pale and fluffy.

8. Beat in the eggs, a little at a time, along with 1 tsp each time, of the flour. Beat the mixture very briskly to prevent it from curdling.

9. Carefully fold in the remaining flour, the baking powder and any fruit or nuts that may be left over. The fruit and nuts must be chopped before adding with the flour.

10. Stir in the digestive biscuits and carefully spoon the cake mixture evenly over the arranged fruit and syrup in the cake dish.

11. Cook the cake on HIGH for 6-7 minutes, or until it begins to draw away from the sides of the dish and is well risen and springy to the touch. Allow the cake to stand for 5 minutes.

12. Loosen the sides of the cake away from the dish with a round-bladed knife and invert a serving plate over the top of the dish.

13. Carefully turn the dish and the plate completely over, shaking gently as you do so to drop the cake onto the plate. Remove the dish and serve hot.

APRICOT PUDDING
SERVES 4-6

*Served with a rich, fruity sauce, this light sponge pudding
is ideal for chilly winter days.*

410g /14½oz tin apricots
60g /2oz vegetable margarine
60g /2oz caster sugar
1 egg, beaten
120g /4oz self-raising flour
5ml /1 tsp baking powder
45ml /3 tbsps milk
Few drops almond essence
Juice of ½ lemon
15ml /1 tbsp cornflour

---

1. Drain half the tinned apricots, reserving these separately from the remaining juice and apricots.

2. Chop the drained apricots and set them aside to use in the sponge.

3. Soften the margarine for 15 seconds on HIGH, then beat in the sugar, mixing until it becomes light and fluffy.

4. Gradually add the egg, beating well between additions to prevent the mixture from curdling.

5. Sift the flour and baking powder together.

Step 3 Cream together the softened margarine and sugar until the mixture is lightly coloured and fluffy textured.

Step 9 Smoothly blend the cornflour and lemon juice into the fruit purée, making sure that no lumps of cornflour remain.

Fold this into the sugar and egg mixture, along with the chopped apricots and enough milk to produce a soft, dropping consistency batter.

6. Add the almond essence to the cake mixture.

7. Spoon the cake mixture into a well greased 570ml /- pint pudding basin. Cook, uncovered, on HIGH for 3-5 minutes, or until the top is almost set but still moist. Allow the pudding to stand for 5 minutes before serving.

8. To make the sauce, purée the remaining apricots and the juice in a liquidiser or food processor.

9. Add the lemon juice and cornflour, and blend into the fruit purée until the cornflour is smoothly incorporated.

10. Put the fruit purée into a jug or bowl and cook on HIGH for 3-5 minutes, or until it has thickened and the cornflour has cleared slightly.

11. Carefully turn the cooked sponge pudding onto a serving plate and pour a little of the sauce over it for decoration.

12. Serve any remaining sauce separately.

Cook's Notes

TIME: Preparation takes about 10 minutes, microwave cooking takes about 10 minutes with 5 minutes standing time.

VEGETARIAN SUITABILITY: This recipe is suitable for lacto-vegetarians only.

VARIATION: Use any other favourite tinned fruit in place of the apricots in this recipe.

JAMAICAN MOUSSE CAKE
SERVES 6-8

This delectable chocolate mousse cake is sure to tempt even the most strong willed of dieters, so be warned!

180g /6oz plain chocolate
45ml /3 tbsps dark rum
280ml /½ pint double cream
15ml /1 tbsp strong black coffee
15g /½oz soft brown sugar
2 large bananas, peeled and mashed until
    smooth
3 eggs, separated
Chocolate curls to decorate

1. Put the chocolate into a bowl and melt it on HIGH for 2-3 minutes.

2. Stir the rum and 140ml /¼ pint of the cream into the melted chocolate and beat thoroughly until it is smooth.

3. Put the coffee and the sugar into a small bowl and heat on HIGH for 30 seconds to 1 minute, stirring occasionally until the sugar has completely melted.

4. Put the mashed bananas into a large bowl and beat in the coffee and sugar mixture.

Step 2 Stir the rum and half of the cream into the melted chocolate, beating thoroughly to produce a smooth cream.

Step 7 Quickly, but carefully fold the egg whites into the chocolate mixture with a metal spoon, taking care not to over mix the mousse and lose the texture of the eggs.

5. Add the egg yolks to the banana mixture and beat well. Continue beating and add all the chocolate mixture.

6. Whisk the egg whites until they are stiff and form firm peaks.

7. Quickly, but carefully, fold the whisked egg whites into the chocolate and banana mixture.

8. Spoon the mixture into a lightly greased and base-lined springform cake tin. Chill for at least 2 hours, or until completely set and firm.

9. Carefully loosen the sides of the mousse cake with a warmed round bladed knife and unmould the sides of the tin.

10. Carefully slide the mousse off the base of the tin onto a serving plate.

11. Whip the remaining cream until it is thick and pipe a decorative border on the mousse cake.

12. Sprinkle over the chocolate curls and chill well before serving.

Cook's Notes

TIME: Preparation takes about 25 minutes plus chilling time, microwave cooking takes about 4 minutes.

VARIATION: Use carob bars instead of plain chocolate in this recipe if desired.

SERVING IDEA: Serve the cake partially frozen for a chilled summer dessert.

WHITE AND DARK CHOCOLATE BOMBE

SERVES 6-8

A delicious white and dark chocolate iced dessert which is made much more quickly by including the use of a microwave oven in its preparation.

280ml /½ pint dark chocolate ice cream
10ml /2 tsps coffee powder
15ml /1 tbsp hot water
570ml /1 pint vanilla ice cream
120g /4oz white chocolate
60g /2oz ratafia biscuits, coarsely crushed

---

1. Chill a 1150ml / 2-pint bombe mould or basin in the freezer for 2 hours.

2. Put the chocolate ice cream into the microwave oven on soften on HIGH for 1 minute. Ensure the ice cream is just softened and not melted.

3. Mix together the coffee powder and the water and beat this thoroughly into the chocolate ice cream.

4. Re-freeze the chocolate ice cream until it is fairly solid, but still spreadable.

5. Coat the base and the sides of the chilled mould or basin with the chocolate ice cream, leaving a hollow in the centre and re-freezing the ice if it is too soft to stay up the sides of the bowl.

6. Freeze the chocolate ice cream until it is solid.

7. Soften the vanilla ice cream on HIGH for 1 minute.

8. Melt the white chocolate on HIGH for 1

Step 5 Coat the base and the sides with the semi-frozen chocolate ice cream, leaving a hollow in the centre of the dessert.

Step 9 Stir the crushed ratafia biscuits into the white chocolate ice cream, mixing well to incorporate evenly.

Step 10 Fill the centre of the dark chocolate ice cream with the white ice cream, smoothing the top with a round-bladed knife.

minute, and stir this thoroughly into the softened ice cream.

9. Stir in the crushed biscuits, and mix well to distribute evenly.

10. Fill the centre of the lined bombe mould with the white chocolate ice cream, spreading the surface flat with a round bladed knife.

11. Re-freeze the ice cream bombe until it is completely solid.

12. Half an hour before serving, unmould the bombe by heating it for 30 seconds on HIGH.

13. Invert a serving plate over the top of the mould or basin and turn both of them over, shaking the ice cream gently to help it drop onto the plate.

14. Decorate the top with grated white chocolate if desired.

BAKED CARROT CUSTARD
SERVES 4

*The natural sweetness of carrots makes them an ideal ingredient
in desserts as well as their more usual savoury role.*

450g /1lb carrots, peeled
120ml /8 tbsps water
120g /4oz pitted dates
5ml /1 tsp ground cinnamon
2.5ml /½ tsp grated nutmeg
1.25ml /¼ tsp ground ginger
1.25ml /¼ tsp ground cloves
3 large eggs, beaten
430ml /12fl oz milk
60g /2oz chopped pistachio nuts

1. Grate the carrots using the coarse side of a cheese grater.

2. Put the grated carrot and 60ml /4 tbsps of the water into a bowl. Cover the bowl with cling film and pierce this several times with the tip of a sharp knife. Cook the carrots on HIGH for 5 minutes, or until they are soft.

Step 4 Blend the carrots and dates together in a food processor or liquidiser until they form a smooth purée.

Step 8 Cook the custard until the centre is just set and the outer edges are firm.

3. Finely chop the dates and put these into a bowl with the remaining water. Cover this bowl as before and cook the dates on HIGH for 2 minutes.

4. Put the carrots and dates, along with their cooking liquids, into the goblet of a liquidiser or food processor and blend them together until they make a smooth purée.

5. Stir the spices into the carrot mixture and transfer the mixture to a large bowl.

6. Beat together the eggs and milk, and beat this into the spiced carrot mixture.

7. Stir in the chopped pistachios.

8. Spoon the mixture into a shallow serving dish, and cook uncovered, on MEDIUM for 15 minutes, or until the centre is just set.

9. Allow the pudding to stand for 10 minutes before serving warm, or alternatively, chill it completely before serving.

Cook's Notes

TIME: Preparation takes about 10 minutes, microwave cooking takes about 22 minutes plus standing or chilling time.

VEGETARIAN SUITABILITY: This recipe is suitable for lacto-vegetarians only.

PREPARATION: If you do not have a liquidiser or food processor, the purée can be made by rubbing the carrots and dates, along with the cooking liquid, through a wire sieve. This will, however, increase the preparation time.

COOK'S TIP: If you are worried that the custard will curdle, stand the serving dish inside a larger dish into which you have poured 1 pint of warm water. Increase the cooking time by 5 minutes.

BROWN BREAD CRUMBLE
SERVES 4

*The unusual crumble topping on this dessert is simple
to make, highly nutritious and very tasty.*

225g /8oz cooking apples
225g /8oz fresh raspberries
Raw cane sugar, to taste
90g /3oz fresh, wholemeal breadcrumbs
90g /3oz rolled oats
60g /2oz muscovado sugar
60g /2oz vegetable margarine
5ml /1 tsp ground cinnamon
2.5ml /½ tsp ground cardamom

1. Wash and quarter the apples. Remove the cores then thinly slice them with a sharp knife.

2. Arrange the apples in the base of a serving dish and sprinkle over the raspberries and the raw cane sugar.

3. Put the breadcrumbs, oats, muscovado sugar and the spices into a large bowl. Mix them together well to spread the spices evenly.

Step 1 Thinly slice the prepared apples using a sharp knife.

Step 3 Mix the spices thoroughly into the breadcrumbs, oats and sugar mixture, to spread their flavours evenly.

Step 4 Rub the margarine into the breadcrumb mixture with the fingertips, until it is evenly distributed.

4. Add the margarine and rub this into the breadcrumb mixture until it is evenly distributed.

5. Spoon the topping mixture over the prepared fruit in the serving dish and smooth the top with the back of a spoon.

6. Cook the pudding on HIGH for 5 minutes, then allow to stand for a further 5 minutes before serving.

Cook's Notes

 TIME: Preparation takes about 15 minutes, microwave cooking takes about 5 minutes plus 5 minutes standing time.

VEGETARIAN SUITABILITY: This recipe is suitable for vegans.

FREEZING: The crumble can be frozen for up to 2 months, then re-heated on HIGH for 3 minutes after defrosting.

 SERVING IDEA: Serve hot or cold with fresh cream or fruit purée.

 VARIATION: Use the topping over any variety of mixed fruits.

TREASURE RICE

SERVES 4-6

*This is a traditional, colourful Chinese dessert which
can be served either hot or cold.*

225g /8oz pudding rice
5ml /1 tsp salt
870ml /1½ pints water
225g /8oz caster sugar
150g /5oz sweetened red bean paste
15ml /1 tbsp candied lotus seeds (optional)
30g /1oz whole blanched almonds
4 red glacé cherries
4 green glacé cherries
2 rings glacé pineapple
2-3 stoned dates
4 glacé apricots

1. Put the rice, salt and water into a large bowl
and cook on HIGH for 10 minutes, stirring the
mixture several times during this cooking time.

2. Stir the sugar into the rice and cook for a

Step 5 Cover the
red bean sauce
layer with the
remaining rice,
smoothing the
surface with the
back of a spoon.

Step 6 Cut the fruit
into convenient
pieces ready to
decorate the rice.

further 20 minutes on LOW, once again stirring
the rice frequently to dissolve the sugar
completely.

3. Spread half of the cooked rice over the base
of a microwave-proof serving dish.

4. Carefully, so as not to dislodge the rice too
much, spread the red bean paste over the rice in
the serving dish.

5. Spread the remaining half of the cooked rice
over the red bean paste.

6. Cut the fruit into convenient pieces and
arrange the pieces decoratively over the rice in
the serving dish.

7. Cover the dish with cling film and pierce this
several times with the tip of a sharp knife.

8. Cook on MEDIUM for 4-5 minutes, then serve
either hot or cold.

Cook's Notes

PREPARATION: Chinese
desserts are very sweet. The
sugar in this recipe can be halved
if preferred.

SERVING IDEA: Glaze the
dessert with a sugar syrup if
liked.

TIME: Preparation takes about
25 minutes, microwave
cooking takes about 40 minutes.

VEGETARIAN SUITABILITY:
This recipe is suitable for
vegans.

VARIATION: Use any
favourite glacé fruits of your
choice in place of those suggested
in the recipe.

BAKED MANGO AND RICE

SERVES 4

An exotic variation of traditional rice pudding, this recipe demonstrates a delicious way of using mangoes.

2 large ripe mangoes
Juice of 1 lime
120g /4oz pudding rice
570ml /1 pint boiling water
Pinch ground cinnamon
Pinch ground nutmeg
30g /1oz caster sugar
180g /6oz can evaporated milk

1. Cut both the mangoes in half lengthways, through the narrower sides of the fruit, to make it easier to remove the stone.

2. Reserve one mango half for decoration and carefully scoop the flesh from inside the skin of the other 3 halves.

3. Put the mango flesh into a liquidiser or food processor and purée it along with the lime juice.

4. Put the rice, water and spices into a large

Step 3 You may fin‹ it easier to chop the mango flesh before putting it in the liquidiser.

bowl and cook on HIGH for 10 minutes, stirring once or twice during this cooking time.

5. Add the sugar and the evaporated milk to the rice mixture and continue cooking on LOW for a further 15 minutes.

6. Allow the cooked rice to stand for 5-10 minutes.

7. Put a layer of rice into a glass serving dish and cover this with a layer of mango.

8. Repeat this layering process until all the rice and mango purée are used up.

9. Heat the pudding gently for a further 5 minutes on LOW.

10. Thinly slice the reserved mango half with a sharp knife.

11. Decorate the dessert with the mango slices and serve at once.

Step 1 Cut both mangoes in half lengthways, through the narrower sides of the fruit, to make it easier to remove the large stone.

Cook's Notes

 PREPARATION: If you do not have a liquidiser or food processor, the fruit purée can be made by rubbing the mango flesh through a metal sieve.

SERVING IDEA: Serve with crisp biscuits.

VEGETARIAN SUITABILITY: This recipe is suitable for lacto-vegetarians only, but could be used for vegans if the evaporated milk was replaced with the same quantity of extra fruit purée.

TIME: Preparation takes about 20 minutes, microwave cooking takes about 30 minutes, plus standing time.

SWEET FRUIT PILAU

SERVES 6

*Fragrantly spiced and served with fresh fruit, this unusual
dessert is a delicious way of serving rice.*

60g /2oz vegetable margarine
225g /8oz pudding rice
30g /1oz cashew nuts
30g /1oz flaked almonds
570ml /1 pint hot milk
120g /4oz caster sugar
9 cardamom pods, lightly crushed
4 cloves
2.5ml /½ tsp grated nutmeg
Finely grated rind, of 1 orange
Few drops orange flower water
60g /2oz black sesame seeds
1 small mango, sliced
60g /2oz white grapes, halved, seeds removed
    and peeled
1 orange, peeled and segmented
1 kiwi fruit, peeled and sliced

1. Put the margarine, rice and nuts into a large,
deep bowl and cook, uncovered, on HIGH for 3
minutes.

2. Stir the rice mixture once or twice during the
cooking time to ensure that the nuts become
evenly browned.

Step 7 Stir the
sesame seeds into
the prepared rice,
mixing well to
incorporate
thoroughly.

3. Pour the milk onto the rice mixture and stir in
the sugar until it has dissolved.

4. Add the cardamoms, cloves, nutmeg, orange
rind and flower water.

5. Cover the bowl with cling film and pierce
this several times with the tip of a sharp knife.

6. Cook the rice for 12 minutes on HIGH,
stirring it occasionally to prevent it from sticking.

7. Allow the rice to stand for 5 minutes, then stir
in the sesame seeds.

8. Spoon the rice into a serving dish and
decorate with the prepared fruit before serving
hot or cold.

Cook's Notes

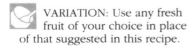 VARIATION: Use any fresh
fruit of your choice in place
of that suggested in this recipe.

SERVING IDEA: Serve with
sponge biscuits.

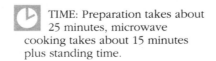 TIME: Preparation takes about
25 minutes, microwave
cooking takes about 15 minutes
plus standing time.

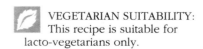 VEGETARIAN SUITABILITY:
This recipe is suitable for
lacto-vegetarians only.

POACHED PEARS WITH RASPBERRY COULIS

SERVES 4

This simple to prepare dessert is lightly perfumed with the fragrance of fresh hyssop.

140ml /¼ pint water
30ml /2 tbsps clear honey
10ml /2 tsps lemon juice
2 sprigs fresh hyssop
4 pears
225g /8oz fresh raspberries
5ml /1 tsp fresh chopped hyssop
Few extra hyssop leaves for decoration

1. Put the water and honey into a large bowl and cook, uncovered, on HIGH for 1-2 minutes or until the honey has dissolved.

2. Stir in the lemon juice and hyssop sprigs and cook for a further 1 minute on HIGH.

3. Peel the pears and carefully cut them in half lengthways with a sharp knife.

4. Keeping the stalks intact, carefully remove the cores with a grapefruit knife.

Step 4 Keeping the stalks intact, carefully remove the cores from the pears using a grapefruit knife.

Step 7 Blend the raspberries with the chopped hyssop for a few minutes, or until the fruit has been broken down.

5. Put the pears into the honey syrup. Cover the bowl with cling film and pierce this several times with the tip of a sharp knife.

6. Cook the pears on HIGH for 7-10 minutes, or until they are tender.

7. Put the raspberries into a liquidiser or food processor along with the chopped hyssop. Blend for a few seconds until the fruits have been well broken down.

8. Push the puréed fruit through a metal sieve into a small bowl, to remove all the pips.

9. Sweeten the raspberry purée with a little of the honey syrup if desired.

10. Arrange the pears on four serving dishes and pour over a little of the coulis. Decorate with the extra hyssop leaves.

11. Serve the remaining sauce separately.

Cook's Notes

 VEGETARIAN SUITABILITY: This recipe is suitable for vegans.

 SERVING IDEA: Serve with crisp biscuits.

PREPARATION: The fruit can be puréed by rubbing it through a sieve from its whole state, but the initial blending does speed up this process.

TIME: Preparation takes about 20 minutes, microwave cooking takes about 10 minutes.

APPLEMINT PUDDING
SERVES 4-6

*This fragrant variation of a traditional apple hat pudding makes excellent
use of the herb applemint, which is so often neglected in the garden.*

225g /8oz cooking apples
Small knob of butter
30g /1oz sugar
15ml /1 tbsp chopped applemint
120g /4oz soft vegetable margarine
120g /4oz soft brown sugar
2 eggs
120g /4oz self-raising flour
5ml /1 tsp baking powder
10ml / 2 tsps golden syrup
30ml / 2 tbsps milk

1. Peel the apples, quarter and core them.
Thinly slice the apple quarters with a very sharp
knife.

2. Put the apples, butter and sugar into a lightly
greased 1150ml /2-pint pudding basin. Cover the
bowl with cling film and pierce this several times
with the tip of a sharp knife.

Step 4 Cream
together the
margarine and the
brown sugar until
the colour has
begun to pale and
the texture is light
and fluffy.

Step 6 Gently fold
the remaining
applemint into the
cake mixture with a
metal spoon.

3. Cook the apples on HIGH for 5 minutes. Stir
in 5ml /1 tsp of the applemint, then continue
mixing the apples until they form a thick purée.

4. Put the margarine and the brown sugar into a
mixing bowl and cream them together until they
are soft and fluffy in texture.

5. Beat in the eggs, flour and baking powder,
along with the golden syrup and the milk to
form a dropping consistency cake batter.

6. Gently fold in the remaining applemint.

7. Spoon the cake mixture over the apple purée
in the pudding bowl.

8. Cook the pudding, uncovered, on HIGH for
6-7 minutes, or until the cake is well risen and
just dry on top.

9. Invert a serving plate over the top of the
basin and carefully turn both over, gently
shaking the pudding to ease it out onto the plate.

10. Spoon any apple that may remain in the
basin onto the top of the pudding and serve hot.

Cook's Notes

 TIME: Preparation takes about
10 minutes, microwave
cooking takes about 12 minutes.

VEGETARIAN SUITABILITY:
This recipe is suitable for
lacto-vegetarians only.

COOK'S TIP: When using
mint of any variety, never boil
or cook it too quickly, otherwise it
will lose its flavour.

SERVING IDEA: Serve with
fresh cream or ice cream.

PREPARATION: If the
pudding sticks in the basin,
loosen it by running a round-
bladed knife around its edge,
before turning it onto the serving
plate.

Vegetarian Microwave Cooking

Chapter ~ 8

· Cakes · Biscuits · and · Sweets ·

FRUIT AND ALMOND CAKE

MAKES 1 CAKE

This delicious cake is sure to please every generation of the family.

180g /6oz vegetable margarine
60g /2oz caster sugar
180g /6oz light, soft muscovado sugar
3 eggs, beaten
180g /6oz self-raising flour
2-3 drops almond essence
30g /1oz ground almonds
30ml /2 tbsps milk
60g /2oz seedless raisins
60g /2oz glacé cherries, chopped

1. Lightly grease a 22.5cm /9-inch circular ring mould with vegetable margarine.

2. Sprinkle 2-3 tsps caster sugar into the mould and shake gently with a rotating action to coat the surface evenly.

3. Put the margarine into a large bowl and soften it on MEDIUM for 30 seconds if necessary.

4. Add the muscovado sugar and beat with a wooden spoon until the mixture is fluffy and light in texture.

5. Add the eggs gradually, adding 1 tbsp of flour with each addition and beating well to prevent the mixture from curdling.

6. Beat in the almond essence, ground almonds and the milk, mixing well to blend thoroughly.

Step 7 Fold the remaining flour and fruit into the cake mixture with a metal spoon.

7. Fold in the remaining flour, then quickly stir in the fruit.

8. Carefully spoon the mixture into the prepared dish and spread the top smooth with a metal knife.

9. Cook the cake on MEDIUM for 12-14 minutes, then increase the power setting to HIGH and cook for a further 1-2 minutes, or until the cake is set, but still moist on top.

10. Allow the cake to stand for 15 minutes before turning it out onto a wire rack to cool completely.

11. Dust with a little extra caster sugar before serving.

Cook's Notes

COOK'S TIP: If you do not have a turntable in your microwave oven, give the cake a quarter turn after each 4 minutes of cooking time.

SERVING IDEA: For a special treat, drizzle a little almond flavoured icing over the cake before serving.

PREPARATION: If the cake has not cooked properly after the specified cooking time, continue cooking on MEDIUM for further 1 minute intervals, checking the cake after each time. The cake should be firm, but the top not quite set, as the cake will continue cooking during the standing period.

TIME: Preparation takes about 20 minutes, microwave cooking takes about 13-16 minutes, plus 15 minutes standing time.

VEGETARIAN SUITABILITY: This recipe is suitable for lacto-vegetarians only.

RICH FRUIT CAKE

MAKES 1 X 22.5cm /9-inch CAKE

As with conventionally baked fruit cakes, this recipe improves both in flavour and texture if stored in an airtight container for one month before eating.

120g /4oz vegetable margarine
120g /4oz dark, soft muscovado sugar
30ml /2 tbsps black treacle
3 eggs, beaten
45ml /3 tbsps milk
225g /8oz self-raising flour
5ml /1 tsp mixed spice
450g /1lb mixed dried fruit
60g /2oz glacé cherries, washed and chopped
30g /1oz flaked almonds
45ml /3 tbsps sherry or brandy

1. Lightly grease a 22.5cm /9-inch round cake dish and line the base with a circle of silicone paper.

2. Put the margarine, sugar and treacle into a large bowl and beat together well until the mixture is fluffy and light in texture.

Step 1 Base-line a lightly greased cake dish with a circle of silicone paper.

Step 4 Fold in the remaining flour with a metal spoon, mixing well to ensure that it is evenly blended in.

3. Beat the eggs into the milk and gradually add these to the sugar mixture, adding a tablespoon of the flour with each addition to prevent the mixture from curdling.

4. Fold in the remaining flour with a metal spoon, mixing well to ensure that it is evenly blended in.

5. Stir in the spice, fruit and nuts, then spoon the mixture into the prepared dish.

6. Cook the cake on DEFROST for 40 minutes, or until the cake has set but the top is still moist. Allow to stand for 20 minutes before turning out of the dish.

7. When the cake is cold, sprinkle over the sherry or brandy and allow this to soak into the cake before sealing in an airtight container and storing until required.

Cook's Notes

COOK'S TIP: If your microwave oven does not have a turntable, give the cake a quarter turn after each eight minutes of cooking time.

TIME: Preparation takes about 30 minutes, microwave cooking takes about 40 minutes, plus 20 minutes standing time.

SERVING IDEA: Cover with almond paste and royal icing for a special celebration.

CHOCOLATE PEAR SPONGE

MAKES 1 X 18cm /7-inch CAKE

Chocolate and pears make a delicious combination and this cake sets both flavours off to their best advantage.

120g /4oz vegetable margarine
120g /4oz caster sugar
15ml /1 tbsp milk
90g /3oz self-raising flour
15g /½oz cocoa powder
2.5ml /½ tsp baking powder
5ml /1 tsp mixed spice
120g /4oz ripe pear, peeled, cored and diced

1. Soften the margarine in the microwave oven on DEFROST for 15 seconds.

2. Add the sugar and milk and beat until the mixture is light and fluffy.

3. Stir in the flour, cocoa, baking powder and mixed spice, mixing well to blend the cocoa in evenly.

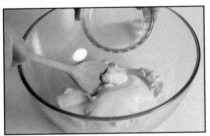

Step 2 Add the sugar and milk to the softened margarine and beat well until the mixture is fluffy and light textured.

Step 3 Stir the flour, cocoa, baking powder and spice into the creamed mixture, mixing well to blend the cocoa in evenly.

4. Fold in the pear.

5. Lightly grease and base-line a deep sided cake dish with silicone paper.

6. Carefully spoon the cake mixture into the cake dish, spreading it evenly with the back of a metal spoon.

7. Cook the cake on MEDIUM for 4 minutes, then increase the power setting to HIGH and continue cooking for a further 2 minutes, or until the cake is firm but the top is still moist.

8. Allow the cake to cool in the dish for 10 minutes before turning out onto a wire rack.

9. Dust the cake with a little extra caster sugar before serving.

Cook's Notes

COOK'S TIP: If your microwave oven does not have a turntable, give the cake a quarter turn after each one minute of cooking time to make sure it cooks evenly.

SERVING IDEA: Serve hot with chocolate sauce or pear purée for a delicious dessert.

PREPARATION: If the cake has not cooked completely after the specified cooking time, continue cooking on HIGH for 30 second intervals, checking the cake after each time. Remember that the cake will continue cooking whilst it is standing in the dish, so do not over-cook it.

TIME: Preparation takes about 15 minutes, microwave cooking takes about 6 minutes.

VEGETARIAN SUITABILITY: This recipe is suitable for vegans.

LEMON ICED TREACLE COOKIES

MAKES 48

Children in particular will love these colourful little biscuits.

120g /4oz dark, soft brown sugar
120g /4oz butter or vegetable margarine
1 egg
30ml /2 tbsps treacle
10ml /2 tsps baking powder
5ml /1 tsp ground allspice
2.5ml /½ tsp ground ginger
225g /8oz wholemeal flour
Pinch salt
450g /1lb icing sugar
140ml /¼ pint hot water
Juice and finely shredded rind of 1 lemon
Yellow food colouring, optional

1. Put the sugar and the butter into a large bowl and cream them together with a wooden spoon until they become fluffy and light textured.

2. Beat the egg, and add this gradually to the sugar mixture, mixing well between additions to prevent it from curdling.

3. Beat in the treacle, continuing to stir

Step 1 Cream the sugar and butter together in a large bowl until they become fluffy and light in texture.

Step 7 Remove the biscuits, still on the paper, to a flat surface to cool completely.

thoroughly with the wooden spoon until it is well incorporated.

4. Using a metal spoon, fold in the baking powder, spices, flour and salt.

5. Line a microwave-proof baking sheet with silicone paper, and drop teaspoonfulls of the treacle mixture onto it in a circle of eight spoonfuls at a time.

6. Cook the biscuits, eight at a time, for 2-3 minutes on MEDIUM, or until the tops look set.

7. Remove the biscuits, still on the paper, to a flat surface to cool completely.

8. Re-line the baking dish and continue cooking the biscuits, eight at a time, in the same way, until all the mixture is used up.

9. When all the biscuits are cooled, mix together the remaining ingredients in a bowl or jug.

10. Coat each cookie with an equal amount of the lemon icing and leave to set completely before serving.

Cook's Notes

VARIATION: Use 2 tbsps of orange juice and the finely shredded rind of half an orange in place of the lemon in this recipe.

TIME: Preparation takes about 20 minutes, microwave cooking takes about 12-18 minutes.

VEGETARIAN SUITABILITY: This recipe is suitable for lacto-vegetarians only.

303

LEMON GLAZED GINGERBREAD

SERVES 6-8

Spicy, traditional gingerbread soaked in a lovely lemony glaze, this cake is both quick and easy to make in the microwave oven.

90g /3oz vegetable margarine
90g /3oz light, soft brown sugar
180g /6oz self-raising flour
Pinch salt
5ml /1 tsp baking soda
1.25ml /¼ tsp ground cloves
2.5ml /½ tsp ground cinnamon
5ml /1 tsp ground ginger
90ml /3fl oz treacle
60ml /2fl oz hot water
1 lemon
90g /3oz caster sugar
30g /1oz vegetable margarine
200ml /6fl oz water

1. Put the margarine into a large bowl and beat until it is softened.

2. Stir in the brown sugar and continue beating until the mixture is fluffy and light in texture.

3. Add the flour, salt, soda and spices, and blend until the mixture looks like coarse breadcrumbs.

4. Mix together the treacle and the hot water in a jug or bowl, and beat this into the flour and spice mixture. Continue beating until the mixture resembles a thick, smooth batter.

5. Spread the cake mixture into a lightly greased and base-lined 20cm /8-inch round baking dish. Cook on MEDIUM for 6 minutes, then increase to HIGH and cook for a further 1-4 minutes, or until set.

Step 4 Beat the treacle and water mixture into the flour with a wooden spoon until it forms a thick, smooth batter.

6. Cool the cake for 10 minutes in the dish before turning onto a wire rack to cool completely.

7. Thinly pare the rind from the lemon with a potato peeler and cut this into very fine shreds with a sharp knife.

8. Squeeze the juice from the lemon and put this, along with the sugar, margarine and water, into a jug or bowl.

9. Cook on HIGH for 2 minutes, then stir in the pared lemon rind.

10. Continue cooking for a further 1-2 minutes, stirring frequently until the sauce begins to thicken and the lemon rind is well blanched.

11. Whilst the lemon glaze is still hot, put the cake onto a serving plate and prick it all over with a trussing needle or skewer.

12. Spoon the sauce evenly over the cake and allow it to soak in and cool before serving.

Cook's Notes

 PREPARATION: If you have an electric beater, this can be used to prepare the cake mixture.

 SERVING IDEA: Serve with sour cream for a delicious dessert.

VEGETARIAN SUITABILITY: This recipe is suitable for vegans.

VARIATION: Use an orange in place of the lemon in this recipe.

TIME: Preparation takes about 20 minutes, microwave cooking takes about 13 minutes, plus 10 minutes standing time.

COCONUT TEACAKE

MAKES 1 x 22.5cm /9-inch CAKE

A delicious light sponge topped with a buttery nut crunch, this unusual cake is sure to become a favourite teatime treat.

225g /8oz butter or vegetable margarine
90g /3oz soft, dark brown sugar
90g /3oz flaked coconut
60g /2oz walnuts, chopped
180g /6oz caster sugar
3 eggs, beaten
180g /6oz plain flour
10ml /2 tsps baking powder
2-3 tbsps milk

1. Grease and base-line with silicone paper, a 22.5cm /9-inch round microwave-proof baking dish.

2. Put 60g /2oz of the butter or margarine into a dish and cook on HIGH for 1 minute to melt.

3. Stir in the brown sugar, coconut and walnuts, and spread this mixture evenly over the base of the dish. Set aside.

4. Put the remaining butter or margarine into a bowl and beat until it has softened.

5. Stir in the caster sugar and continue beating until the mixture is light in colour and fluffy.

Step 5 Cream the sugar into the softened butter until it is light in colour and fluffy.

Step 8 Use a spatula or palette knife to spread the cake mixture over the nut mixture in the dish.

6. Beat in the eggs, a little at a time, mixing well between additions to ensure that the mixture does not curdle.

7. Quickly fold in the flour and baking powder, followed by just enough of the milk to produce a soft dropping consistency mixture.

8. Carefully spread the cake mixture over the coconut mixture in the baking dish, spreading it evenly with a spatula or palette knife.

9. Cook the cake on MEDIUM for 6 minutes, turning the dish one half turn halfway through the cooking time if your microwave oven does not have a turntable.

10. Increase the power setting to HIGH and continue cooking the cake for a further 2-4 minutes, or until the cake is firm to touch.

11. Allow the cake to stand in the dish for 5 minutes before turning it out onto a wire rack to cool completely.

12. Scrape any topping that may be left in the dish back onto the cake and spread it evenly before serving.

Cook's Notes

 SERVING IDEA: Serve this cake warm, with cream, for an unusual dessert.

 VEGETARIAN SUITABILITY: This recipe is suitable for lacto-vegetarians only.

 VARIATION: Use pecans or almonds instead of walnuts in this recipe.

SPICY TREACLE COOKIES

MAKES 24 COOKIES

*Treacle cookies are always a treat, with added
spices they are even more delectable.*

120g /4oz butter or vegetable margarine
120g /4oz soft, dark brown sugar
1 egg, beaten
30ml /2 tbsps black treacle
10ml /2 tsps baking powder
225g /8oz wholemeal flour
Pinch salt
5ml /1 tsp mixed spice
5ml /1 tsp ground ginger

1. Put the butter into a large bowl and soften on DEFROST for 1 minute.

2. Beat the sugar into the softened butter until it is fluffy and light in texture.

3. Add the egg and treacle to the creamed

Step 5 Arrange eight balls at a time well apart on a silicone paper lined baking sheet.

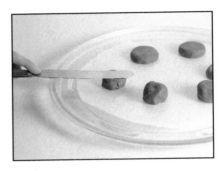

Step 6 Flatten each cookie with the tines of a damp fork or palette knife before baking.

mixture, mixing it well to prevent it from curdling.

4. Quickly stir in the baking powder, flour, salt and spices, mixing until all the ingredients are well blended.

5. Using lightly floured hands, roll the mixture into 2.5cm /1-inch balls and put eight of these at a time on a silicone paper lined baking sheet.

6. Press each ball down lightly to flatten slightly and cook for 2-3 minutes per batch on MEDIUM, or until they have spread slightly and the tops look set.

7. Cool the biscuits on the paper for 10 minutes, before removing them to cool completely on a wire rack.

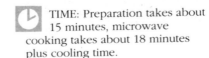

Cook's Notes

VARIATION: Use golden syrup in place of the treacle and cinnamon in place of the mixed spice and ginger in this recipe.

TIME: Preparation takes about 15 minutes, microwave cooking takes about 18 minutes plus cooling time.

SERVING IDEA: Serve the biscuits dusted with a little icing sugar mixed with ground ginger.

MUESLI COOKIES

MAKES 36

These simple-to-make biscuits are full of wholesome ingredients.

120g /4oz vegetable margarine
120g /4oz muscovado sugar
1 egg
5ml /1 tsp vanilla essence
225g /8oz wholemeal flour
2.5ml /½ tsp baking soda
2.5ml /½ tsp baking powder
120g /4oz sugarless muesli
60g /2oz dried currants
Pinch salt

1. Put the margarine and sugar into a bowl, and cream together with a wooden spoon until the mixture is fluffy and light in texture.

2. Mix in the egg and vanilla essence, beating well to prevent the mixture from curdling.

Step 3 Mix the dry ingredients and fruit into the egg mixture to form a stiff dough.

Step 4 Drop teaspoonfuls of the biscuit mix around the edge of a lined plate or circular baking dish.

3. Add the flour, soda and baking powder along with the muesli, currants and salt, mixing well to make a stiff dough.

4. Line a plate or circular baking dish with silicone paper and drop rounded teaspoonfuls of the mix around the edge.

5. Leave a good gap between each spoonful of mix and cook only one single layer of cookies each time.

6. Cook each batch for 2 minutes on HIGH and allow to stand for 1 minute before transferring to a wire rack to cool completely.

7. Continue cooking the remaining mixture in this way.

Cook's Notes

VEGETARIAN SUITABILITY: This recipe is suitable for lacto-vegetarians only.

PREPARATION: If the biscuit mixture is not stiff enough after the flour has been added, stir in a little extra flour to make it firm enough to heap into piles.

TIME: Preparation takes about 15 minutes, microwave cooking takes about 8-10 minutes in total, with 4-5 minutes standing time.

SERVING IDEA: Dip the cookies into melted chocolate or carob.

COOK'S TIP: This recipe can be frozen, uncooked. Make a double batch, then cook as many biscuits as you need and freeze the remaining mixture in batches until required.

APPLE SPICE RING

MAKES 1 x 20cm /8-inch RING CAKE

For those who are trying to cut down their sugar intake, this cake can be made without the sugar and is equally delicious.

450g /1lb dessert apples
90g /3oz ground hazelnuts
120g /4oz wholemeal flour
30g /1oz bran
60g /2oz muscovado sugar (optional)
7.5ml /1½ tsp baking powder
5ml /1 tsp ground cinnamon
Pinch ground nutmeg
Pinch ground cardamom
30g /1oz vegetable margarine
120ml /8 tbsps milk

1. Grate the apples on the coarse side of a cheese grater.

2. Put the grated apple into a bowl along with the hazelnuts and mix well.

3. Add the flour, bran, sugar if used, baking

Step 5 Mix the apple mixture into a fairly stiff batter with the milk.

Step 7 Smooth the top of the cake even with the back of a metal spoon.

powder and spices to the apple mixture and stir well to blend the ingredients thoroughly.

4. Rub the margarine into the apple and flour mixture until it is evenly blended and there are no large lumps remaining.

5. Stir in the milk and mix to a fairly stiff batter.

6. Carefully spoon the batter into a lightly greased 15cm /6-inch ring mould.

7. Smooth the top even with a metal spoon and allow the cake to stand in the tin for about 5 minutes before baking.

8. Cook the cake on HIGH for 3 minutes, then reduce the power setting to MEDIUM and continue cooking for a further 4 minutes. After this time, the cake should be set, but still moist.

9. Allow the cake to cool in the dish for about 5 minutes before turning onto a wire rack to cool completely.

Cook's Notes

 VEGETARIAN SUITABILITY: This recipe is suitable for vegans.

 FREEZING: This cake can be frozen for up to two months, and will become more moist during this process.

 VARIATION: Use almonds instead of the hazelnuts in this recipe.

 SERVING IDEA: Serve hot as a dessert with a custard sauce if desired, or a hot apple purée.

 TIME: Preparation takes about 20 minutes, microwave cooking takes about 7 minutes, plus 15 minutes standing time.

SUNFLOWER CAROB COOKIES

MAKES 4 DOZEN

Cookies come alive with the addition of sunflower seeds.

225g /8oz vegetable margarine
225g /8oz muscovado sugar
2 eggs, beaten
10ml / 2 tsps vanilla essence
5ml /1 tsp baking soda
5ml /1 tsp salt
60g /2oz bran
180g /6oz rolled oats
225g /8oz wholemeal flour
120g /4oz sunflower seeds
225g /8oz carob drops

Step 6 Leave plenty of space between each biscuit placed around the edge of the plate.

1. Cream the margarine and the sugar together in a large bowl, until fluffy and light in texture.

2. Beat in the eggs and the essence, mixing briskly to prevent the sugar from curdling.

3. Quickly stir in the soda, salt, bran, oats and the flour, mixing well until a firm dough is produced.

4. Finally stir in the sunflower seeds and the carob drops.

5. Line a large, circular plate or dish with silicone paper and arrange heaped teaspoonfuls of the biscuit mixture in a single layer around the edge of the plate.

6. Leave a good space between each biscuit to allow the mixture to spread.

7. Bake the biscuits on HIGH for 2 minutes, then allow to stand for 1 minute before transferring to a wire rack to cool completely.

Cook's Notes

COOK'S TIP: Form the dough into 5cm /2-inch diameter log, and freeze this uncooked. Whenever a few cookies are required, simply cut off the desired number into 6mm /¼-inch thick slices and bake as described above for 2 minutes, 15 seconds.

TIME: Preparation takes about 20 minutes, microwave cooking takes about 16-20 minutes, plus 8-10 minutes standing time.

VEGETARIAN SUITABILITY: This recipe is suitable for lacto-vegetarians only.

VARIATION: Use plain chocolate drops instead of carob drops in this recipe.

SERVING IDEA: Serve dusted with a little sieved icing sugar.

COLLETTES

MAKES 12

*These attractive home-made sweets are ideal for serving at
the end of a dinner party or formal meal.*

180g /6oz plain chocolate
60g /2oz milk chocolate
15g /½oz butter or vegetable margarine
10ml /2 tsps brandy of coffee essence
60ml /4 tbsps double cream

1. Arrange 12 paper sweet cases on a tray or plate.

2. Break the plain chocolate into pieces and put these into a microwave-proof jug or bowl. Cook on DEFROST for 4-5 minutes, stirring the chocolate occasionally until it has melted.

3. Using a small paintbrush or teaspoon, coat the inside base and sides of each paper sweet case with an even layer of the plain chocolate.

4. Thicken this layer gradually as the chocolate sets inside the case, by brushing extra thin layers over the top of the previous one.

5. Continue making the chocolate cases until all the melted plain chocolate has gone. Chill the lined sweet cases in a refrigerator until the chocolate has completely set.

6. Put the milk chocolate and the butter into a bowl and cook on DEFROST for 2-2½ minutes, or until they have both melted.

7. Gently mix the butter and chocolate together

Step 9 Whip the cream until it is just softly stiff.

Step 13 Using a rosette nozzle, pipe swirls of the chocolate and cream mixture into each chocolate shell.

for a few minutes, taking great care not to overbeat the chocolate.

8. Stir in the brandy or coffee essence.

9. Whip the cream until it is just softly stiff.

10. Carefully fold the half-whipped cream into the milk chocolate mixture using a metal spoon. Mix well to blend evenly.

11. Chill the milk chocolate mixture in a refrigerator until it is just firm enough to pipe.

12. Carefully peel away the paper cases from the plain chocolate shell and put these into fresh paper cases ready to serve.

13. Using a rosette nozzle, pipe swirls of the milk chocolate mixture into each plain chocolate shell. Refrigerate the collettes until you are ready to serve them.

Step 3 Using a small paintbrush or teaspoon, coat the base and sides of each paper sweet case with an even layer of the melted chocolate.

MICROWAVE MERINGUES

MAKES 10 SANDWICHED MERINGUES

How simple the microwave oven makes the preparation of meringues, and how delicious the end result!

1 egg white
180ml /6oz icing sugar, sieved
Pink food colouring, optional
180g /6oz chocolate flavour buttercream
Chocolate vermicelli

1. Put the egg white into a large mixing bowl and whisk until it becomes frothy, but not too stiff.

2. Gradually work in the icing sugar, mixing it well to form a really stiff fondant.

3. Colour the fondant with a few drops of food colouring if desired, kneading it well to blend the colour evenly.

4. Divide the fondant into 20 pieces and roll each piece into a small ball about the size of a marble.

5. Line a baking sheet or dinner plate with silicon paper and arrange four of the fondant

Step 2 Mix the icing sugar into the egg whites to form a stiff fondant.

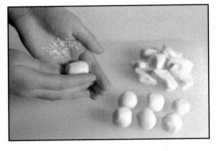

Step 4 Roll the pieces of fondant into 20 even-sized balls using lightly dusted hands.

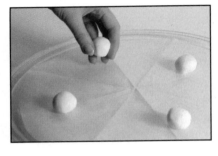

Step 5 Arrange four of the fondant balls well apart on a baking sheet or dinner plate.

balls onto this, keeping them well apart to allow the mixture to rise.

6. Cook on HIGH for 1½ minutes. Allow to stand on the plate for 2 minutes before removing to a cooling rack.

7. Continue cooking the remaining balls in the same way until all the fondant has been used up.

8. When the meringues are cold, sandwich them together with the buttercream and sprinkle a little vermicelli over them to decorate.

Cook's Notes

SERVING IDEA: Omit the buttercream and serve with fresh cream and fruit for a luxury summer tea.

TIME: Preparation takes about 20 minutes, microwave cooking takes about 8 minutes, plus 10 minutes standing time.

VARIATION: Add a few drops of strong coffee essence to the fondant before dividing into balls.

CRANBERRY BARS

MAKES 12-16 BARS

Cranberries have a delicious flavour but never seem to be used to their full potential. This recipe certainly rectifies this situation, and these delicious bars are sure to become a firm family favourite.

120g /4oz butter or vegetable margarine
150g /5oz soft brown sugar
120g /4oz plain flour
Pinch salt
90g /3oz rolled oats
1209g /4oz cranberry sauce
60g /2oz walnuts, chopped

1. Put the butter and sugar into a bowl and cream them together until they are fluffy and light in texture.

2. Stir in the flour, salt and oats, mixing all the ingredients together until the mixture resembles coarse breadcrumbs.

3. Press ⅔ of the oat mixture into the base of a well-greased 20cm /8-inch square baking dish.

4. Stand the baking dish in the microwave oven on a rack or inverted saucer to prevent the base from cooking too quickly.

5. Cook on MEDIUM for 5 minutes, or until the oat base is just firm.

6. Put the cranberry sauce and the nuts into a small bowl and mix them together well.

Step 2 Mix the dry ingredients carefully into the butter mixture, stirring until they resemble coarse breadcrumbs.

Step 7 Spread the cranberry and nut mixture evenly over the oat base with a round-bladed knife.

Step 8 Crumble the remaining oat mixture over the top of the cranberries to make an even topping.

7. Spread this cranberry mixture over the cooked oat base.

8. Crumble the remaining oat mixture evenly over the cranberry sauce, gently spreading it with a round-bladed knife to produce an even finish.

9. Continue cooking the cranberry bars on HIGH for a further 5 minutes.

10. Allow the mixture to cool for about 10 minutes, then cut into bars and leave in the dish to cool completely.

11. Do not remove from the dish until the biscuits are completely cold.

CHOCOLATE TRUFFLES

MAKES 30

*These delectable truffles are ideal for serving after dinner,
or for giving as an unusual home-made present.*

180g /6oz chocolate chips
15g /½oz butter or vegetable margarine
2 egg yolks
10ml /2 tsps single cream
10ml /2 tsps brandy or instant coffee for
    coating
45ml /3 tbsps each cocoa and ground blanched
    almonds

1. Put the chocolate chips into a bowl along with the butter. Melt on MEDIUM for 3-4 minutes, stirring two or three times during this period to create a smooth cream.

2. Lightly beat the egg yolks and add these to the melted chocolate mixture, stirring them in well to incorporate them completely.

3. Blend in the cream and brandy, once again mixing well to incorporate smoothly.

Step 2 Stir the lightly beaten egg yolks into the chocolate mixture, mixing well to blend thoroughly.

Step 5 Roll each piece of truffle mixture into a small ball with your hands.

Step 6 Gently roll the truffle-coated balls in either the cocoa or the ground almonds to coat them before serving.

4. Chill the chocolate mixture in a refrigerator for at least 1 hour, or until it is firm.

5. Divide the mixture into 30 even-sized pieces and roll these into small balls using your hands.

6. Put the cocoa and the ground almonds onto separate plates and gently roll half the chocolate balls in one coating and half in the other.

7. Put the coated truffles into individual paper sweet cases and refrigerate until ready to serve.

Cook's Notes

TIME: Preparation takes about 20 minutes, microwave cooking takes about 4-5 minutes.

VEGETARIAN SUITABILITY: This recipe is suitable for lacto-vegetarians only.

VARIATION: Use white chocolate in place of the chocolate chips and a fruit liqueur in place of the coffee or brandy.

SERVING IDEA: Serve with coffee or liqueurs.

PREPARATION: If the chocolate balls become too soft whilst you are rolling them into shape, put them back into the refrigerator for a few minutes to set and then continue.

CHERRY NUT BALLS

MAKES 16

*These crunchy textured sweets are a delicious treat and
a favourite with children.*

120g /4oz butter or vegetable margarine
180g /6oz caster sugar
225g /8oz glacé cherries
1 egg, beaten
30ml /2 tbsps evaporated milk
60g /2oz crisp rice cereal, crushed
60g /2oz walnuts, chopped
3-4 tbsps desiccated coconut

1. Put the butter and sugar into a bowl and cook on HIGH for 4 minutes, stirring after each minute to dissolve the sugar.

2. Rinse the cherries and chop them finely using a sharp knife.

3. Mix the chopped cherries into the melted butter and sugar. Stir well and cook for 1 minute on HIGH.

4. Beat the egg into the milk and then add gradually to the hot cherry mixture, stirring well between additions.

Step 2 Chop the rinsed cherries into small pieces using a sharp knife.

Step 5 Cook the cherry mixture until it comes together to form a ball when stirred.

Step 8 Roll each cherry ball in the coconut, pressing it on with your fingers to coat evenly.

5. Cook the cherry mixture on MEDIUM for 5-8 minutes, or until it comes together in a ball when stirred.

6. Mix the cereal and nuts into the hot cherries and divide the mixture into 16 even pieces.

7. Roll each piece into a small ball.

8. Toss each cherry ball into the desiccated coconut and cover evenly, pressing the coconut on with your fingers if necessary.

9. Chill well before serving in individual paper sweet cases.

Cook's Notes

COOK'S TIP: Make sure that you do not overcook the sweet mixture after adding the eggs and milk, by stirring after each minute of cooking time.

VARIATION: Use any combination of glacé fruit and nuts in place of those suggested in this recipe.

TIME: Preparation takes about 20 minutes, microwave cooking takes about 10-13 minutes.

ROCKY ROAD FUDGE

MAKES 1LB

Home made fudge is always welcome and this easy to prepare microwave fudge is no exception.

60g /2oz plain chocolate
450g /1lb caster sugar
200ml /6fl oz milk
60g /2oz butter, or vegetable margarine
10ml /2 tsps vanilla essence
60g /2oz walnuts, chopped
30g /1oz crisp rice cereal

1. Grate or finely chop the chocolate using the coarse side of a cheese grater, or a very sharp knife.

2. Put the chocolate into a bowl along with the sugar and the milk.

3. Cover the bowl with cling film and pierce this several times with the tip of a sharp knife. Cook the chocolate on HIGH for 5 minutes.

4. Uncover the bowl and stir the chocolate mixture well to dissolve the sugar completely.

5. Continue cooking the fudge mixture on MEDIUM for about 15 minutes, stirring very

Step 4 Stir the chocolate mixture slowly until the sugar has completely dissolved.

Step 5 To test, drop a small amount of the mixture into cold water. If it forms a soft ball, it is ready to be cooled.

frequently during this cooking time. To test, drop a small amount of the mixture into cold water, if it forms a soft ball it is ready to be cooled.

6. This cooking time may be extended if required, until this 'soft ball' stage is reached.

7. Allow the fudge to cool for about 10 minutes, then beat in the vanilla essence.

8. Continue beating the fudge until it begins to lose its shiny appearance and starts to become grainy and thick.

9. Quickly beat in the nuts and cereal, mixing them well to distribute them evenly.

10. Spread the fudge mixture evenly into a 20cm /8-inch square dish or tin which has been lined with silicone or wax paper.

11. Mark the fudge into squares and refrigerate until it is completely cold before removing from the dish and breaking up.

Cook's Notes

 TIME: Preparation takes about 20 minutes, microwave cooking takes about 20 minutes.

 VEGETARIAN SUITABILITY: This recipe is suitable for lacto-vegetarians only.

 VARIATION: Use a carob bar instead of the plain chocolate in this recipe.

 SERVING IDEA: Serve in individual paper cases.

PREPARATION: Stir the fudge frequently during the cooking period to prevent the sugar from burning and tainting the flavour of the fudge.

HONEYCOMB

MAKES 1lb

*As well as being a great family favourite, this traditional
sweet is also fascinating to watch being prepared.*

225g /8oz granulated sugar
280ml /8fl oz golden syrup
15ml /1 tbsp wine vinegar
15ml /1 tbsp baking soda
225g /8oz plain or milk chocolate for coating,
   optional

1. Line a 20cm /8-inch square dish or tin with
well oiled aluminium foil, pressing this well into
the corners of the dish and pressing it as
smoothly as possible against the base and sides.

2. Put the sugar, syrup and vinegar into a large,
deep-sided bowl. Cover this with cling film and
pierce this several times with the tip of a sharp
knife.

3. Cook the sugar mixture on HIGH for 3
minutes. Remove the cling film and stir well to
dissolve the sugar.

4. Continue cooking the sugar, uncovered, for a
further 4-10 minutes on HIGH, stirring after
every minute to prevent the sugar from burning,
until the mixture reaches 150°C /300°F on a
sugar thermometer.

Step 1 Line a
square dish
carefully with
aluminium foil,
pressing this well
into the corners and
onto the sides of
the dish to remove
as many creases as
possible.

Step 5 Stir the
baking soda quickly
into the sugar
mixture to make it
foam up the sides
of the bowl.

Step 7 Break the
honeycomb into
irregular shaped
pieces after peeling
off the aluminium
foil.

5. Quickly add the baking soda to the hot sugar
mixture and stir it well. The mixture will foam
very quickly once the soda is added.

6. Pour the foaming sugar into the prepared
dish or tin and leave in a cool place until it has
set.

7. Remove the honeycomb from the foil and
break it up into small, irregular shaped pieces.

8. If used, melt the chocolate in a bowl on
MEDIUM for 3 minutes and coat about half of
the honeycombe with this.

9. Allow the chocolate to set completely before
serving.

BANANA, DATE AND WALNUT LOAF

MAKES 1 LOAF

Banana cakes are an ideal way of using up over-ripe bananas. The riper they are, the more flavour they seem to lend to the finished cake.

60ml /4 tbsps milk
15ml /1 tbsp treacle
120g /4oz vegetable margarine
90g /3oz soft, light brown sugar
2 eggs, beaten
180g /6oz self-raising flour
90g /3oz chopped dates
1 small banana, peeled and sliced
60g /2oz shelled walnuts, chopped

1. Put the milk, treacle, margarine and sugar into a jug or bowl, and cook on HIGH for 2 minutes.

2. Stir well until the sugar has dissolved, cooking for a further 2 minutes if necessary.

3. Cool the treacle mixture slightly then beat in the eggs.

4. Put the flour, fruit and nuts into a large bowl and make a well in the centre.

5. Put in the egg and treacle mixture and beat

Step 4 Put the flour, fruit and nuts into a large bowl and make a well in the centre.

Step 5 Beat the egg and treacle mixture thoroughly into the flour and fruit, mixing until a thick batter is produced.

Step 2 Stir the sugar thoroughly with the treacle and margarine, until it has completely dissolved.

well until the flour is completely incorporated and the cake mixture is a thick batter.

6. Pour the batter into a greased and base-lined microwave proof 1.75-litre /3-pint bread dish and cook on HIGH for 6 minutes, turning the dish one half turn after 3 minutes if your microwave oven does not have a turntable.

7. Leave the cake to stand in the dish for 10 minutes before turning out onto a wire rack to cool completely.

Cook's Notes

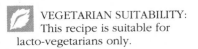 VEGETARIAN SUITABILITY: This recipe is suitable for lacto-vegetarians only.

 VARIATION: Use honey in place of the treacle in this recipe.

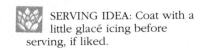 SERVING IDEA: Coat with a little glacé icing before serving, if liked.

GINGER NUTS

MAKES 36

*These spicy biscuits are given a delicious texture by
the nuts that are included in this recipe.*

180g /6oz vegetable margarine or butter
120g /4oz dark, soft brown sugar
120ml /4fl oz treacle
10ml /2 tsps vinegar
30ml /2 tbsps milk
3 eggs, beaten
675g /1½lbs wholemeal flour
7.5ml /1½ tsps baking soda
10ml /2 tsps ground ginger
2.5ml /½ tsp ground cinnamon
Pinch ground cloves
60g /2oz hazelnuts, chopped

1. Put the margarine, sugar, treacle and vinegar
into a bowl and beat together well until they are
smooth and well blended.

2. Beat in the milk and eggs.

3. Add the flour, soda and spices to the treacle
mixture, mixing well until all the ingredients are
blended and form a firm dough.

4. Stir in the hazelnuts.

5. Line a baking dish with silicone paper and

Step 1 Beat the margarine, sugar, treacle and vinegar together in a large bowl until they are smooth and well blended.

Step 3 Make a firm dough by beating the dry ingredients into the treacle mixture and mixing well with a wooden spoon.

Step 6 Press the biscuits down gently with the tines of a fork to flatten them slightly.

pour teaspoons of the biscuit mixture, well apart,
onto it. Cook the biscuits in batches of 6-8 at a
time.

6. Press the biscuits down gently with a fork
and cook on HIGH for 1-3 minutes per batch.

7. Allow the biscuits to cool for 3-5 minutes
before removing them from the paper and
transferring them to a wire rack to cool
completely.

8. Continue cooking the biscuits in this way
until all the mixture is used up.

Cook's Notes

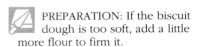

TIME: Preparation takes about 20 minutes, microwave cooking takes about 5-10 minutes plus standing time.

COOK'S TIP: If the treacle is difficult to measure out, warm it gently for 30 seconds on HIGH to soften it.

PREPARATION: If the biscuit dough is too soft, add a little more flour to firm it.

DATE AND WALNUT CAKE
MAKES 1 LOAF

This traditional fruit loaf is made wonderfully quick and easy by using the microwave oven.

140ml /¼ pint water
90g /3oz vegetable margarine
120g /4oz sugarless or fresh dates, stoned and
  chopped
120g /4oz wholemeal flour
10ml /2 tsps baking powder
2.5ml /½ tsp baking soda
5ml /1 tsp ground cinnamon
60g /2oz shelled walnuts, chopped
60ml /4 tbsps demerara sugar

1. Put the water, margarine and dates into a bowl and cook on HIGH for 3 minutes, or until the dates have softened.

2. Using a fork, mash the dates coarsely into the cooking liquid.

3. Put the flour, baking powder, baking soda, cinnamon and walnuts into a bowl. Make a well in the centre and beat in the date mixture.

Step 3 Beat the date mixture into the dry ingredients, mixing well to incorporate thoroughly.

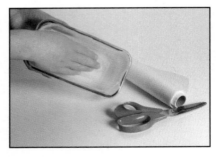

Step 5 Line a loaf dish with silicone paper, making sure that it is folded smoothly into each corner.

Step 2 Use a fork to mash the chopped dates coarsely into the cooking liquid.

4. Stir the walnuts into the cake mixture, beating well to mix them in evenly.

5. Line a 450g /1lb loaf dish with silicone paper and spoon the cake mixture into this.

6. Cook the loaf on MEDIUM for 5 minutes then allow to stand for a further 5 minutes before turning out onto a wire rack to cool completely.

7. Sprinkle the cake with demerara sugar before serving.

Cook's Notes

 VARIATION: Use apricots instead of dates, and almonds instead of the walnuts in this recipe.

SERVING IDEA: Serve with morning coffee.

PREPARATION: If the cake still feels sticky to touch, after the cooking and standing times combined, microwave it on HIGH for a further 1-2 minutes, then allow it to stand for a further 5 minutes.

TIME: Preparation takes about 15 minutes, microwave cooking takes about 8 minutes, plus 5 minutes standing time.

335

PEANUT BUTTER BRAN COOKIES

MAKES 5 DOZEN

*These rich, crumbly cookies are just the thing for hungry
children, mid-morning, with a glass of milk.*

120g /4oz vegetable margarine
120g /4oz muscovado sugar
1 egg
225g /8oz crunchy peanut butter
60g /2oz bran
120g /4oz wholemeal flour
2.5ml /½ tsp salt
2.5ml /½ tsp baking soda
2.5ml /½ tsp vanilla essence

1. Put the margarine and sugar into a large bowl and cream them together until fluffy and light in texture.

2. Quickly beat in the egg and peanut butter, mixing well to prevent the biscuit mix from curdling.

3. Stir in the bran, flour, salt, soda and essence, mixing well to form a stiff dough.

4. Line a large, circular dish or plate with silicone paper, and arrange 6-8 heaped

Step 1 Cream the margarine and sugar together in a large bowl with a wooden spoon until fluffy and light in texture.

Step 3 Add the bran, flour, salt, soda and essence to the peanut mixture, stirring well to make a stiff dough.

Step 5 Flatten each cookie with the tines of a damp fork or palette knife before baking.

teaspoonfuls of the biscuit mixture, well apart, in a single layer around the edge.

5. Flatten each cookie slightly with a damp fork before baking for 2 minutes on HIGH.

6. Allow the biscuits to cool for 1 minute on the plate before transferring to a wire rack to cool completely.

7. Cook the remaining mixture in the same way.

Cook's Notes

 VEGETARIAN SUITABILITY: This recipe is suitable for lacto-vegetarians only.

 PREPARATION: If the biscuit dough is too soft, add extra flour to stiffen it.

 FREEZING: These biscuits freeze well for up to 3 months.

 SERVING IDEA: Serve for tea or with a packed lunch.

TIME: Preparation takes about 20 minutes, microwave cooking takes about 2 minutes per batch, plus 1 minute standing time.

HAZELNUT BROWNIES

MAKES 16

*These moist, cake-like brownies are an irresistible treat
and so easily made in the microwave oven.*

120g /4oz vegetable margarine
180g /6oz muscovado sugar
2 eggs
2.5ml /½ tsp vanilla essence
90g /3oz wholemeal flour
2.5ml /½ tsp baking powder
Pinch salt
60g /2oz chopped hazelnuts

1. Cut the margarine into small dice and put these into a bowl. Melt on HIGH for 1-2 minutes.

2. Add the sugar to the melted margarine, mix well until it is smooth, and then cool slightly.

3. Add the eggs and essence and beat well to prevent the mixture from curdling.

4. Stir in all the remaining ingredients, mixing well to blend evenly.

5. Line a 20cm /8-inch square dish with silicone paper and cover the corners with aluminium foil.

Step 2 Mix the sugar into the melted margarine, stirring until it is smooth.

Step 4 Add the dry ingredients and the nuts to the egg and sugar mixture, mixing thoroughly to blend evenly.

Step 5 Cover just the corners of the silicone paper lined square dish with aluminium foil to prevent the cakes from burning on these edges.

6. Pour the cake mixture into the dish and smooth the top with a metal spoon.

7. Stand the dish on a rack inside the microwave oven and cook on HIGH for 5 minutes. Reduce the power setting to MEDIUM and continue cooking for a further 1-2 minutes, or until set but still moist.

8. Allow the cake to cool in the dish for 15 minutes before turning onto a wire rack to cool completely.

9. Cut the cake into 16 squares before serving.

Cook's Notes

 FREEZING: This recipe freezes well for up to six weeks.

 SERVING IDEA: Serve with coffee or afternoon tea.

TIME: Preparation takes about 15 minutes, microwave cooking takes 6-7 minutes, plus 15 minutes standing time.

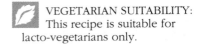 VEGETARIAN SUITABILITY: This recipe is suitable for lacto-vegetarians only.

VEGETARIAN MICROWAVE COOKING

CHAPTER ~ 9

· BREADS AND SCONES ·

CHEESE AND PAPRIKA SCONES

MAKES ABOUT 10 SCONES

*These moreish savoury scones are best eaten
warm on the same day that they are made.*

225g /8oz self-raising flour
5ml /1 tsp paprika
Pinch salt
60g /2oz vegetable margarine
60g /2oz vegetarian red Leicester cheese, grated
5ml /1 tsp made mustard
1 egg
45ml /3 tbsps milk
5ml /1 tsp Marmite or yeast extract
Little boiling water for mixing

1. Put the flour into a bowl and stir in the paprika and salt.

2. Add the margarine to the flour and rub in with fingertips until the mixture resembles breadcrumbs.

3. Stir the cheese into the flour with a fork, mixing well to distribute evenly.

Step 2 Rub the margarine into the flour with your fingers until the mixture resembles fine breadcrumbs.

Step 8 Carefully brush the tops of each scone with the yeast extract mixture before baking.

4. Beat the mustard, egg and milk together in a small bowl. Pour this mixture into the flour and cheese and mix well to form a soft dough, adding a little extra milk if necessary.

5. Turn the dough onto a lightly floured board and knead it gently until smooth.

6. Roll the dough out to about 1cm /½ inch thick and cut into 10 rounds with a 5cm /2-inch pastry cutter.

7. Line a large circular plate or dish with silicone paper and arrange 5 scones at a time in a circle around the edge.

8. Mix together the yeast extract and some boiling water, and brush the tops of the scones with this mixture.

9. Cook the scones for 5-6 minutes on MEDIUM, then allow to stand for 3 minutes before serving.

10. Cook the remaining five scones in the same way.

Cook's Notes

VARIATION: Omit the yeast extract from this recipe and sprinkle the tops of the scones with a mixture of sesame seeds and a little extra grated cheese.

TIME: Preparation takes about 20 minutes, microwave cooking takes about 10-12 minutes for both batches, plus about 6 minutes standing time.

PREPARATION: Use six tbsps of natural yogurt instead of the egg in this recipe if preferred.

CINNAMON FRUIT PLAIT

MAKES 1 LOAF

*An attractive fruit bread which would be equally delicious
served with coffee in the morning or with afternoon tea.*

285-340g /10-12oz strong plain flour
30g /1oz caster sugar
5ml /1 tsp salt
60ml /4 tbsps water
15ml /1 tbsp active dried yeast
140ml /¼ pint milk
60ml /4 tbsps vegetable oil
1 egg
90g /3oz vegetable margarine
120g /4oz muscovado sugar
3 cooking apples, peeled, cored and roughly
    chopped
180g /6oz raisins
90g /3oz chopped glacé citrus fruits
90g /3oz chopped dried apricots
30g /1oz plain flour
5ml /1 tsp ground mixed spice
15ml /1 tbsp granulated sugar
5ml /1 tsp ground cinnamon

1. Put the flour, caster sugar and salt into a large bowl and make a well in the centre.

2. Put the water into a jug or bowl and heat on HIGH for 30 seconds, or until hand hot. Stir in yeast, milk and vegetable oil.

3. Whisk the egg until it is foamy, then whisk it into the yeast mixture. Stir until the yeast has completely dissolved.

4. Heat the flour on HIGH for 1 minute, then pour in the yeast mixture all at once. Beat the liquid into the warm, dry ingredients until it is well incorporated and forms a soft, but not too sticky, dough.

5. Turn the dough onto a well floured board and knead for about 10 minutes, or until it is soft, smooth and very elastic.

6. Put the dough into a lightly floured bowl and cover with cling film or a clean damp tea towel.

Microwave on MEDIUM for 1 minute then allow to stand for 15 minutes.

7. Continue this process until the dough has doubled in bulk.

8. Turn the dough out once again onto a floured board and knead for a further 2 minutes.

9. Roll out the dough to a rectangle 20cm x 25cm /8 inches x 10 inches.

10. Cut the longer edges at 2.5cm /1-inch intervals into 7.5cm /3-inch strips on the diagonal.

11. Put 60g /2oz of the margarine into a large bowl along with the muscovado sugar. Heat on HIGH for 1 minute, or until the margarine is melted. Stir well to partially dissolve the sugar.

12. Put the fruit, flour and spice into the margarine and sugar mixture and mix well to coat evenly.

13. Pile the filling mixture down the centre of the cut dough.

14. Fold over the side strips, from alternating sides, down the length of the loaf.

15. Cover the plait loosely with cling film or a damp cloth and heat on MEDIUM for 1 minute. Allow to stand for 15 minutes.

16. Melt the remaining margarine on HIGH for 30 seconds. Brush the plait with this and sprinkle over the granulated sugar and the cinnamon.

17. Put the plait onto a baking sheet which has been lined with silicone paper and bake on MEDIUM for 6 minutes, turning the tray one quarter turn after each minute.

18. Increase the power setting to HIGH and continue cooking for a further 2 minutes. Allow the loaf to stand for 5 minutes before removing to a wire rack to cool completely.

HOLIDAY FRUIT BRIOCHE

MAKES 1 LOAF

A brioche is a traditionally shaped French sweet bread, baked in a shaped mould. If you do not have one, use a 20cm /8-inch round cake dish instead.

285-340g /10-12oz strong plain flour
30g /1oz caster sugar
5ml /1 tsp salt
60ml /4 tbsps water
15ml /1 tbsp active dried baking yeast
140ml /¼ pint milk
60ml /4 tbsps vegetable oil
1 egg
180g /6oz glacé fruits
90g /3oz flaked almonds
Icing sugar for dusting

---

1. Put the flour, sugar and salt into a large bowl and make a well in the centre.

2. Heat the water in a jug or bowl on HIGH for 30 seconds, or until it is hand hot. Stir in the baking yeast, milk and oil.

3. Whisk the egg until it is frothy, then add this to the yeast liquid, stirring well to incorporate thoroughly.

4. Heat the flour on HIGH for 1 minute, then pour in the yeast liquid all at once, mixing well to form a soft dough.

5. Add the fruit and almonds, and knead the dough gently in the bowl until they are well incorporated.

6. Turn the dough onto a lightly floured board and continue kneading for a further 10 minutes, or until the dough is soft and very elastic.

7. Put the dough into a lightly floured bowl and cover with cling film. Heat on MEDIUM for 1

Step 10 Put the smaller dough ball onto the top of the milk-brushed large ball in the dish.

Step 11 Push the handle of a wooden spoon down through the centre of both the pieces of dough to seal them together.

minute then allow to stand for 15 minutes. Continue this process until the dough has doubled in bulk.

8. Turn the dough out once again onto a lightly floured board and knead for a further 2 minutes. Cut the dough into two pieces, one piece being twice the size of the other.

9. Shape the larger piece of dough into a ball and put this into the base of a well greased 22.5cm /9-inch brioche dish, or a 20cm /8-inch cake dish.

10. Brush the top of the large ball with a little milk. Shape the smaller piece of dough into another ball and put this on top of the larger piece in the mould.

11. Push the handle of a wooden spoon down through the centre of both pieces of dough to seal them together.

12. Heat the dough on MEDIUM for 1 minute then allow to stand for 15 minutes. Repeat this procedure until the brioche has doubled in bulk.

13. Brush the top of the brioche with a little more milk and cook on MEDIUM for 6 minutes. Increase the power setting to HIGH and cook for a further 1-2 minutes, or until the top of the brioche springs back when lightly pressed.

14. Allow the brioche to stand in its dish for 5 minutes. Turn out and cool completely on a wire rack, before dusting with the icing sugar and serving.

CHEESE AND CHIVE SPIRAL LOAF

MAKES 1 LARGE LOAF

This flavoursome bread is best eaten warm and freshly made.

400-450g /14-16oz strong plain flour
30g /1oz caster sugar
5ml /1 tsp salt
30ml /2 tbsps water
140ml /¼ pint milk
15ml /1 tbsp active dried yeast
45ml /3 tbsps vegetable oil
120g /4oz vegetarian Cheddar cheese, grated
60g /2oz fresh breadcrumbs
45g /1½oz fresh chives, finely chopped
30g /1oz vegetable margarine, melted
30g /1oz cheese biscuits, crushed

Step 13 Sprinkle the greased surfaces of the loaf dish with about ⅔ of the crushed cheese biscuits, tipping and rotating the dish to produce an even coating.

1. Put the flour, sugar and salt into a large bowl and heat on HIGH for 1 minute to warm.

2. Put the water and the milk into a jug or bowl and heat on HIGH for 30 seconds, or until hand hot.

3. Stir in the yeast and the oil and mix well until the yeast has dissolved completely.

4. Make a well in the centre of the warmed flour and pour in the yeast mixture all at once.

5. Beat thoroughly until a soft, smooth dough is formed.

6. Continue beating until the dough forms a ball and is very elastic.

7. Turn the dough onto a floured board and knead for 10 minutes.

8. Put the dough into a large bowl and cover with floured cling film or a damp cloth. Heat on LOW for 4 minutes then allow to stand for 10 minutes. Continue this process until the dough has doubled in size.

9. Turn the dough once again onto a floured board and knead for a further 2 minutes. Roll the dough out to a rectangle approximately 20 x 30cm /8 x 12 inches.

10. Put the breadcrumbs and chives into a bowl and mix them together thoroughly.

11. Sprinkle the cheese mixture evenly over the rectangle of dough, leaving a 1cm /½-inch border all around the edge.

12. Roll up the dough, starting from the narrow end, in a Swiss roll fashion. Tuck in the narrow edges to seal in the filling.

13. Brush a 900g /2lb loaf tin with half of the melted margarine. Sprinkle the greased surface of the loaf tin with about ⅔ of the crushed biscuits.

14. Put the uncooked bread, seam side down, into the loaf dish. Heat on LOW for 4 minutes then allow to stand for 10 minutes. Repeat this process one more time, until the loaf has doubled in size.

15. Gently brush the surface of the loaf with the remaining margarine and sprinkle the remaining crushed biscuits evenly over the surface.

16. Cook the bread on MEDIUM for 6 minutes, then increase the power setting to HIGH, and continue cooking for a further 1-2 minutes, or until the top of the loaf springs back when gently pressed.

17. Allow the loaf to stand in the dish for 5 minutes before turning out and cooling on a wire rack.

CARAWAY RYE STICKS

MAKES 16 ROLLS

*These unusual bread rolls make a delicious addition
to a picnic or informal supper.*

350g /12oz rye flour
120g /4oz strong plain flour
5ml /1 tsp salt
5ml /1 tsp soft brown sugar
280ml /½ pint milk
15ml /1 tbsp active dried yeast
30ml /2 tbsps vegetable oil
30ml /2 tbsps caraway seeds
Extra 30ml /2 tbsps milk
Extra 15ml /1 tbsp caraway seeds
10ml /2 tsps coarse sea salt

1. Put the flours into a large bowl and add the salt and sugar. Mix them together thoroughly and make a well in the centre. Heat on HIGH for 1 minute to warm.

2. Put the milk into a jug and heat on HIGH for 30 seconds or until hand hot. Stir in the yeast and blend until it has completely dissolved.

3. Stir the oil into the yeast mixture and add this to the warmed flour along with the 30ml /2 tbsps of caraway seeds. Mix well to form a soft dough.

4. Continue beating the dough until it forms a ball and is very elastic.

Step 4 Beat the dough thoroughly until it forms a soft ball.

Step 8 Shape the sixteen pieces of dough into sticks which are slightly thicker at the centres than at the ends.

5. Turn the dough onto a floured board and knead for 10 minutes.

6. Put the dough into a bowl and cover with lightly floured cling film or a damp tea towel. Heat on LOW for 4 minutes then stand for 10 minutes. Continue this process until the dough has doubled in size.

7. Turn the dough once again onto a floured surface and knead for a further 2 minutes.

8. Divide the dough into 16 equal-sized pieces and shape these pieces into sticks which are slightly thicker at the centre than at the ends.

9. Arrange the rolls on a lightly greased baking sheet and cover loosely with cling film or a damp tea towel. Warm the rolls on LOW for 4 minutes, then allow to stand for 10 minutes. Repeat this process one more time, or until the rolls have doubled in size.

10. Brush each roll with a little of the extra milk, then sprinkle them with equal amounts of the extra caraway seeds and the coarse sea salt.

11. Cook the rolls, eight at a time, on HIGH for 3-4 minutes, or until they are firm to touch.

Cook's Notes

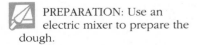

PREPARATION: Use an electric mixer to prepare the dough.

SERVING IDEA: Serve with salads or spicy casseroles.

FREEZING: These rolls freeze very well for up to six weeks.

WHOLEMEAL LOAF

MAKES 1 LOAF

Nothing can beat the flavour of freshly made wholemeal bread, so do not expect this loaf to last for long once you have taken it out of the oven!

350g /12oz wholemeal flour
120g /4oz strong plain flour
5ml /1 tsp salt
5ml /1 tsp soft brown sugar
280ml /½ pint milk
15ml /1 tbsp active dried yeast
30ml /2 tbsps vegetable oil
Extra milk for brushing

1. Sift the flours into a bowl. The bran from the wholemeal flour will remain in the sieve. Add half of this to the flour in the bowl and reserve the other half for the top of the loaf.

2. Add the salt and sugar to the flour in the bowl and make a well in the centre.

3. Heat the flour on HIGH for 1 minute.

4. Put the milk into a jug or basin and heat on HIGH for 30 seconds, or until it is at body temperature.

5. Stir the yeast into the milk and mix until it has completely dissolved.

6. Add the oil to the yeast mixture and pour this all at once into the warmed flour. Mix well to form a soft dough.

7. Continue beating the dough until it forms a ball and is very elastic.

8. Turn the dough out onto a floured surface and knead it for 10 minutes. Put the dough into

Step 1 After sifting the flours, the bran from the whole-meal flour will remain in the sieve.

Step 14 Sprinkle the reserved bran evenly over the top of the milk-brushed loaf.

a bowl and cover it with lightly floured cling film or a damp tea towel.

9. Heat the dough on LOW for 4 minutes, then allow to stand for 10 minutes. Repeat this procedure until the dough has doubled in size.

10. Turn the dough out once again onto a floured surface and knead for further 2 minutes.

11. Roll out the dough to a rectangle 20 x 30cm / 8 x 12 inches. Roll up the rectangle, starting from a narrower end, Swiss roll fashion.

12. Turn the ends under and put the loaf into a greased 900g /2lb loaf dish.

13. Cover the loaf with lightly floured cling film or a damp tea towel and heat on LOW for 4 minutes. Allow to stand for 10 minutes. Repeat this procedure until the loaf has once again doubled in size.

14. Brush the top of the loaf with the milk and sprinkle the reserved bran evenly over the top.

15. Cook the loaf on MEDIUM for 6 minutes, turning it one quarter turn after each two minute interval if your microwave oven does not have a turntable.

16. Increase the power setting to HIGH and cook for a further 2 minutes, or until the loaf is firm and springs back when the top is pressed.

17. Allow the loaf to stand in the tin for 5 minutes before turning out to cool completely on a wire rack.

PUMPERNICKEL ROLLS

MAKES 16 ROLLS

Pumpernickel is a dark bread which is very popular in Germany and America. It is usually served in slices, but these rolls make an interesting variation.

350g /12oz dark rye or wholemeal flour
120g /4oz strong plain flour
5ml /1 tsp dill seed
5ml /1 tsp salt
140ml /¼ pint water
15ml /1 tbsp active dried yeast
60ml /4 tbsps vegetable oil
140ml /¼ pint black treacle
1 egg, beaten
60g /2oz vegetable margarine, melted
Sesame seeds for sprinkling

1. Put the flours into a large bowl and stir in the dill seed and the salt. Make a well in the centre of the flour and heat on HIGH for 1 minute to warm.

2. Put the water into a jug or bowl and heat on HIGH for 30 seconds. Stir in the yeast and mix until well blended.

3. Add the oil and the treacle to the yeast mixture, stirring until the treacle has completely blended into the liquid, then pour the whole amount into the flour.

4. Add the egg and mix well to form a soft dough. Continue beating this dough until it forms a ball and is soft and very elastic.

5. Turn the dough out onto a floured board and knead for 10 minutes.

6. Shape the dough into a ball and put it into a lightly floured bowl. Cover the bowl loosely with cling film or a damp tea towel, and heat on LOW for 4 minutes. Leave to stand for 15 minutes.

Step 14 After two minutes cooking time, turn the rolls completely over on the baking sheet, to ensure that they are evenly cooked.

7. Repeat this process until the dough has risen to double its original size.

8. Turn the dough out once again onto the floured surface and continue kneading for a further 2 minutes.

9. Divide the dough into 16 even-sized pieces and form each piece into a roll shape of your choice. Knots and rounds are particularly successful.

10. Arrange the rolls, 8 per sheet, on two lightly greased microwave-proof baking sheets.

11. Cover the rolls as the dough before, and leave in a warm place for 30 minutes, or until they have doubled their size.

12. Brush the tops of each roll carefully with the melted margarine and sprinkle over equal amounts of the sesame seeds.

13. Bake the rolls in two batches, for 3-4 minutes per batch on HIGH.

14. Turn the rolls over after two minutes of cooking time to ensure that they are evenly baked.

15. Leave on a wire rack to cool completely.

Cook's Notes

 FREEZING: These rolls will freeze successfully for up to two months.

 SERVING IDEA: Serve with salad or strong vegetarian cheese and pickles.

 VEGETARIAN SUITABILITY: This recipe is suitable for vegans.

POPPY SEED PLAIT

MAKES 1 LOAF

This ever-popular bread looks so pretty and is best eaten warm and freshly made.

450g /1lb strong plain flour
5ml /1 tsp salt
280ml /½ pint milk
5ml /1 tsp caster sugar
15ml /1 tbsp active dried yeast
45g /1½oz vegetable margarine, melted
1 egg, beaten
Poppy seeds for sprinkling

1. Put the flour and the salt into a large bowl and make a well in the centre. Heat on HIGH for 1 minute to warm.

2. Put the milk into a jug or bowl, and heat on HIGH for 45 seconds, or until hand hot. Stir in the sugar and the yeast, mixing well until the yeast has completely dissolved.

3. Stir in the melted margarine and add the yeast liquid, all at once, to the flour.

4. Mix well to blend to a soft dough, then continue beating until the dough forms a ball and is very elastic.

5. Turn the dough out onto a floured surface and knead for 10 minutes.

6. Put the dough into a floured bowl and cover it loosely with cling film or a damp tea towel. Heat on LOW for 4 minutes then stand for 15 minutes.

7. Repeat this procedure until the dough has doubled in size.

8. Turn the dough out once again onto the floured surface and knead for a further two minutes.

Step 9 Roll each of the three pieces of dough into a long sausage shape.

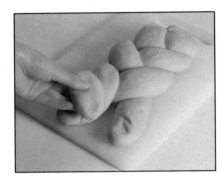

Step 10 Loosely plait the three pieces of dough together.

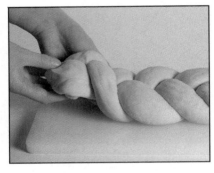

Step 11 Fold the loose ends of the plait underneath the finished loaf to secure them.

9. Divide the dough into three equal pieces and roll each piece into a fairly long sausage shape.

10. Join the three pieces of dough at one end and loosely plait them together.

11. Fold the other loose ends under, and place the loaf onto a lightly greased microwave-proof baking sheet. Cover it loosely as before and stand in a warm place for about 30 minutes, or until doubled in size.

12. Carefully brush the top of the loaf with beaten egg and sprinkle liberally with poppy seeds.

13. Cook the loaf for 1 minute on HIGH, then reduce the power setting to LOW and cook for a further 9 minutes, or until the top of the loaf springs back when lightly touched.

14. Leave the bread to stand on the baking sheet for 5 minutes before serving, or allow to cool completely on a wire rack.

COFFEE ALMOND RING
MAKES 1 RING

*This very attractive bread makes an impressive
and welcome addition to afternoon tea.*

340g /12oz strong plain flour
30g /1oz caster sugar
5ml /1 tsp salt
60ml /4 fl oz water
15ml /1 tbsp active dried yeast
60g /2oz vegetable margarine, melted
1 egg, beaten
225g /8oz almond paste
225g /8oz soft glacé or royal icing
Glacé cherries, angelica and toasted almonds for
    decoration

1. Put the flour, sugar and salt into a large bowl and make a well in the centre. Heat on HIGH for 1 minute to warm.

2. Put the water and milk into a jug or basin and heat on HIGH for 45 seconds, or until hand hot.

3. Stir in the yeast and blend until it has completely dissolved.

4. Add the yeast mixture, melted margarine and egg all at once to the warmed flour and mix to a soft dough. Continue beating this dough until it forms a ball and is very elastic.

5. Turn the dough out onto a floured surface and knead for 10 minutes.

6. Put the dough into a lightly floured bowl and cover loosely with cling film or a damp tea towel. Heat on LOW for 4 minutes, then allow to stand for 15 minutes. Continue with this process until the dough has doubled in size.

Step 11 Bring the two ends of the roll together to form a ring.

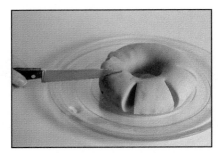

Step 12 Cut the circle all around at 5cm /2-inch intervals, turning each section on its side as you go to reveal the almond paste.

7. Turn the dough out once again onto the floured surface and knead for a further 2 minutes.

8. Roll out the dough to a rectangle 20 x 30cm / 8 x 12 inches.

9. Thinly roll out the almond paste to a similar size and place this carefully onto the dough rectangle.

10. Carefully roll up the dough, Swiss roll fashion, but starting with the longer edge.

11. Place the roll carefully onto a microwave-proof baking sheet and bring the two ends together to form a ring. Seal the two ends carefully.

12. Cut the circle all round at 5cm /2-inch intervals and turn each section on its side so that the spiral of almond paste shows.

13. Cover the ring lightly with cling film, or a damp tea towel and leave in a warm place for 30 minutes, or until doubled in size.

14. Cook the ring on MEDIUM for 6 minutes, then increase the power setting to HIGH and continue cooking for a further 1-2 minutes or until the top of the ring springs back when lightly pressed.

15. Allow to stand for five minutes before cooling completely on a wire rack.

16. Drizzle the icing thickly over the ring and decorate with the cherries, angelica and almonds before serving.

HONEY WHOLEMEAL MUFFINS
MAKES 8-10 MUFFINS

Although these are not what are traditionally understood to be muffins in England, they are a delicious tea bread and well worth making in the microwave oven.

120g /4oz wholemeal flour
10ml /2 tsps baking powder
Pinch salt
Pinch ground ginger
30g /1oz soft, dark brown sugar
60ml /4 tbsps clear honey
90ml /3 fl oz milk
60ml /4 tbsps vegetable oil
1 egg, beaten
30g /1oz chopped toasted almonds

1. Put the flour, baking powder, salt and ginger into a bowl.

2. Stir in the brown sugar and make a well in the centre.

3. Mix together the honey, milk, oil and egg in a basin or jug.

4. Pour this honey mixture, all at once, into the flour mixture.

5. Beat the mixture thoroughly to form a fairly soft batter.

Step 5 Beat the mixture thoroughly until it forms a fairly soft consistency batter.

Step 7 Fill each paper case approximately half full with the honey batter. Do not overfill the cases as the muffins will rise during the cooking.

Step 8 Sprinkle equal amounts of the chopped almonds evenly over the top of each muffin.

6. Arrange 8-10 individual bun paper cases into a deep-sided microwave-proof dish.

7. Fill each paper case approximately half full with the honey batter.

8. Sprinkle the chopped almonds evenly over the top of each muffin.

9. Cook on HIGH for 3-5 minutes, or until the muffins are set, but the tops are still soft.

10. Allow the cakes to stand for 10 minutes, to dry out completely before serving warm, or serve when completely cooled.

Cook's Notes

 VEGETARIAN SUITABILITY: This recipe is suitable for lacto-vegetarians only.

 VARIATION: Stir 30g /1oz chopped almonds into the batter for a nutty variation.

 SERVING IDEA: Serve for afternoon tea.

WHOLEMEAL SODA BREAD

MAKES 1 ROUND LOAF

*Soda bread is an excellent alternative to yeast baked bread,
and can be made in a fraction of the time. It does need to be eaten
very fresh, preferably straight from the oven!*

225g /8oz wholemeal flour
225g /8oz plain flour
10ml /2 tsps baking soda
10ml /2 tsps cream of tartar
30g /1oz vegetable margarine
10ml /2 tsps soft brown sugar
280ml /½ pint milk
15ml /1 tbsp lemon juice or vinegar
15g /½oz coarse oatmeal or rolled oats

1. Put the wholemeal flour into a large bowl and sift in the plain flour, mixed with the baking soda and the cream of tartar.

2. Cut the margarine into small dice and mix these into the flours with a round-bladed knife.

3. Rub the margarine into the flours with the fingertips until the mixture resembles fine breadcrumbs.

4. Stir in the sugar, mixing thoroughly to distribute it evenly.

Step 3 Rub the margarine into the flours with your fingertips until the mixture resembles fine breadcrumbs.

Step 10 Score a deep cross into the top of the bread round with a sharp knife, to mark into four sections.

5. Put the milk into a jug or basin and warm on HIGH for 30 seconds.

6. Stir in the lemon juice or vinegar and mix until the milk sours and curdles.

7. Make a well in the centre of the flour mixture and pour in all the milk.

8. Mix well to produce a soft dough.

9. Turn the dough out onto a lightly floured board and knead lightly until it is smooth.

10. Shape the dough into a round and score a deep cross into the top of the round with a sharp knife, to mark into four sections.

11. Put the loaf onto a microwave-proof baking sheet and sprinkle over the oatmeal.

12. Cook on MEDIUM for 5 minutes, then increase the power setting to HIGH and cook for a further 3 minutes, or until the loaf is well risen and firm to touch.

13. Allow the loaf to stand for 10 minutes, before serving.

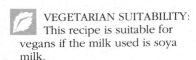

Cook's Notes

TIME: Preparation takes about 15 minutes, microwave cooking takes about 9 minutes, plus 10 minutes standing time.

VEGETARIAN SUITABILITY: This recipe is suitable for vegans if the milk used is soya milk.

PREPARATION: Mixing the dough can be made much easier by using an electric mixer or food processor.

CHEESE AND DILL BREAD
MAKES 1 LOAF

*This delicious variation of a traditional soda bread is
best eaten warm, as part of a lunch or supper.*

225g /8oz plain flour
10ml /2 tsps baking powder
2.5ml /½ tsp baking soda
5ml /1 tsp salt
10ml /2 tsps soft brown sugar
90g /3oz vegetable margarine
30ml /2 tbsps fresh chopped dill weed
60g /2oz vegetarian Red Leicester cheese, grated
180ml /6 fl oz milk
15ml /1 tbsp lemon juice or vinegar
30g /2oz dry breadcrumbs
30g /2 tbsps vegetarian Cheddar cheese, finely
   grated

1. Sift the flour, baking powder, baking soda, salt and sugar together, into a large bowl.

2. Cut the margarine into small dice and mix these into the flour using a round bladed knife.

3. Rub in the margarine with fingertips until the mixture resembles fine breadcrumbs.

4. Stir in the dill and the Red Leicester cheese, mixing well to incorporate evenly.

Step 8 Spread the soft bread dough carefully into the lined cake dish.

Step 10 Cover a rim, 2.5cm /1-inch wide all around the edge of the bread dough with aluminium foil to prevent the edges from burning during the cooking.

5. Put the milk into a jug or basin and heat on HIGH for 30 seconds.

6. Stir in the lemon juice or vinegar and mix until the milk sours and curdles.

7. Pour the soured milk into the flour mixture and beat until it forms a soft dough.

8. Line a 20cm /8-inch round cake dish with silicone paper and spread the bread dough into this.

9. Mix together the breadcrumbs and the Cheddar cheese, and sprinkle this mixture evenly over the top of the dough in the dish.

10. Cover 2.5cm /1 inch around the edge of the bread dough with aluminium foil, to prevent it from overcooking.

11. Bake on on MEDIUM for 10 minutes. Increase the power to HIGH and continue cooking for a further 3-5 minutes, or until the loaf is firm. Remove the foil from the edge of the loaf for this final cooking period.

12. Allow the bread to stand in the dish for 10 minutes, before turning out and serving still warm.

Cook's Notes

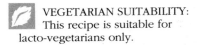

VEGETARIAN SUITABILITY: This recipe is suitable for lacto-vegetarians only.

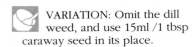

VARIATION: Omit the dill weed, and use 15ml /1 tbsp caraway seed in its place.

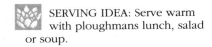

SERVING IDEA: Serve warm with ploughmans lunch, salad or soup.

PUMPKIN RAISIN BREAD

MAKES 1 LOAF

*An unusual spicy, sweet soda bread, this recipe is simple
and very quick to make using the microwave oven.*

120g /4oz plain flour
5ml /1 tsp salt
5ml /1 tsp baking powder
5ml /1 tsp baking soda
5ml /1 tsp ground allspice
5ml /1 tsp ground cinnamon
5ml /1 tsp ground ginger
180g /6oz soft brown sugar
140ml /¼ pint vegetable oil
2 eggs, beaten
120g /4oz raisins
225g /8oz puréed pumpkin

1. Sift the flour, salt, baking powder, baking soda and spices into a large bowl.

2. Stir in the sugar, mixing well to distribute evenly.

Step 5 Carefully line the sides and base of a microwave-proof loaf dish with silicone paper.

Step 6 Cover a 2.5cm /1-inch rim around the edge of the batter in the dish with aluminium foil, to prevent overcooking.

3. Make a well in the centre of the flour mixture and pour in the oil and the eggs. Beat this mixture very thoroughly to make a soft dough.

4. Stir in the raisins and the pumpkin, beating thoroughly once again to form a firm batter.

5. Line a 22.5 x 12.5cm /9 x 5 inch loaf dish with silicone paper.

6. Spread the batter into this prepared dish and cover just 2.5cm /1 inch around the edge of the batter with aluminium foil.

7. Bake the loaf on MEDIUM for 10 minutes, then remove the foil and continue cooking the loaf for a further 5 minutes on HIGH.

8. Leave the loaf to stand in the dish for 10 minutes before turning out on a wire rack to cool completely.

Cook's Notes

VARIATION: Use sultanas in place of the raisins, and stir in 30g /1oz of chopped pecans when you add the pumpkin.

SERVING IDEA: Serve spread with butter for tea.

PREPARATION: The preparation of this recipe can be made quicker and easier if you use an electric mixer or a food processor.

TIME: Preparation takes about 20 minutes, microwave cooking takes about 15-16 minutes, plus 10 minutes standing time.

367

FRUIT SCONES

MAKES 6-8 SCONES

These traditional teatime favourites are best served freshly made and warm.

225g /8oz plain flour
15ml /1 tbsp baking powder
60g /2oz vegetable margarine
30g /1oz caster sugar
30g /1oz sultanas
1 egg, beaten
60ml /4 tbsps milk
Little extra milk for brushing
30g /1oz granulated sugar
15ml /1 tbsp ground cinnamon

1. Put the flour and the baking powder into a large bowl. Add the margarine and rub together until the mixture resembles fine breadcrumbs.

2. Stir in the caster sugar and the sultanas, mixing well to distribute these ingredients evenly.

3. Beat the egg and the milk together in a small bowl and stir this into the flour mixture to form a

Step 5 Cut 5cm /2 inch rounds out of the scone mixture with a biscuit cutter.

Step 6 Arrange the scones in a single layer around the edge of the lined plate or dish.

soft dough. Add a little more milk if the dough is too stiff.

4. Turn the dough onto a lightly floured board and knead gently until it is evenly blended.

5. Roll the dough out to about 1cm /^{1}/$_2$-inch thick and cut into rounds with a 5cm /2-inch biscuit cutter.

6. Line a circular dish or plate with silicone paper and arrange the scones in a single layer around the edge.

7. Brush the tops of the scones with extra milk.

8. Mix together the sugar and cinnamon and sprinkle this evenly over the tops of the brushed scones.

9. Bake the scones on HIGH for 3-4 minutes, then allow to stand for 2-3 minutes before either serving warm or cooling on a wire rack.

Cook's Notes

PREPARATION: If your microwave oven does not have a turntable, turn the dish one quarter turn after each one minute of cooking time.

SERVING IDEA: Serve cut in half and spread with a fruit preserve.

VARIATION: Use 6 tbsps of natural yogurt in place of the egg in this recipe.

FREEZING: These scones freeze successfully for up to two months. Defrost and re-heat for 1 minute on HIGH before serving.

TIME: Preparation takes about 15 minutes, microwave cooking takes about 3-4 minutes, plus 2-3 minutes standing time.

VEGETARIAN SUITABILITY: This recipe is suitable for lacto-vegetarians only.

BOSTON BROWN BREAD

MAKES 1 LARGE LOAF

This traditional American bread is served in Boston with baked beans. However, it is equally good served spread with butter for a sweet tea bread.

15g /½oz vegetable margarine
280ml /½ pint natural yogurt
90ml /3oz black treacle
70g /2½oz wholemeal flour
70g /2½oz plain flour
90g /3oz cornmeal
5ml /1 tsp baking powder
5ml /1 tsp salt
60g /2oz raisins

1. Put the margarine into a bowl and melt on HIGH for 30 seconds.

2. Stir in the yogurt and treacle, mixing well until they are completely blended.

3. Put the flours, baking powder and salt into a large bowl.

4. Stir in the raisins and then the yogurt mixture. Mix thoroughly until a soft dough is formed.

Step 2 Stir the yogurt and treacle into the melted margarine, mixing well to blend thoroughly.

Step 4 Mix the raisins and yogurt mixture into the flour mixture, stirring well to form a soft batter.

Step 6 Spoon the bread batter into the prepared dish, making sure that it does not fill the dish more than half full.

5. Lightly grease and base line a 900g /2lb loaf dish.

6. Carefully spoon the bread dough into the dish, making sure that it does not come more than halfway up the inside of the container.

7. Cover the dish with cling film and pierce this several times with the tip of a sharp knife.

8. Bake the bread for 10 minutes on HIGH, then allow to stand for a further 10 minutes before turning onto a wire rack to cool completely.

Cook's Notes

VARIATION: For a vegan recipe, use 200ml /7fl oz of water or soya milk instead of the yogurt in this recipe, and increase the flours by 15g /½oz each if necessary.

TIME: Preparation takes about 15 minutes, microwave cooking takes about 10 minutes, with 10 minutes standing time.

VEGETARIAN SUITABILITY: This recipe is suitable for lacto-vegetarians only. See variation for vegan alternative.

CITRUS SCONES

MAKES 12

*Served warm or cold, these scones are delicious for tea
and make a very nice breakfast treat as well.*

120g /4oz wholemeal flour
5ml /1 tsp baking powder
2.5ml /½ tsp ground cinnamon
60g /2oz bran
Pinch salt
60g /2oz vegetable margarine
30g /1oz soft brown sugar
60g /2oz preserved mixed citrus peel
120ml /4fl oz milk or water

1. Put the flour, baking powder, cinnamon, bran and salt into a large bowl.

2. Cut the margarine into dice and add these to the dry ingredients. Rub the margarine into the flour mixture until it resembles fine breadcrumbs.

3. Stir in the sugar, mixing well to distribute evenly.

4. Add the peel and mix this in thoroughly also.

5. Pour the milk or water into the flour and peel mixture all at once and mix to form a fairly stiff dough.

Step 5 Mix the liquids into the flour mixture, beating thoroughly to form a fairly stiff dough.

Step 8 Arrange the scones, 6 at a time, in a single layer around the edge of a silicone paper lined circular dish or plate.

Step 2 Rub the margarine into the flour with your fingertips until the mixture resembles fine breadcrumbs.

6. Transfer the dough onto a lightly floured board and knead gently until it is well combined.

7. Roll out the dough to approximately 1cm /½ inch thick and cut into 12 scones with a 5cm / 2 inch round cutter.

8. Arrange the scones, six at a time, around the edge of a large circular dish or plate which has been covered with silicone paper.

9. Cook the scones on HIGH for 3 minutes per batch, or until they are well risen. Serve warm or cold.

Cook's Notes

VEGETARIAN SUITABILITY: This recipe is suitable for vegans if water is used. Soya milk could also be substituted if desired.

VARIATION: Use any combination of dried mixed fruit instead of the peel in this recipe.

TIME: Preparation takes about 20 minutes, microwave cooking takes about 6 minutes.

CORNBREAD

MAKES 1 LARGE ROUND LOAF

This South American style bread is quickly and easily made in the microwave oven.

180g /6oz cornmeal
60g /2oz wholemeal flour
5ml /1 tsp baking soda
2.5ml /½ tsp salt
1 egg
30ml /2 tbsps clear honey
240ml /8 fl oz natural yogurt

1. Put the cornmeal, flour, baking soda and salt into a large bowl and stir well.

2. Beat together the egg, honey and yogurt in a jug or bowl.

3. Make a well in the centre of the dry ingredients and pour in the egg mixture all at once.

4. Mix together thoroughly to blend evenly.

5. Carefully line a 22.5cm /9-inch round cake dish with silicone paper.

Step 1 Mix the cornmeal, flour, baking soda and salt together in a large bowl.

Step 4 Carefully blend the egg mixture into the flour mixture, starting to beat from the centre of the bowl and gradually incorporating dry ingredients from the edge.

Step 5 Line a lightly greased cake dish with silicone paper.

6. Pour the cornbread mixture into the dish and bake on HIGH for 3 minutes. Reduce the power setting to MEDIUM and continue cooking for a further 10 minutes, or until the bread is well risen and firm to touch.

7. Carefully turn out the bread onto a wire rack to cool, peeling away the silicone paper from the sides and base of the loaf.

Cook's Notes

 TIME: Preparation takes about 15 minutes, microwave cooking takes about 13 minutes.

VEGETARIAN SUITABILITY: This recipe is suitable for lacto-vegetarians only.

FREEZING: Cornbread can be frozen for up to six weeks.

SERVING IDEA: Cornbread can be served equally well with a spicy dish such as barbeque beans, with a sweet preserve.

PREPARATION: The cornbread mixture will be quite soft when it is mixed, but this moisture will be absorbed by the cornmeal during cooking.

VEGETARIAN MICROWAVE COOKING

CHAPTER ~ 10

·HEALTHY·DRINKS·

RASPBERRY CORDIAL

MAKES 900ml-1200ml /1½-2 PINTS

*This delicious cordial makes a refreshing change
from conventional squashes or soft drinks.*

900g /2lbs fresh or frozen raspberries
180ml /7 fl oz water
5cm /2-inch piece cinnamon stick
340g /12oz white sugar
15ml /1 tbsp lemon juice

---

1. Wash the berries and put them into a large bowl along with the water and the cinnamon stick. Cover the bowl with cling film and pierce this several times with the tip of a sharp knife.

2. Cook the raspberries on HIGH for 3 minutes. Mash the berries with a fork or potato masher, then allow them to stand until they have cooled and the juice has seeped out.

3. Strain the berries into another bowl through a nylon sieve, stirring them gently to release all the juice, but taking care to retain and discard all the pips and fibres.

Step 2 Gently mash the raspberries with a fork or potato masher to allow the juice to seep out of the fruit.

Step 3 Strain the juice from the berries into another bowl through a nylon sieve.

Step 4 Stir the raspberry juice and sugar together until the sugar has completely dissolved.

4. Stir the sugar into the raspberry juice and cook on HIGH for 7 minutes, stirring after each minute of cooking time, until the mixture has boiled but not caramelised.

5. Stir in the lemon juice and pour into bottles or jars. Seal well and keep in a refrigerator until served.

Cook's Notes

 TIME: Preparation takes about 5 minutes, microwave cooking takes about 10 minutes.

VARIATION: Use strawberries or any other soft fruit in place of the raspberries in this recipe.

 VEGETARIAN SUITABILITY: This recipe is suitable for vegans.

BLUEBERRY CORDIAL

MAKES ABOUT 900ml /1½ PINTS

Until recently, blueberries were not readily available, but now larger supermarkets and greengrocers often have them in stock, and they are well worth hunting out, if just to make this delicious cordial.

675g /1½lbs fresh or frozen blueberries
140ml /¼ pint water
225g /8oz white sugar
15ml /1 tbsp lemon juice

---

1. Wash the blueberries and put them into a bowl with the water.

2. Cover the bowl with cling film and pierce this several times with the tip of a sharp knife.

3. Cook the blueberries on HIGH for 3-5 minutes, or until the berries begin to break up.

4. Roughly mash the berries with a fork or potato masher, and allow the berries to cool slightly and their juice to seep out.

5. Strain the juice from the berries into another bowl through a nylon sieve, gently stirring the berries in the sieve so that they release all their juice, but the pips and fibres are retained and can be discarded.

Step 3 Cook the berries until they begin to burst their skins and break up.

Step 4 Roughly mash the berries with a fork or potato masher to allow the juice to seep out.

Step 5 Stir the fruit in the nylon sieve gently to release the juice but retain the pips and fibres.

6. Mix the sugar into the fruit juice and cook on HIGH for 6-7 minutes, stirring after each 1 minute of cooking time so that the sugar dissolves completely but does not caramelise.

7. Stir in the lemon juice and pour the syrup into clean screw top bottles or jars for storing in a refrigerator until required.

Cook's Notes

SERVING IDEA: Serve diluted with soda water or dry white wine, or undiluted over ice cream or desserts.

 VARIATION: Use cranberries or damsons in place of the blueberries in this recipe.

TIME: Preparation takes about 5 minutes, microwave cooking takes about 10 minutes.

IRISH COFFEE

MAKES 4 GLASSES

*Irish coffee makes the perfect ending for a meal, and is also excellent
for warming the spirits on cold, wet winter days.*

700ml /1¼ pints hot water
25ml /1½ tbsps instant coffee
60ml /4 tbsps Irish whiskey
30ml /2 tbsps granulated sugar
120ml /8 tbsps whipping cream

1. Put the water into a large jug and heat on
HIGH for 6-8 minutes or until boiling.

2. Stir in the coffee, mixing well until it has
completely dissolved.

3. Return the coffee to the microwave oven and
heat for a further 2 minutes on HIGH, or until
almost re-boiled.

4. Divide the whiskey equally between 4
heat-proof glasses and add the sugar to the
whiskey in the glasses.

5. Divide the coffee between the four glasses
and stir each one until the sugar has dissolved.

Step 4 Add the
sugar to the
whiskey in the
glasses.

Step 6 Whip the
cream until it is just
softly stiff. Take
care not to over-
whip it, otherwise it
will not float.

Step 7 Carefully
float equal amounts
of the softly
whipped cream
onto the coffee in
the glasses.

6. Put the cream into a small bowl and whip it
until it is softly stiff.

7. Carefully place equal amounts of the cream
on top of the coffee in the glasses, making sure
that you do not stir the beverage as this will
make the cream sink.

8. Serve at once.

Cooks Notes

TIME: Preparation takes about
5 minutes, microwave
cooking takes about 8-10 minutes.

VEGETARIAN SUITABILITY:
This recipe is suitable for
lacto-vegetarians only.

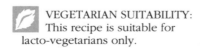

SERVING IDEA: Serve with
truffles, mints or other after
dinner sweets.

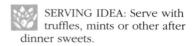

MULLED WINE

MAKES 4 GLASSES

This warming beverage is traditionally served at Christmas, but is so easy to prepare using a microwave oven that it is ideal for serving on any cold winters evening.

½ lemon
570ml /1 pint red wine
2 cinnamon sticks
6 cloves
60ml /4 tbsps brandy

1. Using a potato peeler, carefully pare away the rind from the lemon half, keeping it in one piece if possible.

2. Put the lemon rind, wine, sugar, cinnamon sticks and cloves into a large bowl. Cover the bowl with cling film and pierce this several times with the tip of a sharp knife.

3. Heat the wine and spices on HIGH for 4 minutes, or until it is just boiling.

4. Remove the cling film and stir the wine mixture until the sugar has completely dissolved.

Step 1 Carefully pare away just the rind from the lemon half using a potato peeler or very sharp knife.

Step 4 Stir the wine, spices and sugar mixture until the sugar has completely dissolved.

Step 5 Strain the wine mixture into a large jug to remove the lemon rind and spices.

Allow the wine to stand for 5 minutes to infuse the flavour of the spices and lemon rind.

5. Strain the wine mixture into a large microwave-proof jug and discard the lemon rind and the spices.

6. Re-heat the wine for 2 minutes on HIGH, but do not allow it to re-boil.

7. Stir in the brandy and serve at once.

Cook's Notes

 COOK'S TIP: Only use whole spices in this recipe, as ground spices will impart a stronger flavour and will make the mulled wine cloudy and grainy when drinking.

 VARIATION: Use cider instead of wine in this recipe.

SERVING IDEA: Serve each glass of wine with a small cinnamon stick placed in it.

 TIME: Preparation takes about 5 minutes, microwave cooking takes about 6 minutes, plus 5 minutes standing time.

SPICED ORANGE TEA

MAKES 4 CUPS

This refreshing tea-based drink makes a delicious change from the traditional cuppa!

Half an orange
700ml /1¼ pints hot water
3 whole cloves
1 stick cinnamon
2 tea bags, Assam or Darjeeling variety

---

1. Using the fine side of a cheese grater, carefully grate the rind from the orange, taking care not to get any of the white pith into the peel.

2. Put the grated rind into a large jug or bowl and pour over the water. Stir in the spices.

3. Cover the jug with cling film and pierce this several times with the tip of a sharp knife.

4. Heat the water on HIGH for 6-10 minutes, or until it is boiling.

Step 1 Carefully grate the rind from the orange half using the fine side of a cheese grater.

Step 5 Stir the tea bags into the flavoured water.

Step 6 Strain the tea through a nylon sieve into another jug to remove the spices and tea bags.

5. Uncover the water and add the tea bags. Stir well and leave to stand for 5 minutes.

6. Using a nylon sieve, strain the tea into another jug or bowl to remove the spices, tea bags, and some of the coarser pieces of peel.

7. Serve the tea hot, re-heating it for 1 minute on HIGH if necessary, or chill it completely and serve very cold.

Cook's Notes

VARIATION: Use lemon rind in place of the orange rind and allspice berries instead of cloves.

SERVING IDEA: Serve warm with twists of thinly pared orange rind floating in the tea, or very cold on ice.

TIME: Preparation takes about 5 minutes, microwave cooking takes about 6-11 minutes, plus 5 minutes standing time.

VEGETARIAN SUITABILITY: This recipe is suitable for vegans.

COOK'S TIP: Only use whole spices in this recipe, as ground spices will impart a stronger flavour and will leave the tea cloudy and grainy to drink.

EAU DE FRAMBOISE

MAKES 570ml /1 PINT

*Raspberry liqueurs are delicious and just that little bit
different to serve to friends after dinner.*

450g /1lb fresh or frozen raspberries
340g /12oz white sugar
430ml /¾ pint vodka

---

1. Put the raspberries into a large bowl and
cover with cling film.

2. Puncture the film several times with the tip of
a sharp knife, and cook the raspberries for 4-5
minutes on MEDIUM, to release the juices.

3. Lightly crush the berries with a fork and
strain the juice through a nylon sieve into large
bowl. Set the berries to one side.

4. Stir the sugar into the juice and cover the
bowl with cling film as before. Cook on HIGH
for 3-5 minutes, or until just boiling, stirring the

Step 3 Strain the
juice from the
lightly crushed
berries through a
nylon sieve into a
large bowl.

Step 4 Stir the sugar
into the juice and
then cover the bowl
with cling film.

syrup after each minute to dissolve the sugar
completely. Re-cover the bowl with the film after
each time.

5. Cool the syrup completely, then stir in the
reserved berries and the vodka, mixing well to
blend thoroughly.

6. Put the liqueur into a large-necked crock or
bottle and seal it well.

7. Stand the bottle in a cool, dark place for 1
month, stirring it occasionally to blend the
flavours completely.

8. After this time strain the liqueur through a
nylon sieve into a jug. Discard the fruit and pour
the liqueur into a coloured bottle. Seal this with
a cork or screw top and serve as required.

Cook's Notes

PREPARATION: Take care not
to caramelise the sugar when
initially preparing the syrup as this
will discolour the liqueur and spoil
the finished flavour.

VARIATION: Use strawberries
or redcurrants in place of the
raspberries in this recipe.

TIME: Preparation takes about
10 minutes, plus one month
standing time, microwave cooking
takes about 7-10 minutes.

VEGETARIAN SUITABILITY:
This recipe is suitable for
vegans.

COOK'S TIP: Do not crush
the raspberries too much
once they have been added to the
syrup as this will result in a cloudy
liqueur.

LIQUEUR À L'ORANGE

MAKES 850ml /1½ PINTS

*This delicious liqueur should be made no less than one month before
it is required. Although it sounds expensive, you only drink a small quantity
at a time and it can be made with cheaper varieties of brandy.*

3 oranges
225g /8oz sugar
570ml /1 pint brandy

1. Using a potato peeler, thinly pare off the rind from one of the oranges, taking care not to remove any of the bitter white pith with it.

2. Cut all the oranges in half and squeeze the juice.

3. Put the orange juice into a bowl and stir in the pared orange rind and the sugar.

4. Cover the bowl with cling film and pierce this several times with the tip of a sharp knife.

5. Cook on HIGH for 4 minutes, stirring the mixture after each minute and re-covering each time.

6. Allow the mixture to cool, then strain it through a nylon sieve to remove the orange rind and any membrane that may be in the syrup.

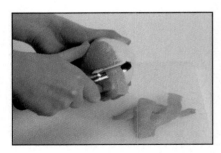

Step 1 Thinly pare off the rind from one of the oranges with a potato peeler, taking care not to remove any of the white pith as you peel.

Step 3 Stir the orange rind and the sugar into the orange juice, mixing well to begin dissolving the sugar.

Step 6 Strain the orange syrup through a nylon sieve to remove the orange rind and any membranes that may have been in the juice.

7. Mix the orange syrup and the brandy together in a large jug, then carefully pour the mixture into a clean, coloured bottle.

8. Seal the bottle with a cork or screw top and leave in a cool, dark place for at least a month, shaking the bottle vigorously occasionally to mix thoroughly.

Cook's Notes

 TIME: Preparation takes about 15 minutes, microwave cooking takes about 4 minutes.

VEGETARIAN SUITABILITY: This recipe is suitable for vegans.

COOK'S TIP: Using a coloured bottle greatly improves the colour of this liqueur. Always store liqueurs of any type in cool, dark places to preserve colour and flavour.

 VARIATION: Use 175g /6oz fresh raspberries or strawberries in place of the oranges in this recipe.

CRÈME DE MENTHE

MAKES 570ml / 1 PINT

This favourite liqueur is easily made using a microwave oven, and is deliciously different when prepared with fresh ingredients.

340g /12oz white sugar
280ml /½ pint water
6-8 large sprigs of fresh mint, *or*
    5ml /1 tsp natural mint essence
Few drops of green food colouring, optional
430ml /¾ pint vodka

1. Put the sugar into a large bowl and pour the water over.

2. Cover the bowl with cling film and pierce this several times with the tip of a sharp knife.

3. Heat the sugar and water on HIGH for 4-5 minutes, or until just boiling. Stir the mixture after each minute of cooking time to dissolve the sugar. Re-cover the bowl each time.

4. Add the mint sprigs to the hot sugar syrup and allow the flavour to infuse for 10 minutes. If you are using the mint essence, add it at this stage but do not bother to allow the mixture to

Step 3 Stir the sugar and water together until the sugar has completely dissolved and a clear syrup is produced.

Step 4 Stir the mint sprigs into the hot syrup to infuse their flavour.

Step 5 Add the food colouring and the vodka to the flavoured syrup and stir well to blend thoroughly.

stand for 10 minutes, just cool slightly before proceeding.

5. Remove the mint sprigs and stir in the food colouring if used. Add the vodka to the syrup and stir well to make sure that it is well blended.

6. Pour the liqueur into a clean, coloured bottle, and allow to stand in a cool dark place for at least 1 month before serving.

Cook's Notes

 TIME: Preparation takes about 10 minutes, microwave cooking takes about 9-10 minutes, plus 10 minutes standing time.

VEGETARIAN SUITABILITY: This recipe is suitable for vegans.

COOK'S TIP: Never boil fresh mint in a mixture, as the boiling process destroys the delicate flavour. Allow the flavour to infuse slowly, and if the liquid does cool too quickly, re-heat it gently, but do not boil.

PREPARATION: Take care not to caramelise the sugar when initially preparing the syrup in this recipe, as this will discolour the liqueur and the final flavour will be spoiled.

VEGETARIAN MICROWAVE COOKING

CHAPTER ~ 11

· JAMS · JELLIES · AND · CHUTNEYS ·

PICKLED ORANGE SLICES
MAKES 670g /1½lbs

*These orange slices make a luxurious accompaniment for a nut roast
or an elegant garnish to many other main courses.*

3-4 large oranges
340g /12oz granulated sugar
280ml /½ pint water
280ml /½ pint white wine vinegar
1 stick cinnamon
2 whole allspice berries
4 whole cloves

1. Carefully slice the tops and bottoms off each of the oranges and discard these.

2. Slice the remaining fruit into 5mm /¼-inch-thick rounds, keeping these as even as possible.

3. Put the rest of the ingredients into a large jug and cook, uncovered, on HIGH for 6 minutes, stirring after each minute to ensure that the sugar has completely dissolved.

Step 2 Slice the oranges into 5mm /¼-inch-thick rounds, keeping these as even as possible.

Step 4 Put the orange slices into jars, arranging a few of them to face outwards in a decorative manner.

Step 5 Pour the vinegar mixture over the oranges in the jars so that they are just covered.

4. Put the orange slices into clean, sterilised jars, arranging a few of them to face outwards in a decorative manner.

5. Pour the vinegar mixture over the oranges in the jars, so that they are just covered.

6. Seal and cover the jars whilst the vinegar mixture is still warm.

Cook's Notes

TIME: Preparation takes about 10 minutes, microwave cooking takes about 16 minutes.

VEGETARIAN SUITABILITY: This recipe is suitable for vegans.

PREPARATION: If preferred, the vinegar mixture can be strained before pouring over the oranges to remove the spices.

SERVING IDEA: Serve with nut roasts or as a garnish to other dishes.

397

SWEET PICKLED ONIONS

MAKES 900g /2lbs

Nothing can compare with the flavour of home-made pickled onions, and this recipe is so quick and easy that there will be no excuse not to make your own!

675g /1½lbs pickling onions
340g /12oz soft, light brown sugar
570ml /1 pint cider, malt or white wine vinegar
140ml /¼ pint water
15ml /1 tbsp mustard seed
½ cinnamon stick
Pinch salt

---

1. Put the onions into a large bowl and pour over enough water to just cover them. Cook on HIGH for 1 minute.

2. Drain the onions and carefully peel away all the brown skins. Rinse the peeled onions in cold water.

3. Put the sugar, vinegar, water, mustard seed, cinnamon and salt into a large bowl and cook, uncovered, on HIGH for 5 minutes, stirring after each minute.

4. Continue stirring until the sugar has completely dissolved.

Step 2 Carefully peel away all the brown skin from the blanched onions.

Step 5 Strain the vinegar into a large bowl or jug through a nylon sieve to remove the spices.

Step 6 Pack the onions into clean, sterilised jars, packing them down well to prevent them from rising up when the vinegar is poured over.

5. Strain the vinegar through a nylon sieve into a large bowl or jug to remove the mustard seeds and the cinnamon stick.

6. Pack the onions into clean, sterilised jars, pressing them down well to prevent them from rising when the vinegar is poured over.

7. Pour the vinegar over the onions in the jars.

8. Arrange the jars on a microwave-proof baking sheet and cook on HIGH for 5 minutes before covering and sealing in the usual way.

Cook's Notes

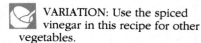

TIME: Preparation takes about 20 minutes, microwave cooking takes about 15 minutes.

VARIATION: Use the spiced vinegar in this recipe for other vegetables.

SERVING IDEA: Serve these onions with fresh bread and cheese for a delicious lunch.

THREE FRUIT MARMALADE
MAKES 2.75kg /6lbs

*This marmalade recipe can be made at any time of the year,
unlike those which include Seville oranges in their ingredients.*

4 limes
2 oranges
2 grapefruits
850ml /1½ pints boiling water
1.5kg /3½lbs granulated sugar

1. Using a potato peeler or sharp knife, thinly pare only the rind from the citrus fruit.

2. Cut the fruit in half and squeeze out all the juice, setting this aside until required.

3. Put the fruit shells and any pips and membranes into a muslin or cheesecloth bag and tie the top securely.

4. Carefully shred the citrus rind into small, thin strips.

5. Put the strips of rind, the juice and the bag of pips and pith into a large bowl. Pour in the water and leave to stand for 30 minutes.

Step 4 Shred the citrus fruit rinds into very small, thin strips.

Step 9 The marmalade is ready when the surface of a small spoonful is almost set after it has been allowed to cool for 2 minutes on a well chilled plate.

6. Cover the bowl with cling film and pierce this several times with the tip of a sharp knife. Cook the fruit and liquid on HIGH for 25 minutes.

7. Uncover the bowl and remove the muslin bag. Squeeze out any juice and discard.

8. Stir the sugar into the frui t liquid and cook, uncovered, on HIGH for 20-25 minutes, stirring after each 5 minutes.

9. Test for setting point by putting a small amount of the hot marmalade onto a well chilled plate and leaving it for 2 minutes. If after this time the surface of the marmalade wrinkles when it is pushed lightly with a finger, then setting point has been reached.

10. If necessary, continue cooking the marmalade until this point is achieved, testing after each 3 minutes.

11. Pour the hot marmalade into clean, sterilised jars, covering and sealing these in the usual way.

Cook's Notes

TIME: Preparation takes about 20 minutes, plus 30 minutes standing time. Microwave cooking takes about 50 minutes to an hour.

VEGETARIAN SUITABILITY: This recipe is suitable for vegans.

VARIATION: Use any combination of citrus fruit in place of that suggested in this recipe.

SERVING IDEA: Serve with hot buttered toast for breakfast.

COOK'S TIP: To get the maximum amount of juice from any citrus fruit, heat the fruits in a microwave oven on HIGH for a few seconds before squeezing.

RHUBARB AND RASPBERRY JAM

MAKES 900g /2lbs

Raspberries can be expensive, but when mixed with rhubarb, which is both cheap and plentiful when in season, just a few will produce a delicious fruity jam.

340g /12oz rhubarb
340g /12oz raspberries
900g /2lb granulated sugar
45ml /3 tbsps lemon juice
60ml /4 tbsps pectin for each 600ml /1 pint
    cooked fruit and juice

---

1. Wash the rhubarb and cut it into 1.25cm /½-inch pieces.

2. Put the rhubarb into a large bowl and cover it with cling film. Puncture this several times with the tip of a knife.

3. Cook the rhubarb for 2 minutes on HIGH.

4. Add the raspberries to the rhubarb, re-cover and cook for a further 1 minute on HIGH.

5. Stir the sugar and lemon juice into the raspberry mixture and mix well.

6. Cook, uncovered, on HIGH for 10 minutes, stirring the jam after each 2 minutes of cooking time to completely dissolve the sugar.

Step 5 Add the sugar and the lemon juice to the raspberry mixture and stir well to dissolve the sugar.

Step 8 Setting point has been reached when a channel is left in the surface of the jam after it has been stirred with a wooden spoon.

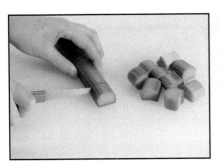

Step 1 Cut the washed rhubarb into even-sized pieces approximately 1.25cm /½-inch long.

7. Measure the cooked fruit and liquid into another bowl and stir in the required amount of pectin. Cook for a further 1 minute on HIGH.

8. Test the jam for setting point by drawing a spoon across the surface. If it leaves a channel, the setting point has been reached. If not, continue cooking for a further 2-3 minutes, or until the jam sets.

9. Pour the jam into clean, sterilised jars, and cover and seal in the usual way.

Cook's Notes

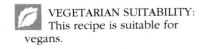 TIME: Preparation takes about 10 minutes, microwave cooking takes about 13-15 minutes.

VEGETARIAN SUITABILITY: This recipe is suitable for vegans.

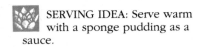 SERVING IDEA: Serve warm with a sponge pudding as a sauce.

TARRAGON VINEGAR PICKLES

MAKES 900g /2lbs

Make sure that you use the aromatic French tarragon in this recipe, as the more common Russian tarragon does not have the same delicious flavour.

675g /1½lbs whole small pickling cucumbers
Salt
225g /8oz granulated sugar
420ml /¾ pint white wine vinegar
140ml /¼ pint water
45ml /3 tbsps fresh chopped tarragon
6 black peppercorns

1. Cut the cucumbers into quarters, lengthways and sprinkle liberally with salt.

2. Put into a bowl or dish and leave the cucumber to stand for 30 minutes.

3. Rinse the cucumbers in clear water and drain thoroughly to remove any excess saltiness.

Step 7 Pack the cooked cucumbers evenly in 2 450g / 1lb glass jars, before pouring over the pickling vinegar.

Step 6 Cook the cucumbers in the vinegar mixture, until they have lost their bright green colour.

4. Pat the drained cucumbers as dry as possible using absorbent kitchen paper.

5. Put the sugar, vinegar, water, tarragon and peppercorns into a large jug or bowl and cook on HIGH for 10 minutes, stirring after each 2 minutes to ensure that the sugar dissolves completely.

6. Add the cucumbers to the vinegar mixture and cook, uncovered, for a further 3 minutes on HIGH, or until the cucumbers lose their bright green colour.

7. Divide the pickled cucumbers evenly between 2 450g /1lb jars and pour over the vinegar liquor.

8. Cover and seal in the usual way.

Cook's Notes

 TIME: Preparation takes about 15 minutes, microwave cooking takes about 13 minutes.

 VEGETARIAN SUITABILITY: This recipe is suitable for vegans.

 VARIATION: Use the tangy vinegar mixture to pickle any other vegetables of your choice.

 SERVING IDEA: Use as you would pickled onions.

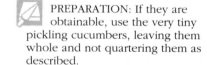 PREPARATION: If they are obtainable, use the very tiny pickling cucumbers, leaving them whole and not quartering them as described.

ORANGE AND GRAPEFRUIT MARMALADE WITH WHISKY

MAKES APPROXIMATELY 450g /1lb

This delicious breakfast marmalade could be used as a very welcome home-made present for Christmas or New Year.

2 large oranges
2 small grapefruit
425ml /14fl oz water
450g /1lb brown sugar
60ml /4 tbsps Scotch whisky

1. Using a potato peeler or very sharp knife, carefully pare off the skins from the oranges and grapefruit, making sure that none of the bitter white pith is removed as you peel.

2. Cut the peel into very fine shreds using a sharp knife.

3. Cut the fruit in half and squeeze out the juice. Put the juice into a large bowl along with the shredded fruit peel.

4. Put the fruit pith and any pips into a cheesecloth or muslin bag and tie the top securely. Put this bag into the bowl with the juice.

5. Heat the water on HIGH for 3-4 minutes, or until it is boiling. Pour the water into the bowl with the fruit juice and peel, and allow to stand for 30 minutes to infuse.

6. Cover the bowl with cling film and pierce this several times with the tip of a sharp knife. Cook on HIGH for 20 minutes.

Step 1 Pare off the skins from the oranges and grapefruit, using a potato peeler or very sharp knife. Avoid cutting any of the bitter white pith away from the fruit with the rind.

Step 2 Using a very sharp knife, cut the citrus rind into very fine shreds.

Step 4 Tie the fruit pith and any pips into a cheesecloth or muslin bag.

7. Uncover the bowl, squeeze the juice from the muslin bag, then remove the bag and stir in the sugar. Continue stirring until the sugar has completely dissolved.

8. Cook the marmalade for a further 20 minutes on HIGH, stirring frequently and allowing it to boil rapidly.

9. Put a little of the marmalade on to a cold plate and leave to stand for 2-3 minutes. If after this time the marmalade has begun to set, it is ready; if not, continue cooking on HIGH for a further 2-3 minutes and then re-test.

10. Stir in the whisky and pour the hot marmalade into sterilised jars. Seal and store in the usual way.

LEMON LIME CURD

MAKES APPROXIMATELY 675g /1½lbs

There is nothing which can quite equal the fresh taste of home-made citrus fruit curds. They can be time consuming to make in the conventional manner; made in the microwave oven however, they are simplicity itself, so treat the family and enjoy this tangy recipe.

2 lemons
1 lime
40g /1½oz unsalted butter
225g /8oz caster sugar
3 eggs

1. Using the fine side of a cheese grater, grate the rind only from both the lemons and the lime.

2. Put the lemons and lime into the microwave oven and heat on HIGH for 30 seconds to release the juices.

3. Cut the citrus fruits in half and squeeze out all the juice.

4. Put the grated rind and the juice into a large bowl and add the butter. Cook, uncovered, on HIGH for 3 minutes, or until the butter has completely melted.

5. Add the sugar to the butter mixture and stir it well until it begins to dissolve.

6. Cook on HIGH for 2 minutes, then continue stirring until the sugar has completely dissolved.

7. Whisk the eggs in a bowl until they begin to froth.

8. Pour the whisked eggs onto the lemon and

Step 1 Using the fine side of a cheese grater, finely grate the rind only from the lemons and the lime.

Step 8 Pour the whisked eggs onto the lemon and sugar mixture through a nylon sieve, to remove any lumps.

Step 11 The lemon lime curd has finished cooking when the mixture evenly coats the back of a wooden spoon.

sugar mixture through a nylon sieve to remove any lumps.

9. Stir well to blend thoroughly.

10. Cook the lemon and egg mixture on LOW for 12-14 minutes, stirring after each 2 minutes to prevent curdling. DO NOT ALLOW THE MIXTURE TO BOIL.

11. Continue cooking and stirring until the mixture evenly coats the back of a wooden spoon.

12. Pour the lemon lime curd into clean, sterilised jars, and cover and seal in the usual way. Store in a refrigerator until required.

WHOLE STRAWBERRY CONSERVE WITH GRAND MARNIER

MAKES APPROXIMATELY 900g /2lbs

This luxury preserve will make an attractive and delicious gift for a 'foodie' friend or relative. Make sure, however, that you use only firm, unblemished berries, as any marks will show.

900g /2lbs fresh strawberries
900g /2lbs white, granulated sugar
15ml /1 tbsp lemon juice
30ml /2 tbsps Grand Marnier

1. Hull the strawberries carefully, wash them and leave them to dry.

2. Put the strawberries into a large bowl and add the sugar. Gently toss the berries in the sugar, taking care not to mark the fruit.

3. Leave the strawberries to stand in the sugar for 30 minutes to 1 hour, or until the juice begins to flow.

4. Cook the strawberries, uncovered, on HIGH for 5 minutes, or until they are boiling. Stir gently and add the lemon juice.

Step 3 After one hour the juice should be beginning to flow from the strawberries.

Step 7 Setting point is reached when the surface of the jam wrinkles slightly when a little is cooled on a plate.

5. Continue cooking on HIGH for a further 10 minutes, stirring occasionally until the syrup clears and thickens.

6. Put a small spoonful of the syrup on a cold plate and allow it to stand for 2-3 minutes.

7. If the syrup forms a skin and the surface wrinkles when the plate is tilted, setting point has been reached.

8. If the setting point has not been reached at this stage, continue cooking on HIGH, testing after each 2 minute interval until it is ready.

9. Cool the jam slightly, then gently stir in the Grand Marnier, taking care not to break or spoil the berries.

10. Pour the conserve into sterilised jars, then seal and cover in the usual way.

Cook's Notes

VARIATION: Use whole, stoned cherries instead of the strawberries in this recipe, and Kirsch instead of the Grand Marnier.

TIME: Preparation takes about 10 minutes plus 30 minutes to one hour standing time. Microwave cooking takes about 15-20 minutes.

PREPARATION: Take great care not to overstir this conserve, otherwise the berries will break and the attractive appearance will be spoilt.

GINGER PEAR JAM
MAKES APPROXIMATELY 900g /2lb

Often, a glut of pears leaves you wondering how you can ever use them up. This recipe is an ideal way, allowing you to savour the flavour of fresh pears right through the winter.

900g /2lbs firm pears
1 lemon
45g /1½oz fresh ginger root, grated
450g /1lb granulated sugar

1. Peel and core the pears. Reserve the peelings, cores and pips, and cut the flesh into thick slices with a sharp knife.

2. Carefully pare off the rind from the lemon, using a potato peeler or very sharp knife. Do not get any white pith on the lemon rind.

3. Cut the lemon in half, and squeeze out the juice. Put the juice into a large bowl and mix in the pear slices.

4. Cut the lemon rind into short, very thin strips with a small sharp knife.

5. Stir the lemon strips into the pears along with the grated ginger. Stir to mix well.

6. Put the pear peelings, cores, lemon skins and any pips or seeds into a muslin or cheesecloth bag. Tie the top of the bag firmly and put this into the bowl along with the pears and lemon juice mixture.

Step 1 Cut the pear flesh into thick slices with a sharp knife.

Step 4 Carefully cut the pared lemon rind into short, very thin strips.

Step 6 Tie the pear peelings, the cores, lemon skins and any pips or seeds into a muslin or cheesecloth bag.

7. Cover the bowl of pears with cling film and puncture this twice with the tip of a knife. Cook the pears on HIGH for 15 minutes, stirring them frequently to break them up.

8. Uncover the pears, remove the muslin bag and stir in the sugar. Continue stirring until the sugar has completely dissolved.

9. Cook the pear mixture, still uncovered, for a further 20 minutes on HIGH, or until it has thickened and setting point has been reached.

10. Continue cooking and checking for setting point at 2 minute intervals if necessary.

11. Pour the jam into warmed, sterilised jars, then seal and cover them before storing.

KUMQUATS IN COINTREAU
MAKES 675g /1½lb

Preserved whole fruit look and taste deliciously exotic. This recipe is an ideal way of using kumquats, which are now easily available from most supermarkets and greengrocers.

340g /12oz whole kumquats
450g /1lb granulated sugar
350ml /³⁄₄ pint water
30ml /2 tbsps Cointreau

1. Using a sharp knife, cut a small cross in the rounded end of each kumquat.

2. Put the sugar and water into a large jug or bowl, and cook, uncovered, for 4 minutes on HIGH.

3. Stir to completely dissolve the sugar, then cook again on HIGH, until boiling.

Step 1 Cut a small cross in the rounded end of each kumquat with a sharp, pointed knife.

Step 4 Pack the kumquats into 2 450g /1lb heat-proof glass jars, pressing them down to prevent them from floating when the syrup is poured over.

4. Put the kumquats into 2 450g /1lb heat-proof glass jars, packing them down quite firmly to prevent them from floating when the syrup is added.

5. Pour the sugar syrup into the jars until the kumquats are just covered.

6. Cover the jars with cling film and cook for 18 minutes on HIGH, or until the kumquats begin to look clear.

7. Remove the cling film and pour in the Cointreau.

8. Cover and seal the jars immediately, then store for at least one month before using.

Cook's Notes

 PREPARATION: Put 1 or 2 lime or other citrus leaves into the jars with the kumquats for an attractive decoration.

SERVING IDEA: Serve with ice cream or as part of a fruit salad.

 TIME: Preparation takes about 15 minutes, microwave cooking takes about 25 minutes.

VEGETARIAN SUITABILITY: This recipe is suitable for vegans.

VARIATION: Small clementines or tangerines can be preserved in place of the kumquats.

PINEAPPLE GRAPEFRUIT MARMALADE

MAKES APPROXIMATELY 900g /2lbs

The flavours of pineapple and grapefruit complement each other wonderfully as highlighted in this delicious and unusual recipe.

1 fresh pineapple
1 large grapefruit
500ml /1 pint water
225g /8oz granulated sugar

1. Peel the pineapple and remove any brown 'eyes' with a sharp knife or the tip of a potato peeler.

2. Cut the pineapple flesh into small pieces with a sharp knife, cutting away and setting aside the tough inner core.

3. Pare off just the rind from the grapefruit using a potato peeler. Take care not to leave any of the bitter white pith on the rind.

4. Cut the grapefruit peel into short, fine shreds with a sharp knife.

5. Cut the grapefruit in half and squeeze out the juice. Put the juice into a large bowl along with the shredded peel and chopped pineapple flesh.

6. Put the grapefruit pith, any pips and the pineapple core into a cheesecloth or muslin bag. Tie securely and put this into the bowl along with the pineapple.

7. Bring the water to the boil on HIGH for 4 minutes and stir this into the pineapple mixture.

Step 1 Remove the brown 'eyes' from the peeled pineapple using the end of a potato peeler, or a very sharp knife.

Step 4 Cut the grapefruit peel into short, fine shreds with a sharp knife.

Step 6 Tie the grapefruit pith and pips into a muslin or cheesecloth bag, along with the pineapple cores.

Allow to stand for 30 minutes to infuse.

8. Cover the bowl with cling film and pierce this several times with the tip of a sharp knife. Cook for 20 minutes on HIGH.

9. Remove the bag of pith and pips from the bowl and squeeze out any juice.

10. Stir the sugar into the pineapple and grapefruit mixture, mixing well until it has dissolved.

11. Cook, uncovered, for a further 20 minutes, stirring frequently, until setting point is reached.

12. Pour the marmalade into hot, sterilised jars and cover and seal in the usual way.

CHRYSANTHEMUM AND GREEN PEPPERCORN JELLY

MAKES 675g /1½lbs

This exotic-flavoured jelly is best made with the old-fashioned type of chrysanthemums, often found in gardens.

500ml /1 pint unsweetened clear apple juice
340g /12oz granulated sugar
15ml /1 tbsp lemon juice
90ml /5 tbsps pectin
15ml /1 tbsp green peppercorns in brine, drained
Good handful of chrysanthemum petals

1. Put the apple juice into a large bowl and heat on HIGH for 3 minutes.

2. Stir in the sugar and lemon juice and continue stirring until the sugar has completely dissolved.

3. Cover the bowl with cling film and pierce this several times with the tip of a sharp knife. Cook on HIGH for 10 minutes.

4. Stir the pectin and peppercorns into the fruit

Step 5 To test for setting point, put a small spoonful of the jelly onto a cold plate and allow to stand for two minutes.

Step 8 Add the chrysanthemum petals to the jelly, stirring them well to distribute evenly.

syrup and continue cooking, uncovered, on HIGH for a further 10 minutes, making sure that the jelly boils rapidly.

5. After this time, setting point should have been reached. To test for setting point, put a small spoonful of the jelly onto a cold plate and after 2 minutes tilt it gently from side to side.

6. If setting point has been reached, the jelly will have formed a skin which will wrinkle as the plate is tipped.

7. If this does not happen, continue cooking the jelly on HIGH and testing after each 2 minutes, until it does.

8. Stir the chrysanthemum petals into the jelly, stirring well to distribute them evenly.

9. Pour the jelly into sterilised jars and cover and seal in the usual way.

Cook's Notes

 TIME: Preparation takes about 10 minutes, microwave cooking takes about 25 minutes.

VEGETARIAN SUITABILITY: This recipe is suitable for vegans.

VARIATION: Use nasturtium or carnation petals in this recipe instead of the chrysanthemum petals.

SERVING IDEA: Serve with salads.

COOK'S TIP: To speed up the test for setting point, put the plate to be used into the deep freeze for about 10 minutes before putting the jelly onto it.

APPLE CIDER JELLY

MAKES 450g /1lb

This delicious fruit jelly can be made at any time, as cider is always available.

570ml /1 pint dry, still cider
450g /1lb granulated sugar
5ml /1 tsp lemon juice
90ml /5 tbsps pectin

---

1. Put the cider into a large bowl along with the sugar and the lemon juice.

2. Cook on HIGH for 4 minutes, then stir well to dissolve the sugar completely.

3. Cover the bowl with cling film, and continue cooking on HIGH for a further 8 minutes.

4. Remove the covering and stir in the pectin. Boil the jelly rapidly by cooking once again on HIGH for another 10 minutes.

5. After this time, setting point should have been reached.

6. To test for setting point, put a little of the jelly onto a cold plate. After 2 minutes, tilt the plate gently from side to side.

Step 4 Stir the pectin into the cider and sugar mixture with a wooden spoon.

Step 6 Put a small spoonful of the jelly onto a cold plate and stand for 2 minutes.

Step 7 If setting point has been reached, the surface of the jelly will wrinkle when the plate is tilted.

7. If the jelly is sufficiently set, a skin will have formed on top and this will wrinkle as the plate is tipped.

8. If setting point has not been reached, continue cooking on HIGH for 2 minute intervals, checking after each time until the jelly is sufficiently set.

9. Pour the jelly into warmed, sterilised jars and cover and seal in the usual way.

Cook's Notes

 VARIATION: Add a good handful of freshly chopped mint leaves for a delicious variation.

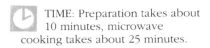 TIME: Preparation takes about 10 minutes, microwave cooking takes about 25 minutes.

 SERVING IDEA: Serve on warm buttered bread or scones.

PINEAPPLE, MANGO AND MINT CHUTNEY

MAKES 900g /2lbs

This fresh-tasting chutney makes an ideal accompaniment for salads, or is equally delicious served simply with cheese and home-made bread.

450g /1lb fresh, skinned pineapple
Salt
1 small piece of fresh root ginger
1 large mango
180g /6oz sultanas
570ml /1 pint distilled white vinegar
30ml /2 tbsps fresh chopped mint
Large pinch ground nutmeg
225g /8oz granulated sugar

1. Cut the pineapple into bite-sized pieces and sprinkle liberally with salt. Put the pineapple in a bowl and leave to stand for 30 minutes.

2. Drain the pineapple, then rinse it thoroughly to remove the excess saltiness.

3. Peel the piece of ginger and cut it into very fine slivers with a sharp knife.

4. Peel the mango and roughly chop the flesh. Discard the large stone.

5. Put the pineapple, ginger and mango into a large bowl and stir in the raisins, vinegar, mint and nutmeg. Mix well.

6. Cover the bowl with cling film and pierce this several times with the tip of a sharp knife.

7. Cook the pineapple mixture on HIGH for 15 minutes, stirring frequently during the cooking time.

Step 10 The chutney is ready when a channel is left in its surface when a wooden spoon is drawn through it.

8. Add the sugar to the cooked fruit and stir until it has completely dissolved.

9. Continue cooking the chutney on HIGH for another 15 minutes, stirring after each 3 minutes to prevent the chutney from burning.

10. After this time, run a wooden spoon through the chutney. If a channel is left behind the spoon when it has been withdrawn then the chutney is ready. If not, continue cooking for a further 5 minutes, testing after each minute until setting point is reached.

11. Pour the chutney immediately into hot, sterilised jars, and cover and seal in the usual way.

Cook's Notes

COOK'S TIP: If fresh pineapples are not available, use the equivalent amount of drained, tinned pineapple, but make sure that the fruit has been tinned in natural juice and not in sugar syrup.

TIME: Preparation takes about 20 minutes, microwave cooking takes about 30-35 minutes.

VEGETARIAN SUITABILITY: This recipe is suitable for vegans.

VARIATION: Use peaches in place of the mango in this recipe.

SERVING IDEA: Serve with curries, ploughman's lunches, or cold pies.

FENNEL PRESERVES WITH AQUAVIT

MAKES 900g /2lbs

*This highly flavoured, aniseed preserve would make an
unusual accompaniment for cold nut roasts or vegetable pies.*

2-3 bulbs Florentine fennel
225g /8oz granulated sugar
280ml /½ pint distilled white wine vinegar
280ml /½ pint water
15ml /1 tbsp caraway seeds
Salt
140ml /¼ pint aquavit

1. Cut the root ends off the fennel bulbs and slice the bulb into 1.5cm /½-inch pieces, including the green tops as you cut.

2. Put the sugar, vinegar, water, seeds and a small pinch of salt into a large bowl.

3. Cook, uncovered, on HIGH for 10 minutes, stirring after each 2 minutes to make sure the sugar has completely dissolved.

4. Stir the sliced fennel into the sugar syrup and mix well.

5. Cover the bowl with cling film and pierce this several times with the tip of a sharp knife.

Step 6 Cook the fennel slices in the syrup until they look translucent.

Step 8 Place a silicone paper disc into the top of each jar and seal with either a screw top, or with cellophane tops held in place with an elastic band.

Step 1 Slice the trimmed fennel bulbs into even-sized pieces, including the green tops as you cut.

6. Cook the fennel in the syrup for 10 minutes on MEDIUM, or until the fennel slices begin to look translucent.

7. Stir the aquavit into the fennel mixture and pour it straight away into clean, sterilised jars.

8. Cover the top of the preserve with small silicone paper discs and seal the pots with either screw tops or with cellophane tops held in place with an elastic band.

Cook's Notes

 TIME: Preparation takes about 15 minutes, microwave cooking takes about 20-25 minutes.

PREPARATION: If you prefer a less chunky preserve, grate the fennel rather than slicing it.

 SERVING IDEA: Serve with nut roasts or with vegetable pies.

HOT PEPPER JELLY

MAKES APPROXIMATELY 900g /2lbs

*A most unusual savoury jelly, which will add a touch
of spice to any barbeque or picnic.*

---

3 red peppers
1 green pepper
2 hot chilli peppers
240ml /½ pint white wine vinegar
675g /1½lbs granulated sugar
200ml /6fl oz pectin

---

1. Cut all the peppers in half and remove the seeds and white cores.

2. Chop the peppers finely using a sharp knife or a food processor.

3. Put the chopped peppers into a large bowl and pour over the vinegar.

4. Cover the bowl with cling film and pierce this

Step 1 Remove the seeds and white cores from all the halved peppers.

Step 2 Using a sharp knife or food processor, carefully chop the peppers very finely.

several times with the tip of a sharp knife. Cook the peppers in the vinegar for 2 minutes on HIGH.

5. Remove the cling film and stir in the sugar. Continue stirring until the sugar has completely dissolved.

6. Cook the pepper mixture, uncovered, for a further 10 minutes on HIGH, stirring once or twice during cooking time to prevent the sugar from burning.

7. After 7 minutes of the cooking time, stir in the pectin.

8. Pour the jelly into clean, hot, sterilised jars. Cover and seal in the usual way.

Cook's Notes

PREPARATION: Remember, great care must be taken when preparing hot chilli peppers. Avoid getting the juice into your eyes or mouth. If this should happen, rinse with lots of clear, cold water.

TIME: Preparation takes about 10 minutes, microwave cooking takes about 12 minutes.

VEGETARIAN SUITABILITY: This recipe is suitable for vegans.

COOK'S TIP: The juice from chilli peppers will stay on unprotected fingers for several hours, even after washing. Wear rubber gloves to avoid this happening when preparing them.

CURRIED FRUIT

MAKES 900g /2lbs

A rich, spicy chutney which is ideal as an accompaniment to Indian food.

3 apples
180g /6oz drained pineapple chunks
90g /3oz raisins
225g /8oz light brown sugar
140ml /¼ pint distilled white vinegar
140ml /¼ pint water
4 whole cloves
5ml /1 tsp coriander seeds
30ml /2 tbsps mild curry paste
6 apricots, stoned and thickly sliced

1. Peel the apples and remove the cores. Roughly chop the flesh with a sharp knife.

2. If the pineapple chunks are large, cut them into smaller pieces.

3. Put the apples, pineapple and raisins into a large bowl and mix together well.

Step 6 Mix the vinegar and sugar syrup into the fruit in the bowl.

Step 8 Stir the sliced apricots into the partially cooked fruit, taking care not to over-stir the chutney and break up the fruit.

4. Put the sugar, vinegar, water, spices and curry paste into another bowl or large measuring jug.

5. Cook the vinegar mixture on HIGH for 5 minutes, stirring after each minute to ensure that the sugar has dissolved.

6. Pour the vinegar and sugar syrup over the fruit in the bowl and mix well.

7. Cook the fruit, uncovered, on HIGH for 10 minutes, stirring frequently to prevent the sugar from burning.

8. After 7 minutes, stir in the sliced apricots.

9. Pour the chutney into hot, sterilised jars, cover and seal in the usual way.

Cook's Notes

 VARIATION: Use hot curry paste in this recipe in place of the mild one suggested.

 SERVING IDEA: Stir a tablespoon of this chutney into some mayonnaise and serve over hard-boiled eggs for a delicious appetizer.

 TIME: Preparation takes about 15 minutes, microwave cooking takes about 15-18 minutes.

 VEGETARIAN SUITABILITY: This recipe is suitable for vegans.

 PREPARATION: If after the 10 minutes cooking time the apples are still firm and not translucent, continue cooking on HIGH for an additional 2-3 minutes, or until they soften.

·INDEX·